SPRING FRAMEWORK WITH JAVA— A PRACTICAL APPROACH

SPRING FRAMEWORK WITH JAVA— A PRACTICAL APPROACH

By

B. Mohamed Ibrahim

MCA, M.Phil., MBA

Software Solution Architect

UNIVERSITY SCIENCE PRESS

(An Imprint of Laxmi Publications Pvt. Ltd.)

An ISO 9001:2008 Company

BENGALURU • CHENNAI • COCHIN • GUWAHATI • HYDERABAD
JALANDHAR • KOLKATA • LUCKNOW • MUMBAI • RANCHI • NEW DELHI
BOSTON (USA) • ACCRA (GHANA) • NAIROBI (KENYA)

SPRING FRAMEWORK WITH JAVA—A PRACTICAL APPROACH

Printed and bound in India
Typeset at Kalyani Computer Services, Delhi
First Edition : 2016
ISBN 978-93-84872-61-8

Branches

Bengaluru	080-26 75 69 30	
Chennai	044-24 34 47 26,	24 35 95 07
Cochin	0484-237 70 04,	405 13 03
Guwahati	0361-254 36 69,	251 38 81
Hyderabad	040-27 55 53 83,	27 55 53 93
Jalandhar	0181-222 12 72	
Kolkata	033-22 27 43 84	
Lucknow	0522-220 99 16	
Mumbai	022-24 91 54 15,	24 92 78 69
Ranchi	0651-220 44 64	

PUBLISHED IN INDIA BY

UNIVERSITY SCIENCE PRESS
(An Imprint of Laxmi Publications Pvt. Ltd.)

An ISO 9001:2008 Company
113, GOLDEN HOUSE, DARYAGANJ,
NEW DELHI - 110002, INDIA
Telephone : 91-11-4353 2500, 4353 2501
Fax : 91-11-2325 2572, 4353 2528
www.laxmipublications.com info@laxmipublications.com

C—
Printed at:

CONTENTS

SPRING FRAMEWORK WITH JAVA— A PRACTICAL APPROACH

By

B. Mohamed Ibrahim

MCA, M.Phil., MBA

Software Solution Architect

UNIVERSITY SCIENCE PRESS

(An Imprint of Laxmi Publications Pvt. Ltd.)

An ISO 9001:2008 Company

BENGALURU • CHENNAI • COCHIN • GUWAHATI • HYDERABAD
JALANDHAR • KOLKATA • LUCKNOW • MUMBAI • RANCHI • NEW DELHI
BOSTON (USA) • ACCRA (GHANA) • NAIROBI (KENYA)

SPRING FRAMEWORK WITH JAVA—A PRACTICAL APPROACH

Printed and bound in India
Typeset at Kalyani Computer Services, Delhi
First Edition : 2016
ISBN 978-93-84872-61-8

Branches

Bengaluru	080-26 75 69 30	
Chennai	044-24 34 47 26,	24 35 95 07
Cochin	0484-237 70 04,	405 13 03
Guwahati	0361-254 36 69,	251 38 81
Hyderabad	040-27 55 53 83,	27 55 53 93
Jalandhar	0181-222 12 72	
Kolkata	033-22 27 43 84	
Lucknow	0522-220 99 16	
Mumbai	022-24 91 54 15,	24 92 78 69
Ranchi	0651-220 44 64	

PUBLISHED IN INDIA BY

UNIVERSITY SCIENCE PRESS
(An Imprint of Laxmi Publications Pvt. Ltd.)

An ISO 9001:2008 Company
113, GOLDEN HOUSE, DARYAGANJ,
NEW DELHI - 110002, INDIA
Telephone : 91-11-4353 2500, 4353 2501
Fax : 91-11-2325 2572, 4353 2528
www.laxmipublications.com info@laxmipublications.com

C—
Printed at:

PREFACE

The Spring Framework, simply Spring is an open-source application framework which provides excellent features such as Inversion of Control (IoC), support for Aspect Oriented Programming, MVC support for web application development and distributed transact management that simplify the development of Java based enterprise applications, and thus it became as a dominant framework in industry for enterprise computing.

This book is written in such a way that the readers will have the perception of gaining hands-on experience as the concepts are explained with complete illustrating programs and their corresponding screen outputs. This book only covers the important components of the Spring Framework in terms the given 12 chapters, and this book is well suited for the beginners and the intermediates to practice code in Spring Framework with Java.

—Author

CHAPTER 1

SPRING CORE CONCEPTS

The Spring Framework (simply Spring) is a layered open-source application framework for Java platform; simplifying Java Enterprise Edition application development by its excellent features such as Inversion-of-Control (IoC), Aspect Oriented Programming, and Transaction Management.

1.1 SETTING UP THE ENVIRONMENT

You can download the latest version of Spring Framework from Spring Source Community webpage (*http://www.springsource.org/download*). The Spring Framework version 3.2.1 (spring-framework-3.2.1.RELEASE-dist.zip) is used in the demonstration code of this book. And Eclipse IDE (version Juno) with Windows platform is used for code development. You can download the latest Eclipse IDE from its official download page (*http://www.eclipse.org/downloads*).

Create a new Java Project named "SpringDemo" in Eclipse IDE. Choose File ⟶ New ⟶ Other ⟶ Java Project ⟶ Type "SpringDemo" as Project Name ⟶ Accept the defaults ⟶ Finish.

Create a new directory named "lib" under "SpringDemo". Select "SpringDemo" ⟶ Right Click ⟶ New ⟶ Folder ⟶ Type "lib" as Folder name ⟶ Finish.

Include Spring library jar files in CLASSPATH. Copy all the Spring library jars (from spring-framework-3.2.1.RELEASE\libs) to this "lib" directory. Select the project-name "SpringDemo" ⟶ Right click ⟶ Properties ⟶ Java Build Path (left side) ⟶ Libraries Tab ⟶ Add JARs ⟶ Select All Jar files under the lib directory of our project and press OK ⟶ OK. Follow the same procedure to include dependent library files according to your application's need into CLASSPATH.

Create a Package named "com.springdemo". Select "src" directory of the project ⟶ Right Click ⟶ New ⟶ Package ⟶ Type "com.springdemo" as package name ⟶ Finish.

Now the IDE is ready and test Spring applications.

1.2 FIRST APPLICATION: DISPLAYING YOUR NAME

Store the following program under "com.springdemo" package.

```
//File Name: Employee.java
package com.springdemo;

public class Employee {
  private String name;

  public void setName(String name) {
    this.name = name;
  }

  public String getName() {
    return name;
  }
}
```

Store the following program under "com.springdemo" package.

```
//File Name: EmployeeApp.java
package com.springdemo;
import org.springframework.context.ApplicationContext;
import org.springframework.context.support.ClassPathXml
                                          ApplicationContext;
public class EmployeeApp {

  public static void main(String args[]) {
    ApplicationContext context =
                new ClassPathXmlApplicationContext("beans.xml");
    Employee employee = (Employee) context.getBean("employee");
    System.out.println("My name is" + employee.getName());
  }
}
```

Store the following "beans.xml" file in "src" directory of the project.

```
<?xml version="1.0" encoding="UTF-8"?>
<beans xmlns="http://www.springframework.org/schema/beans"
   xmlns:xsi="http://www.w3.org/2001/XMLSchema-instance"
   xsi:schemaLocation="http://www.springframework.org/schema/beans
   http://www.springframework.org/schema/beans/spring-beans.xsd">

  <bean id="employee" class="com.springdemo.Employee">
    <property name="name" value="Mohamed Ibrahim"/>
  </bean>

</beans>
```

Run the EmployeeApp as Java Application. Select "EmployeeApp.java" ⟶ Right Click ⟶ Run As ⟶ Java Application.

The output is shown below.

```
My name is Mohamed Ibrahim
```

1.3 INVERSE OF CONTROL (IoC), DEPENDENCY INJECTION

The Inverse of Control (IoC), also known as Dependency Injection (DI) is a technique where objects define their dependencies. An object defines at runtime what the objects that it will work with them are. The Spring container injects those dependencies (objects) when it creates an object (bean).

The following example demonstrates how to apply IoC.

```
// File Name: DisplayRecord.java
package com.springdemo;

public interface DisplayRecord {
  public void display();
}
```

```
// File Name: Student.java
package com.springdemo;

public class Student implements DisplayRecord {

  @Override
  public void display() {
    System.out.println("STUDENT RECORD");
    System.out.println("Roll Number : 1001");
    System.out.println("Name : Mohamed Ibrahim");
    System.out.println("Result : Pass] ");
  }
}
```

```
// File Name: Employee.java
package com.springdemo;

public class Employee implements DisplayRecord {

  @Override
```

```
  public void display() {
    System.out.println("EMPLOYEE RECORD");
    System.out.println("Employee Number : 1001");
    System.out.println("Employee Name : Mohamed Ibrahim");
    System.out.println("Salary : 10,000.00");
  }

}
```

```
// File Name: AccessRecord.java
package com.springdemo;

public class AccessRecord {

  DisplayRecord displayRecord;

  public void setDisplayRecord(DisplayRecord displayRecord) {
    this.displayRecord = displayRecord;
  }

  public void outputDetails() {
    displayRecord.display();
  }
}
```

```
// File Name: IoCDemo.java
package com.springdemo;

import org.springframework.context.ApplicationContext;
import org.springframework.context.support.ClassPathXmlApplicationContext;

public class IoCDemo {
  public static void main(String args[]) {
    ApplicationContext context =
               new ClassPathXmlApplicationContext("beans.xml");
    AccessRecord accessRecord =
               (AccessRecord) context.getBean("accessRecord");
    accessRecord.outputDetails();
  }
}
```

Store the following *beans.xml* file in the "*src*" directory of the project.

```
<?xml version="1.0" encoding="UTF-8"?>
<beans xmlns="http://www.springframework.org/schema/beans"
    xmlns:xsi="http://www.w3.org/2001/XMLSchema-instance"
   xsi:schemaLocation="http://www.springframework.org/schema/beans
   http://www.springframework.org/schema/beans/spring-beans.xsd">

  <bean id="student" class="com.springdemo.Student"/>
  <bean id="employee" class="com.springdemo.Employee"/>

  <bean id="accessRecord" class="com.springdemo.AccessRecord">
    <property name="displayRecord" ref="employee"/>
  </bean>

</beans>
```

Run the *IoCDemo.java* file. The following will be the result.

```
EMPLOYEE RECORD
Employee Number : 1001
Employee Name : Mohamed Ibrahim
Salary : 10,000.00
```

Now, change the bean configuration as below (change the 'displayRecord' to 'student' object).

```
<?xml version="1.0" encoding="UTF-8"?>
<beans xmlns="http://www.springframework.org/schema/beans"
   xmlns:xsi="http://www.w3.org/2001/XMLSchema-instance"
   xsi:schemaLocation="http://www.springframework.org/schema/beans
   http://www.springframework.org/schema/beans/spring-beans.xsd">

  <bean id="student" class="com.springdemo.Student"/>
  <bean id="employee" class="com.springdemo.Employee"/>

  <bean id="accessRecord" class="com.springdemo.AccessRecord">
    <property name="displayRecord" ref="student"/>
  </bean>

</beans>
```

Now, Run the IoCDemo.java file and the result will be as below.

```
STUDENT RECORD
Roll Number : 1001
Name : Mohamed Ibrahim
Result : Pass
```

Explanation: Depending on the configuration in *beans.xml* file, the *AccessRecord* bean gets *student* or *employee* object for *displayRecord* object. The Spring container injects the dependent object(s) for a bean (Dependency Injection). Normally, the required objects will be assigned to the variables (object references) in a class. But, here objects define their dependencies (through configuration file, hence not tightly coupled), so it is called Inverse of Control.

1.4 SETTER BASED DEPENDENCY INJECTION

Injecting objects/values can be passed through setter methods of a bean.

```
//File Name: Employee.java
package com.springdemo;

public class Employee {
  private int empNumber;
  private String empName;
  private double basicpay;
  private double allowances;
  private double deductions;
  private double netpay;

  public int getEmpNumber() {
    return empNumber;
  }

  public void setEmpNumber(int empNumber) {
    this.empNumber = empNumber;
  }

  public String getEmpName() {
    return empName;
  }

  public void setEmpName(String empName) {
```

```
    this.empName = empName;
  }

  public double getBasicpay() {
    return basicpay;
  }

  public void setBasicpay(double basicpay) {
    this.basicpay = basicpay;
  }

  public double getAllowances() {
    return allowances;
  }

  public void setAllowances(double allowances) {
    this.allowances = allowances;
  }

  public double getDeductions() {
    return deductions;
  }

  public void setDeductions(double deductions) {
    this.deductions = deductions;
  }

  public double getNetpay() {
    return netpay;
  }

  public void setNetpay(double netpay) {
    this.netpay = netpay;
  }

  public String toString() {
    String rStr = " Emp Number    " + empNumber +
                  "\n Emp Name     " + empName +
                  "\n Basic Pay    " + basicpay +
                  "\n Allowances " + allowances +
                  "\n Deductions " + deductions +
                  "\n Netpay       " + netpay;
    return rStr;
  }
}
```

```
//File Name: EmployeeApp.java
package com.springdemo;

import org.springframework.context.ApplicationContext;
import org.springframework.context.support.ClassPathXmlApplicationContext;

public class EmployeeApp {

 public static void main(String args[]) {
  ApplicationContext context =
            new ClassPathXmlApplicationContext("beans.xml");
  Employee employee = (Employee) context.getBean("employee");
  employee.setNetpay(employee.getBasicpay() +
               employee.getAllowances() - employee.getDeductions());
  System.out.println(employee);
 }
}
```

The contents of *beans.xml* file:

```
<?xml version="1.0" encoding="UTF-8"?>
<beans xmlns="http://www.springframework.org/schema/beans"
      xmlns:xsi="http://www.w3.org/2001/XMLSchema-instance"
      xsi:schemaLocation="http://www.springframework.org/schema/beans
      http://www.springframework.org/schema/beans/spring-beans.xsd">

   <bean id="employee" class="com.springdemo.Employee">
     <property name="empNumber" value="1001" />
     <property name="empName" value="Mohamed Ibrahim" />
     <property name="basicpay" value="10000.0" />
     <property name="allowances" value="3000.0" />
     <property name="deductions" value="2000.0" />
   </bean>

</beans>
```

Execute the "*EmployeeApp.java*" file.

```
Emp Number    1001
Emp Name      Mohamed Ibrahim
Basic Pay     10000.0
```

```
Allowances     3000.0
Deductions     2000.0
Netpay         11000.0
```

1.5 CONSTRUCTOR BASED DEPENDENCY INJECTION

Injecting objects / values can be passed through constructors of a bean.

```
//File Name: Employee.java
package com.springdemo;

public class Employee {
 private int empNumber;
 private String empName;
 private double basicpay;
 private double allowances;
 private double deductions;
 private double netpay;

 public Employee(int empNumber,
         String empName,
         double basicpay,
         double allowances,
         double deductions) {
  this.empNumber = empNumber;
  this.empName = empName;
  this.basicpay = basicpay;
  this.allowances = allowances;
  this.deductions = deductions;
 }

 public int getEmpNumber() {
  return empNumber;
 }

 public void setEmpNumber(int empNumber) {
  this.empNumber = empNumber;
 }

 public String getEmpName() {
  return empName;
 }
```

```
public void setEmpName(String empName) {
 this.empName = empName;
}

public double getBasicpay() {
 return basicpay;
}

public void setBasicpay(double basicpay) {
 this.basicpay = basicpay;
}

public double getAllowances() {
 return allowances;
}

public void setAllowances(double allowances) {
 this.allowances = allowances;
}

public double getDeductions() {
 return deductions;
}

public void setDeductions(double deductions) {
 this.deductions = deductions;
}

public double getNetpay() {
 return netpay;
}

public void setNetpay(double netpay) {
 this.netpay = netpay;
}

public String toString() {
 String rStr = " Emp Number   " + empNumber +
               "\n Emp Name    " + empName +
               "\n Basic Pay   " + basicpay +
               "\n Allowances " + allowances +
```

```
        "\n Deductions " + deductions +
        "\n Netpay     " + netpay;
  return rStr;
 }
}
```

```
//File Name: EmployeeApp.java
package com.springdemo;

import org.springframework.context.ApplicationContext;
import org.springframework.context.support.ClassPathXmlApplicationContext;

public class EmployeeApp {

 public static void main(String args[]) {
  ApplicationContext context =
            new ClassPathXmlApplicationContext("beans.xml");
  Employee employee = (Employee) context.getBean("employee");
  employee.setNetpay(employee.getBasicpay() +
            employee.getAllowances() - employee.getDeductions());
  System.out.println(employee);
 }
}
```

The contents of *beans.xml* file:

```
<?xml version="1.0" encoding="UTF-8"?>
<beans xmlns="http://www.springframework.org/schema/beans"
   xmlns:xsi="http://www.w3.org/2001/XMLSchema-instance"
   xsi:schemaLocation="http://www.springframework.org/schema/beans
   http://www.springframework.org/schema/beans/spring-beans.xsd">

  <bean id="employee" class="com.springdemo.Employee">
    <constructor-arg index="0" value="1001" />
    <constructor-arg index="1" value="Mohamed Ibrahim" />
    <constructor-arg index="2" value="10000.0" />
    <constructor-arg index="3" value="3000.0" />
    <constructor-arg index="4" value="2000.0" />
  </bean>

</beans>
```

Execute the "*EmployeeApp.java*" application.

```
Emp Number      1001
Emp Name        Mohamed Ibrahim
Basic Pay       10000.0
Allowances      3000.0
Deductions      2000.0
Netpay          11000.0
```

1.6 DEFINING JAVA COLLECTIONS AS DEPENDENT OBJECTS

The following example demonstrates how to define Java Collection objects such as List and Set as dependent objects. This example uses Setter based dependency injection for its operation.

```
//File Name: Employee.java
//Properties extends Hashtable. HashMap permits null values in it,
//while Hashtable doesn't.
//List permits duplicate values, while Set doesn't.
package com.springdemo;

import java.util.List;
import java.util.Map;
import java.util.Properties;
import java.util.Set;

public class Employee {
 private int empNumber;
 private String empName;
 private Properties doj;      //Date of joining
 private Map<String, String> salaryDetails;
 private List<String> knownLanguages;
 private Set<String> skills;

 public void setEmpNumber(int empNumber) {
  this.empNumber = empNumber;
 }

 public void setEmpName(String empName) {
  this.empName = empName;
 }
```

```
public void setDoj(Properties doj) {
 this.doj = doj;
}

public void setSalaryDetails(Map<String, String> salaryDetails) {
 this.salaryDetails = salaryDetails;
}

public void setKnownLanguages(List<String> knownLanguages) {
 this.knownLanguages = knownLanguages;
}

public void setSkills(Set<String> skills) {
 this.skills = skills;
}

public String toString() {
 String rStr = "Emp Number: " + empNumber + "\nEmp Name: " + empName;
 rStr += "\nDOJ: " + doj.getProperty("day") + "-" +
       doj.getProperty("month") + "-" + doj.getProperty("year");
 rStr += "\nBasic Pay: " + salaryDetails.get("basicpay");
 rStr += "\nAllowances: " + salaryDetails.get("allowances");
 rStr += "\nDeductions: " + salaryDetails.get("deductions");
 double netpay = Double.parseDouble(salaryDetails.get("basicpay")) +
           Double.parseDouble(salaryDetails.get("allowances")) -
           Double.parseDouble(salaryDetails.get("deductions"));
 rStr += "\nNetpay: " + netpay;
 rStr += "\nKnown Languages: " + knownLanguages;
 rStr += "\nSkills: " + skills;
 return rStr;
 }
}
```

```
//File Name: EmployeeApp.java
package com.springdemo;

import org.springframework.context.ApplicationContext;
import org.springframework.context.support.ClassPathXmlApplicationContext;

public class EmployeeApp {
```

```
public static void main(String args[]) {
  ApplicationContext context =
                  new ClassPathXmlApplicationContext("beans.xml");
  Employee employee = (Employee) context.getBean("employee");
  System.out.println(employee);
 }
}
```

The contents of *beans.xml* file:

```
<?xml version="1.0" "encoding="UTF-8"?>
<beans xmlns="http://www.springframework.org/schema/beans"
    xmlns:xsi="http://www.w3.org/2001/XMLSchema-instance"
    xsi:schemaLocation="http://www.springframework.org/schema/beans
    http://www.springframework.org/schema/beans/spring-beans.xsd">

  <bean id="employee" class="com.springdemo.Employee">
   <property name="empNumber" value="1001" />
   <property name="empName" value="Mohamed Ibrahim" />

   <!-- Properties -->
   <property name="doj">
     <props>
          <prop key="day">01</prop>
          <prop key="month">06</prop>
          <prop key="year">2001</prop>
     </props>
   </property>

   <!-- Map -->
   <property name="salaryDetails">
     <map>
          <entry key="basicpay" value="10000.0" />
          <entry key="allowances" value="3000.0" />
          <entry key="deductions" value="2000.0" />
     </map>
   </property>

   <!-- List -->
   <property name="knownLanguages">
     <list>
```

```
          <value>English</value>
          <value>Tamil</value>
          <value>Hindi</value>
      </list>
    </property>

    <!-- results in a setSomeSet(java.util.Set) call -->
    <property name="skills">
      <set>
          <value>Java</value>
          <value>C</value>
          <value>Oracle</value>
          <value>MySQL</value>
      </set>
    </property>
  </bean>

</beans>
```

Execute the "*EmployeeApp.java*" application.

```
Emp Number: 1001
Emp Name: Mohamed Ibrahim
DOJ: 01-06-2001
Basic Pay: 10000.0
Allowances: 3000.0
Deductions: 2000.0
Netpay: 11000.0
Known Languages: [English, Tamil, Hindi]
Skills: [Java, C, Oracle, MySQL]
```

1.7 DEFINING 'NULL' VALUES

The tag <null/> is used to define a null value.

```
//File Name: Employee.java
package com.springdemo;

public class Employee {
 private int empNumber;
 private String empName;
```

```
 private Salary salary;

 public void setEmpNumber(int empNumber) {
  this.empNumber = empNumber;
 }

 public void setEmpName(String empName) {
  this.empName = empName;
 }

 public void setSalary(Salary salary) {
  this.salary = salary;
 }

 public String toString() {
  String rStr = "Emp Number: " + empNumber + "\nEmp Name: " + empName;
  rStr += "\nSalary: " + salary;
  return rStr;
 }
}
```

```
//File Name: Salary.java
package com.springdemo;

public class Salary {
 private double basicpay;
 private double allowances;
 private double deductions;
 private double netpay;

 public void setBasicpay(double basicpay) {
  this.basicpay = basicpay;
 }

 public void setAllowances(double allowances) {
  this.allowances = allowances;
 }

 public void setDeductions(double deductions) {
  this.deductions = deductions;
 }
```

```
 public void setNetpay(double netpay) {
  this.netpay = netpay;
 }

 public void calculateNetpay() {
  netpay = basicpay + allowances - deductions;
 }

 public String toString() {
  calculateNetpay();

  String rStr = "\nBasic Pay: " + basicpay;
  rStr += "\nAllowances: " + allowances;
  rStr += "\nDeductions: " + deductions;
  rStr += "\nNetpay: " + netpay;
  return rStr;
 }
}
```

```
//File Name: EmployeeApp.java
package com.springdemo;

import org.springframework.context.ApplicationContext;
import org.springframework.context.support.ClassPathXmlApplicationContext;

public class EmployeeApp {

 public static void main(String args[]) {
  ApplicationContext context =
                new ClassPathXmlApplicationContext("beans.xml");
  Employee employee = (Employee) context.getBean("employee");
  System.out.println(employee);
 }
}
```

The contents of *beans.xml* file:

```
<?xml version="1.0" encoding="UTF-8"?>
<beans xmlns="http://www.springframework.org/schema/beans"
```

```
    xmlns:xsi="http://www.w3.org/2001/XMLSchema-instance"
    xsi:schemaLocation="http://www.springframework.org/schema/beans
    http://www.springframework.org/schema/beans/spring-beans.xsd">

  <bean id="employee" class="com.springdemo.Employee">
   <property name="empNumber" value="1001" />
   <property name="empName"> <null/> </property>
   <property name="salary"> <null/> </property>
  </bean>

</beans>
```

Execute the "*EmployeeApp.java*" application.

```
Emp Number: 1001
Emp Name: null
Salary: null
```

Change the *beans.xml* file as below. It specifies some values to '*salary*' and '*employee*' objects. It uses setter based DI for setting *salary* object.

```
<?xml version="1.0" encoding="UTF-8"?>
<beans xmlns="http://www.springframework.org/schema/beans"
    xmlns:xsi="http://www.w3.org/2001/XMLSchema-instance"
    xsi:schemaLocation="http://www.springframework.org/schema/beans
    http://www.springframework.org/schema/beans/spring-beans.xsd">

  <bean id="employee" class="com.springdemo.Employee">
   <property name="empNumber" value="1001" />
   <property name="empName" value="Mohamed Ibrahim" />
   <property name="salary" ref="salary" />
  </bean>

  <bean id="salary" class="com.springdemo.Salary">
   <property name="basicpay" value="10000.0" />
   <property name="allowances" value="3000.0" />
   <property name="deductions" value="2000.0" />
  </bean>

</beans>
```

Execute the "*EmployeeApp.java*" application.

```
Emp Number: 1001
Emp Name: Mohamed Ibrahim
Salary:
Basic Pay: 10000.0
Allowances: 3000.0
Deductions: 2000.0
Netpay: 11000.0
```

1.8 SPLITTING BEAN DEFINITIONS INTO MULTIPLE XML FILES

We can also specify bean definitions (like *beans.xml* in earlier examples) in multiple XML files, instead of specifying in a single file.

Keep the same *Employee.java* and *Salary.java* as in the previous example. Change the contents of *EmployeeApp.java* as below. This program uses `ClassPathXmlApplicationContext` with array of configuration XML files as its constructor argument.

```
//File Name: EmployeeApp.java
package com.springdemo;

import org.springframework.context.ApplicationContext;
import org.springframework.context.support.ClassPathXmlApplicationContext;

public class EmployeeApp {

 public static void main(String args[]) {
  ApplicationContext context = new ClassPathXmlApplicationContext(
              new String[] { "employeebean.xml", "salarybean.xml" });

  Employee employee = (Employee) context.getBean("employee");
  System.out.println(employee);
 }
}
```

Add the following configuration file (*employeebean.xml*) in "*src*" of the project.

```
<?xml version="1.0" encoding="UTF-8"?>
<beans xmlns="http://www.springframework.org/schema/beans"
   xmlns:xsi="http://www.w3.org/2001/XMLSchema-instance"
   xsi:schemaLocation="http://www.springframework.org/schema/beans
   http://www.springframework.org/schema/beans/spring-beans.xsd">
```

```
   <bean id="employee" class="com.springdemo.Employee">
    <property name="empNumber" value="1001" />
    <property name="empName" value="Mohamed Ibrahim" />
    <property name="salary" ref="salary" />
   </bean>

</beans>
```

And add the following configuration file (*salarybean.xml*) in "*src*" of the project.

```
<?xml version="1.0" encoding="UTF-8"?>
<beans xmlns="http://www.springframework.org/schema/beans"
    xmlns:xsi="http://www.w3.org/2001/XMLSchema-instance"
    xsi:schemaLocation="http://www.springframework.org/schema/beans
    http://www.springframework.org/schema/beans/spring-beans.xsd">

   <bean id="salary" class="com.springdemo.Salary">
    <property name="basicpay" value="10000.0" />
    <property name="allowances" value="3000.0" />
    <property name="deductions" value="2000.0" />
   </bean>

</beans>
```

Execute the "*EmployeeApp.java*", which will produce the result as given below.

```
Emp Number: 1001
Emp Name: Mohamed Ibrahim
Salary:
Basic Pay: 10000.0
Allowances: 3000.0
Deductions: 2000.0
Netpay: 11000.0
```

We can also use `<import>` tag to import bean definition XML files(s) to a XML file. The following example demonstrates how to import beans definition XML contents to another XML file.

Keep the same *Employee.java* and *Salary.java* as in the previous example. Change the contents of *EmployeeApp.java* as below.

```
//File Name: EmployeeApp.java
package com.springdemo;

import org.springframework.context.ApplicationContext;
import org.springframework.context.support.ClassPathXmlApplicationContext;

public class EmployeeApp {

  public static void main(String args[]) {
   ApplicationContext context =
                  new ClassPathXmlApplicationContext("beans.xml");
   Employee employee = (Employee) context.getBean("employee");
   System.out.println(employee);
  }
}
```

Store the following definition in "*salarybean.xml*" file under "*src*" of the project.

```
<?xml version="1.0" encoding="UTF-8"?>
<beans xmlns="http://www.springframework.org/schema/beans"
    xmlns:xsi="http://www.w3.org/2001/XMLSchema-instance"
    xsi:schemaLocation="http://www.springframework.org/schema/beans
    http://www.springframework.org/schema/beans/spring-beans.xsd">

  <bean id="salary" class="com.springdemo.Salary">
   <property name="basicpay" value="10000.0" />
   <property name="allowances" value="3000.0" />
   <property name="deductions" value="2000.0" />
  </bean>

</beans>
```

Store the following definition (which imports the contents of *salarybean.xml*) in "*beans.xml*" file under "*src*" of the project.

```
<?xml version="1.0" encoding="UTF-8"?>
<beans xmlns="http://www.springframework.org/schema/beans"
    xmlns:xsi="http://www.w3.org/2001/XMLSchema-instance"
    xsi:schemaLocation="http://www.springframework.org/schema/beans
    http://www.springframework.org/schema/beans/spring-beans.xsd">
```

```
  <bean id="employee" class="com.springdemo.Employee">
   <property name="empNumber" value="1001" />
   <property name="empName" value="Mohamed Ibrahim" />
   <property name="salary" ref="salary" />
  </bean>

  <import resource="salarybean.xml"/>

</beans>
```

Execute the "*EmployeeApp.java*", which will produce the result as given below.

```
Emp Number: 1001
Emp Name: Mohamed Ibrahim
Salary:
Basic Pay: 10000.0
Allowances: 3000.0
Deductions: 2000.0
Netpay: 11000.0
```

We can also define a bean definition inside another bean definition (nesting of beans) for specifying beans objects to a bean. The above two example application's bean definition can be written as below.

```
<?xml version="1.0" encoding="UTF-8"?>
<beans xmlns="http://www.springframework.org/schema/beans"
   xmlns:xsi="http://www.w3.org/2001/XMLSchema-instance"
   xsi:schemaLocation="http://www.springframework.org/schema/beans
    http://www.springframework.org/schema/beans/spring-beans.xsd">

  <bean id="employee" class="com.springdemo.Employee">
   <property name="empNumber" value="1001" />
   <property name="empName" value="Mohamed Ibrahim" />
   <property name="salary">
     <bean id="salary" class="com.springdemo.Salary">
          <property name="basicpay" value="10000.0" />
          <property name="allowances" value="3000.0" />
          <property name="deductions" value="2000.0" />
     </bean>
   </property>
  </bean>

</beans>
```

1.9 THE "depends-on" BEAN INITIALIZATION

The `depends-on` attribute of the `<bean>` tag in bean definition explicitly forces the dependent beans (specified in `depends-on` attribute by comma, semicolon or whitespace separated) to be initialized before the bean using this `<bean>` tag (current bean) is to be initialized.

```
//File Name: Employee.java
package com.springdemo;

public class Employee {
 private int empNumber;
 private String empName;
 private Salary salary;

 Employee(int empNumber, String empName, Salary salary) {
  this.empNumber = empNumber;
  this.empName = empName;
  this.salary = salary;
 }

 public String toString() {
  String rStr = "Emp Number: " + empNumber + "\nEmp Name: " + empName;
  rStr += "\nSalary: " + salary;
  return rStr;
 }
}
```

```
//File Name: Salary.java
package com.springdemo;

public class Salary {
 private double basicpay;
 private double allowances;
 private double deductions;
 private double netpay;

 Salary(double basicpay, double allowances, double deductions) {
  this.basicpay = basicpay;
  this.allowances = allowances;
  this.deductions = deductions;
 }
```

```
 public void calculateNetpay() {
  netpay = basicpay + allowances - deductions;
 }

 public String toString() {
  calculateNetpay();

  String rStr = "\nBasic Pay: " + basicpay;
  rStr += "\nAllowances: " + allowances;
  rStr += "\nDeductions: " + deductions;
  rStr += "\nNetpay: " + netpay;
  return rStr;
 }
}
```

```
//File Name: EmployeeApp.java
package com.springdemo;

import org.springframework.context.ApplicationContext;
import org.springframework.context.support.ClassPathXmlApplicationContext;

public class EmployeeApp {

 public static void main(String args[]) {
  ApplicationContext context =
                    new ClassPathXmlApplicationContext("beans.xml");
  Employee employee = (Employee) context.getBean("employee");
  System.out.println(employee);
 }
}
```

Store the following *beans.xml* in the "src" directory of the project.

```
<?xml version="1.0" encoding="UTF-8"?>
<beans xmlns="http://www.springframework.org/schema/beans"
   xmlns:xsi="http://www.w3.org/2001/XMLSchema-instance"
   xsi:schemaLocation="http://www.springframework.org/schema/beans
   http://www.springframework.org/schema/beans/spring-beans.xsd">
```

```
<bean id="employee" class="com.springdemo.Employee" depends-on="salary">
  <constructor-arg index="0" value="1001" />
  <constructor-arg index="1" value="Mohamed Ibrahim" />
  <constructor-arg index="2" ref="salary" />
</bean>

<bean id="salary" class="com.springdemo.Salary">
  <constructor-arg index="0" value="10000.0" />
  <constructor-arg index="1" value="3000.0" />
  <constructor-arg index="2" value="2000.0" />
</bean>

</beans>
```

Execute "EmployeeApp.java" application and the result will be as shown below.

```
Emp Number: 1001
Emp Name: Mohamed Ibrahim
Salary:
Basic Pay: 10000.0
Allowances: 3000.0
Deductions: 2000.0
Netpay: 11000.0
```

1.10 AUTOWIRING COLLABORATORS

The Spring container can automatically make relationships (*autowire*) between collaborating beans. That is, Spring container resolves collaborators (other associated beans) automatically for your bean by inspecting the contents of the `ApplicationContext` and no need to specify bean definitions explicitly. However, explicit dependencies in `property` and `constructor-arg` settings (if specified) always override autowiring.

Autowiring Modes:

`no`	No auto-wiring. Default.
`byName`	Auto-wire a bean whose name is same as the property.
`byType`	Auto-wire a bean whose data type is compatible with the property. The corresponding setter method will be executed.
`constructor`	Auto-wire a bean whose date type is compatible with the property constructor argument. The corresponding constructor will be invoked.
`autodetect`	If a default constructor with no argument is found, it will be auto-wired by data type. Otherwise, it will be auto-wired by constructor.

1.10.1 Autowiring Mode: no

This is the default mode and it instructs the Spring container that no autowiring should be performed, bean references must be defined via a `ref` element in the XML bean definition. Even though the *autowire* is set to `"no"` in the XML bean definition, autowiring will be enforced if `@Autowired` annotation is applied. Note that bean definition can be performed using XML based configurations as well as annotation `(@)` based configurations.

1.10.2 Autowiring Mode: byName

It instructs the Spring container to autowire by property name. That is, Spring container looks for a bean with the same name as the property that needs to be autowired. The property should have its setter method `(set<propertyName>())`.

```
//File Name: Employee.java
package com.springdemo;

public class Employee {
 private int empNumber;
 private String empName;
 private Salary salary;

 Employee() {
  System.out.println("Employee() constructor called");
 }

 Employee(Salary salary) {
  System.out.println("Employee(Salary salary) constructor called");
  this.salary = salary;
 }

 public void setEmpNumber(int empNumber) {
  this.empNumber = empNumber;
 }

 public void setEmpName(String empName) {
  this.empName = empName;
 }

 public void setSalary(Salary salary) {
  System.out.println("setSalary method called");
  this.salary = salary;
 }
```

```
  public String toString() {
   String rStr = "Emp Number: " + empNumber + "\nEmp Name: " + empName;
   rStr += "\nSalary: " + salary;
   return rStr;
  }
}
```

```
//File Name: Salary.java
package com.springdemo;

public class Salary {
 private double basicpay;
 private double allowances;
 private double deductions;
 private double netpay;

 Salary(double basicpay, double allowances, double deductions) {
  this.basicpay = basicpay;
  this.allowances = allowances;
  this.deductions = deductions;
 }

 public void calculateNetpay() {
  netpay = basicpay + allowances - deductions;
 }

 public String toString() {
  calculateNetpay();

  String rStr = "\nBasic Pay: " + basicpay;
  rStr += "\nAllowances: " + allowances;
  rStr += "\nDeductions: " + deductions;
  rStr += "\nNetpay: " + netpay;
  return rStr;
 }
}
```

```
//File Name: EmployeeApp.java
package com.springdemo;
```

```
import org.springframework.context.ApplicationContext;
import org.springframework.context.support.ClassPathXmlApplicationContext;

public class EmployeeApp {

 public static void main(String args[]) {
  ApplicationContext context =
                 new ClassPathXmlApplicationContext("beans.xml");
  Employee employee = (Employee) context.getBean("employee");
  System.out.println(employee);
 }
}
```

Store the following *beans.xml* in the "src" directory of the project.

```
<?xml version="1.0" encoding="UTF-8"?>
<beans xmlns="http://www.springframework.org/schema/beans"
   xmlns:xsi="http://www.w3.org/2001/XMLSchema-instance"
   xsi:schemaLocation="http://www.springframework.org/schema/beans
   http://www.springframework.org/schema/beans/spring-beans.xsd">

  <bean id="employee" class="com.springdemo.Employee" autowire="byName" >
   <property name="empNumber" value="1001" />
   <property name="empName" value="Mohamed Ibrahim" />
  </bean>

  <bean id="salary" class="com.springdemo.Salary">
   <constructor-arg index="0" value="10000.0" />
   <constructor-arg index="1" value="3000.0" />
   <constructor-arg index="2" value="2000.0" />
  </bean>

</beans>
```

Execute "EmployeeApp.java" application and the result will be as shown below.

```
Employee() constructor called
setSalary method called
Emp Number: 1001
Emp Name: Mohamed Ibrahim
```

```
Salary:
Basic Pay: 10000.0
Allowances: 3000.0
Deductions: 2000.0
Netpay: 11000.0
```

In the above case, autowiring is performed for the "*salary*" object in the Employee bean by *Name*. This autowiring mode is specified in the "*employee*" bean definition and the "*salary*" object is defined in the bean definition file.

Now, we will change the Salary object name in Employee bean, and test whether autowiring will be performed or not. Change the "*salary*" field in Employee class to "*empSalary*" and adjust other setting in the file, and keep other files as they are.

The Employee.java file looks as shown below.

```
//File Name: Employee.java
package com.springdemo;

public class Employee {
 private int empNumber;
 private String empName;
 private Salary empSalary;

 Employee() {
  System.out.println("Employee() constructor called");
 }

 Employee(Salary salary) {
  System.out.println("Employee(Salary salary) constructor called");
  this.empSalary = salary;
 }

 public void setEmpNumber(int empNumber) {
  this.empNumber = empNumber;
 }

 public void setEmpName(String empName) {
  this.empName = empName;
 }

 public void setEmpSalary(Salary salary) {
  System.out.println("setEmpSalary method called");
  this.empSalary = salary;
 }
```

```
    public String toString() {
     String rStr = "Emp Number: " + empNumber + "\nEmp Name: " + empName;
     rStr += "\nSalary: " + empSalary;
     return rStr;
    }
}
```

Execute the main application and observe the result that no autowiring *byName* is applied. That is *setEmpSalary()* method is not called since there is no *"empSalary"* object found in the Spring Application Context (no *"empSalary"* object in bean definition in this example. Objects can be created in Spring Application Context in other ways too). The result of the above application is given below for your reference.

```
Employee() constructor called
Emp Number: 1001
Emp Name: Mohamed Ibrahim
Salary: null
```

In our example application, to make autowiring *byName* for *'empSalary'*, we have to define a new instance for the *'empSalary'* in the *beans.xml*; otherwise we have to change the *"salary"* object into *"empSalary"* in the *beans.xml*. A simple way to do is, using aliases.

Aliases create duplicate names (alias) for an object defined in the bean definition file. The following example creates an alias name *"empSalary"* for the defined object *"salary"*.

```
<alias name="salary" alias="empSalary"/>
```

Add the above alias definition in the *beans.xml* file and execute the main application. Now, autowiring will be applied for the object *"empSalary"*.

```
Employee() constructor called
setEmpSalary method called
Emp Number: 1001
Emp Name: Mohamed Ibrahim
Salary:
Basic Pay: 10000.0
Allowances: 3000.0
Deductions: 2000.0
Netpay: 11000.0
```

1.10.3 Autowiring Mode: byType

It instructs the Spring container to autowire by object type. That is, allows a property to be autowired if *exactly one* bean of the property type exists in the Spring container.

Change the content of *Employee.java* as below.

```
//File Name: Employee.java
package com.springdemo;

public class Employee {
 private int empNumber;
 private String empName;
 private Salary empSalary;

 Employee() {
  System.out.println("Employee() constructor called");
 }

 Employee(Salary salary) {
  System.out.println("Employee(Salary salary) constructor called");
  this.empSalary = salary;
 }

 public void setEmpNumber(int empNumber) {
  this.empNumber = empNumber;
 }

 public void setEmpName(String empName) {
  this.empName = empName;
 }

 public void setEmpSalary(Salary salary) {
  System.out.println("setEmpSalary method called");
  this.empSalary = salary;
 }

 public String toString() {
  String rStr = "Emp Number: " + empNumber + "\nEmp Name: " + empName;
  rStr += "\nSalary: " + empSalary;
  return rStr;
 }
}
```

Change the contents of *beans.xml* as below.

```
<?xml version="1.0" encoding="UTF-8"?>
<beans xmlns="http://www.springframework.org/schema/beans"
  xmlns:xsi="http://www.w3.org/2001/XMLSchema-instance"
  xsi:schemaLocation="http://www.springframework.org/schema/beans
  http://www.springframework.org/schema/beans/spring-beans.xsd">

  <bean id="employee" class="com.springdemo.Employee" autowire="byType" >
    <property name="empNumber" value="1001" />
    <property name="empName" value="Mohamed Ibrahim" />
  </bean>

  <bean id="salary" class="com.springdemo.Salary">
    <constructor-arg index="0" value="10000.0" />
    <constructor-arg index="1" value="3000.0" />
    <constructor-arg index="2" value="2000.0" />
  </bean>

</beans>
```

Execute the main application and the result will be as below.

```
Employee() constructor called
setEmpSalary method called
Emp Number: 1001
Emp Name: Mohamed Ibrahim
Salary:
Basic Pay: 10000.0
Allowances: 3000.0
Deductions: 2000.0
Netpay: 11000.0
```

Observe that the only one bean object *"salary"* defined in *beans.xml* file is autowired to *"employee"* object *byType*.

1.10.4 Autowiring Mode: constructor

It instructs the Spring container to autowire by constructor type. That is, autowire a bean whose date type is compatible with the property constructor argument. It is analogous to *byType* autowiring, but applies to constructor arguments.

Keep all the files as in the above example, and change the *beans.xml* file as below to set *constructor* based autowiring.

```
<?xml version="1.0" encoding="UTF-8"?>
<beans xmlns="http://www.springframework.org/schema/beans"
  xmlns:xsi="http://www.w3.org/2001/XMLSchema-instance"
```

```
xsi:schemaLocation="http://www.springframework.org/schema/beans
http://www.springframework.org/schema/beans/spring-beans.xsd">

<bean id="employee" class="com.springdemo.Employee" autowire="constructor">
  <property name="empNumber" value="1001" />
  <property name="empName" value="Mohamed Ibrahim" />
</bean>

  <bean id="salary" class="com.springdemo.Salary">
  <constructor-arg index="0" value="10000.0" />
  <constructor-arg index="1" value="3000.0" />
  <constructor-arg index="2" value="2000.0" />
  </bean>

</beans>
```

Execute the main application and observe from the result that corresponding constructor is invoked for *Salary* object while creating *Employee* object. The result of the application is given below for your reference.

```
Employee(Salary salary) constructor called
Emp Number: 1001
Emp Name: Mohamed Ibrahim
Salary:
Basic Pay: 10000.0
Allowances: 3000.0
Deductions: 2000.0
Netpay: 11000.0
```

1.11 BEAN SCOPES

The scope (range and time to live) of a bean can be defined in the bean definition. The types of supported scopes in Spring container are given below.

singleton	It scopes a single bean definition to exactly single object instance in the Spring container. That is, the Spring container creates exactly one instance of the object defined by the bean definition. This is the default scope also.
prototype	It scopes a single bean definition to any number of object instances in the Spring container. That is, Spring container creates a new instance of the bean every time a request for that bean is made.

request	It scopes a single bean definition to the lifecycle of a single HTTP request. This scope is valid in web-aware Spring ApplicationContext.
session	It scopes a single bean definition to the lifecycle of an HTTP session. This scope is valid in web-aware Spring ApplicationContext.
global session	It scopes a single bean definition to the lifecycle of a global HTTP Session. The global session is used in Portlet context; many portlet applications run on a single portal and this global session applies to all the portlets. This scope is valid in web-aware Spring ApplicationContext.

Example: singleton scope

This example creates three *Employee* objects, and all these three objects share the common *Salary* object (singleton scope). If any one the *Employee* object changes the state of *Salary* object, then change of value will be reflected to other *Employee* objects also.

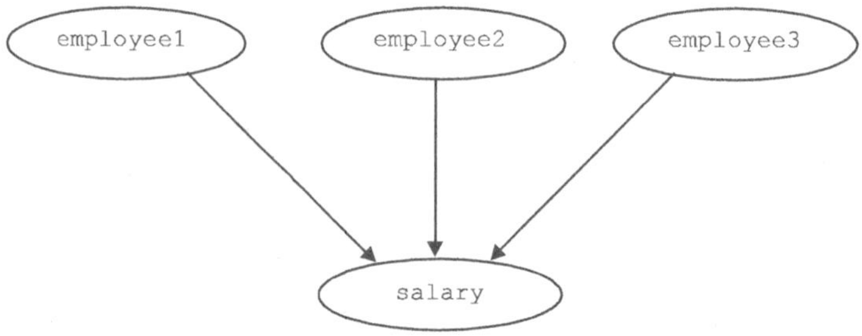


```
//File Name: Employee.java
package com.springdemo;

public class Employee {
 private int empNumber;
 private String empName;
 private Salary salary;

 public void setEmpNumber(int empNumber) {
  this.empNumber = empNumber;
 }

 public void setEmpName(String empName) {
  this.empName = empName;
 }

 public Salary getSalary() {
  return salary;
 }
```

```
public void setSalary(Salary salary) {
 this.salary = salary;
}

public String toString() {
 String rStr = "Emp Number: " + empNumber + "\nEmp Name: " + empName;
 rStr += "\nSalary: " + salary;
 return rStr;
}
}
```

```
//File Name: Salary.java
package com.springdemo;

public class Salary {
 private double basicpay;
 private double allowances;
 private double deductions;
 private double netpay;

 Salary(double basicpay, double allowances, double deductions) {
  this.basicpay = basicpay;
  this.allowances = allowances;
  this.deductions = deductions;
 }

 public void setAllowances(double allowances) {
  this.allowances = allowances;
 }

 public void calculateNetpay() {
  netpay = basicpay + allowances - deductions;
 }

 public String toString() {
  calculateNetpay();

  String rStr = "\nBasic Pay: " + basicpay;
  rStr += "\nAllowances: " + allowances;
  rStr += "\nDeductions: " + deductions;
```

```
  rStr += "\nNetpay: " + netpay;
  return rStr;
 }
}
```

```
//File Name: EmployeeApp.java
package com.springdemo;

import org.springframework.context.ApplicationContext;
import org.springframework.context.support.ClassPathXmlApplicationContext;

public class EmployeeApp {

 public static void main(String args[]) {
  ApplicationContext context =
                new ClassPathXmlApplicationContext("beans.xml");
  Employee employee1 = (Employee) context.getBean("employee1");
  System.out.println(employee1 + "\n");

  Employee employee2 = (Employee) context.getBean("employee2");
  employee2.getSalary().setAllowances(4000.0);
  System.out.println(employee2 + "\n");

  Employee employee3 = (Employee) context.getBean("employee3");
  System.out.println(employee3);
 }
}
```

```
<?xml version="1.0" encoding="UTF-8"?>
<beans xmlns="http://www.springframework.org/schema/beans"
   xmlns:xsi="http://www.w3.org/2001/XMLSchema-instance"
   xsi:schemaLocation="http://www.springframework.org/schema/beans
   http://www.springframework.org/schema/beans/spring-beans.xsd">

  <bean id="employee1" class="com.springdemo.Employee" >
   <property name="empNumber" value="1001" />
   <property name="empName" value="Mohamed Ibrahim" />
   <property name="salary" ref="salary" />
  </bean>
```

```
<bean id="employee2" class="com.springdemo.Employee" >
 <property name="empNumber" value="1002" />
 <property name="empName" value="Keerthi Kumar" />
 <property name="salary" ref="salary" />
</bean>

<bean id="employee3" class="com.springdemo.Employee" >
 <property name="empNumber" value="1003" />
 <property name="empName" value="John" />
 <property name="salary" ref="salary" />
</bean>

<bean id="salary" class="com.springdemo.Salary" scope="singleton" >
 <constructor-arg index="0" value="10000.0" />
 <constructor-arg index="1" value="3000.0" />
 <constructor-arg index="2" value="2000.0" />
</bean>

</beans>
```

Execute the main application, and the result is shown below.

```
Emp Number: 1001
Emp Name: Mohamed Ibrahim
Salary:
Basic Pay: 10000.0
Allowances: 3000.0
Deductions: 2000.0
Netpay: 11000.0

Emp Number: 1002
Emp Name: Keerthi Kumar
Salary:
Basic Pay: 10000.0
Allowances: 4000.0
Deductions: 2000.0
Netpay: 12000.0

Emp Number: 1003
Emp Name: John
Salary:
```

```
Basic Pay: 10000.0
Allowances: 4000.0
Deductions: 2000.0
Netpay: 12000.0
```

Observe from the result that the object *employee2* changed the value of *allowances* field of *Salary* object, and the new value is present while accessing *employee3* object.

Example: prototype scope

This example creates three *Employee* objects, and each object has its own copy of *Salary* object (prototype scope).

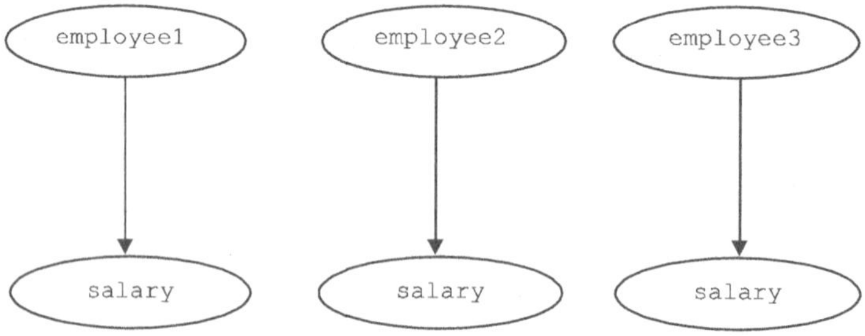

Keep all the files as in the previous example and change the scope of "*salary*" object into "prototype".

```
<bean id="salary" class="com.springdemo.Salary" scope="prototype" >
 <constructor-arg index="0" value="10000.0" />
 <constructor-arg index="1" value="3000.0" />
 <constructor-arg index="2" value="2000.0" />
</bean>
```

Then, the result of the application is as shown below.

```
Emp Number: 1001
Emp Name: Mohamed Ibrahim
Salary:
Basic Pay: 10000.0
Allowances: 3000.0
Deductions: 2000.0
Netpay: 11000.0

Emp Number: 1002
Emp Name: Keerthi Kumar
Salary:
```

```
Basic Pay: 10000.0
Allowances: 4000.0
Deductions: 2000.0
Netpay: 12000.0

Emp Number: 1003
Emp Name: John
Salary:
Basic Pay: 10000.0
Allowances: 3000.0
Deductions: 2000.0
Netpay: 11000.0
```

1.12 LIFECYCLE CALLBACKS

These callback methods are automatically called by the Spring container when appropriate events are occurred.

Initialization Callbacks: The `org.springframework.beans.factory.InitializingBean` interface allows a bean to perform initialization work after all necessary properties on the bean have been set by the container. The `InitializingBean` interface has the following method, which should be overridden by the implementing class.

```
void afterPropertiesSet() throws Exception
```

Alternatively, we can specify a POJO initialization method in a bean class. Specify the name of the method (which should not return/accept any value, i.e. void no-argument method) in the `init-method` attribute of the `<bean>` element, in case of XML based bean definition.

Destruction Callbacks: The `org.springframework.beans.factory.DisposableBean` interface allows a bean to get a callback when the Spring container, which is containing the bean object, is destroyed. The `DisposableBean` interface has the following method, which should be overridden by the implementing class.

```
void destroy() throws Exception
```

Alternatively, we can specify a destruction method in `destroy-method` attribute of `<bean>` element, in case of XML based bean definition (as like `init-method` attribute specifies initialization method).

A note on Shutdown Hook: A shutdown hook is simply a thread that is registered with the JVM and run just before the JVM shuts down. A Shutdown hook should be registered with the current machine JVM for Java standalone applications (non-web applications) which uses Spring IoC container, which ensures destroy callbacks called perfectly. To register a shutdown hook, call the `registerShutdownHook()` method that is declared on the `AbstractApplicationContext` class.

```
//File Name: Employee.java
package com.springdemo;

import org.springframework.beans.factory.DisposableBean;
import org.springframework.beans.factory.InitializingBean;

public class Employee implements InitializingBean, DisposableBean {
 private int empNumber;
 private String empName;

 Employee() {
  System.out.println("Employee() constructor is called");
 }

 Employee(int empNumber) {
  System.out.println("Employee(int empNumber) constructor is called");
  this.empNumber = empNumber;
 }

 public void setEmpName(String empName) {
  System.out.println("setEmpName(String empName) method is called");
  this.empName = empName;
 }

 @Override
 public void afterPropertiesSet() throws Exception {
  System.out.println("afterPropertiesSet() method is called");
 }

 @Override
 public void destroy() throws Exception {
  System.out.println("destroy() method is called");
 }

 public String toString() {
  return "Emp Number: " + empNumber + "\nEmp Name: " + empName;
 }
}
```

```
//File Name: EmployeeApp.java
package com.springdemo;

import org.springframework.context.support.AbstractApplicationContext;
import org.springframework.context.support.ClassPathXmlApplicationContext;

public class EmployeeApp {

 public static void main(String args[]) {
  AbstractApplicationContext context =
                  new ClassPathXmlApplicationContext("beans.xml");
  context.registerShutdownHook();
  Employee employee = (Employee) context.getBean("employee");
  System.out.println(employee);

 // Shutdown hook will be called just prior to the end of this application.
  // so that the destroy() method(s) will be called.
 }
}
```

Store the following *beans.xml* in the "src" directory of the project.

```
<?xml version="1.0" encoding="UTF-8"?>
<beans xmlns="http://www.springframework.org/schema/beans"
  xmlns:xsi="http://www.w3.org/2001/XMLSchema-instance"
  xsi:schemaLocation="http://www.springframework.org/schema/beans
  http://www.springframework.org/schema/beans/spring-beans.xsd">

  <bean id="employee" class="com.springdemo.Employee" >
   <constructor-arg name="empNumber" value="1001" />
   <property name="empName" value="Mohamed Ibrahim" />
  </bean>

</beans>
```

Execute the main application, and the result is shown below.

```
Employee(int empNumber) constructor is called
setEmpName(String empName) method is called
afterPropertiesSet() method is called
Emp Number: 1001
Emp Name: Mohamed Ibrahim
destroy() method is called
```

The above application uses `InitializingBean` and `DisposableBean` interfaces, which are provided by Spring Framework. The same application can be written as below using bean configuration attributes (`init-method`, `destroy-method`), which are not dependent on those two Spring provided interfaces; of course, Spring container is needed to execute this modified application too.

To be meaningful and simple, I named the initialisation method as '*init*' and destruction method as '*destroy*'. However, you can use any method name allowed in Java.

```
//File Name: Employee.java
package com.springdemo;

public class Employee {
 private int empNumber;
 private String empName;

 Employee() {
  System.out.println("Employee() constructor is called");
 }

 Employee(int empNumber) {
  System.out.println("Employee(int empNumber) constructor is called");
  this.empNumber = empNumber;
 }

 public void setEmpName(String empName) {
  System.out.println("setEmpName(String empName) method is called");
  this.empName = empName;
 }

 public void init() {
  System.out.println("init() method is called");
 }

 public void destroy() {
  System.out.println("destroy() method is called");
 }

 public String toString() {
  return "Emp Number: " + empNumber + "\nEmp Name: " + empName;
 }
}
```

```
//File Name: EmployeeApp.java
package com.springdemo;

import org.springframework.context.support.AbstractApplicationContext;
import org.springframework.context.support.ClassPathXmlApplicationContext;

public class EmployeeApp {

  public static void main(String args[]) {
   AbstractApplicationContext context =
                     new ClassPathXmlApplicationContext("beans.xml");
    context.registerShutdownHook();
    Employee employee = (Employee) context.getBean("employee");
    System.out.println(employee);

  // Shutdown hook will be called just prior to the end of this application.
   // so that the destroy() method(s) will be called.
  }
}
```

Store the following *beans.xml* in the "src" directory of the project.

```
<?xml version="1.0" encoding="UTF-8"?>
<beans xmlns="http://www.springframework.org/schema/beans"
   xmlns:xsi="http://www.w3.org/2001/XMLSchema-instance"
   xsi:schemaLocation="http://www.springframework.org/schema/beans
   http://www.springframework.org/schema/beans/spring-beans.xsd">

   <bean id="employee" class="com.springdemo.Employee"
                   init-method="init" destroy-method="destroy" >
    <constructor-arg name="empNumber" value="1001" />
    <property name="empName" value="Mohamed Ibrahim" />
   </bean>

</beans>
```

Execute the main application, and the result is shown below.

```
Employee(int empNumber) constructor is called
setEmpName(String empName) method is called
```

```
init() method is called
Emp Number: 1001
Emp Name: Mohamed Ibrahim
destroy() method is called
```

1.13 ANNOTATION-BASED CONTAINER CONFIGURATION

In the previous examples, we used XML based configuration for defining beans. There is another method for defining beans, which is called Annotation based configuration. Annotations are meta-data information applied to Java elements such as class, interfaces, and fields. These annotations are very easy to use (compared to XML based configuration) and the annotated information are stored in byte code form in a compiled application (results in fast while processing).

Spring can accommodate both styles and even allows mixing them together. Annotation injection is performed before XML injection. So, the later configuration will override the former if *both* approaches are applied for same properties.

Use the following bean definition for applications, those use annotation based configuration. Note that new namespaces are added in global <beans> element.

```
<?xml version="1.0" encoding="UTF-8"?>
<beans xmlns="http://www.springframework.org/schema/beans"
   xmlns:xsi="http://www.w3.org/2001/XMLSchema-instance"
   xmlns:context="http://www.springframework.org/schema/context"
   xsi:schemaLocation="http://www.springframework.org/schema/beans
   http://www.springframework.org/schema/beans/spring-beans-3.0.xsd
   http://www.springframework.org/schema/context
  http://www.springframework.org/schema/context/spring-context-3.0.xsd">

  <context:annotation-config/>
</beans>
```

The element <context:annotation-config/> looks for annotations on beans in the same application context in which it is defined.

1.13.1 @Required –Field should be Populated

This annotation applies to bean property setter methods. This annotation simply indicates that the corresponding bean property must be populated at configuration time, through XML based configuration (value for property set in a bean definition) or autowiring.

```
//File Name: Employee.java
package com.springdemo;

import org.springframework.beans.factory.annotation.Required;
```

```
public class Employee {
 private int empNumber;
 private String empName;

 public void setEmpNumber(int empNumber) {
  this.empNumber = empNumber;
 }

 @Required
 public void setEmpName(String empName) {
  this.empName = empName;
 }

 public String toString() {
  return "Emp Number: " + empNumber + "\nEmp Name: " + empName;
 }
}
```

```
//File Name: EmployeeApp.java
package com.springdemo;

import org.springframework.context.support.AbstractApplicationContext;
import org.springframework.context.support.ClassPathXmlApplicationContext;

public class EmployeeApp {

 public static void main(String args[]) {
  AbstractApplicationContext context =
                     new ClassPathXmlApplicationContext("beans.xml");
  Employee employee = (Employee) context.getBean("employee");
  System.out.println(employee);
 }
}
```

Store the following *beans.xml* in the “src” directory of the project.

```
<?xml version="1.0" encoding="UTF-8"?>
<beans xmlns="http://www.springframework.org/schema/beans"
      xmlns:xsi="http://www.w3.org/2001/XMLSchema-instance"
      xmlns:context="http://www.springframework.org/schema/context"
```

```
      xsi:schemaLocation="http://www.springframework.org/schema/beans
      http://www.springframework.org/schema/beans/spring-beans-3.0.xsd
      http://www.springframework.org/schema/context
   http://www.springframework.org/schema/context/spring-context-3.0.xsd">

   <context:annotation-config />

   <bean id="employee" class="com.springdemo.Employee" >
    <property name="empNumber" value="1001" />
    <property name="empName" value="Mohamed Ibrahim" />
   </bean>

</beans>
```

Execute the main application, and the result is shown below.

```
Emp Number: 1001
Emp Name: Mohamed Ibrahim
```

Now, we will check the behaviour of this `@Required` annotation. Take off the property element, which supplies value for "*empName*" attribute. Keep the bean definition for "*employee*" object as below.

```
   <bean id="employee" class="com.springdemo.Employee" >
    <property name="empNumber" value="1001" />
   </bean>
```

Execute the main application. Then an exception will be raised as shown below.

```
Exception in thread "main"
org.springframework.beans.factory.BeanCreationException:
Error creating bean with name 'employee' defined in class path resource
[beans.xml]: Initialization of bean failed; nested exception is
org.springframework.beans.factory.BeanInitializationException:
Property 'empName' is required for bean 'employee'
...
...
Caused by: org.springframework.beans.factory.BeanInitializationException:
Property 'empName' is required for bean 'employee'
...
...
```

1.13.2 @Autowired –Autowiring Collaborators

The Spring container can automatically make relationships (*autowire*) between collaborating beans. This `@Autowired` annotation is an alternative to XML based autowire configuration, demonstrated in earlier sections.

We can apply the `@Autowired` annotation to (i) setter methods, (ii) arbitrary member methods (not setter methods) with single or multiple arguments, (iii) constructors, and (iv) fields (data members)

This `@Autowired` annotation has a property named '`required`', which is to indicate the value being injected is mandatory or optional. It is default to true (mandatory). By default, the `@Autowired` will perform the dependency checking to make sure the property has been wired properly. When Spring cannot find a matching bean to wire, it will throw an exception. To avoid it, this '`required`' option with the value 'false' should be used.

It is not mandatory to have setter methods for the fields which are declared `@Autowired`. This `@Autowired` annotation can be applied to interfaces also.

1.13.2.1 Autowiring a field

The following application demonstrates how to apply `@Autowired` to a filed in a class.

```
//File Name: Employee.java
package com.springdemo;

import org.springframework.beans.factory.annotation.Autowired;

public class Employee {
 private int empNumber;
 private String empName;

 @Autowired
 private Salary salary;

 public void setEmpNumber(int empNumber) {
  this.empNumber = empNumber;
 }

 public void setEmpName(String empName) {
  this.empName = empName;
 }

 public String toString() {
  String rStr = "Emp Number: " + empNumber + "\nEmp Name: " + empName;
  rStr += "\nSalary: " + salary;
  return rStr;
 }
}
```

```
//File Name: Salary.java
package com.springdemo;

public class Salary {
 private double basicpay;
 private double allowances;
 private double deductions;
 private double netpay;

 Salary(double basicpay, double allowances, double deductions) {
  this.basicpay = basicpay;
  this.allowances = allowances;
  this.deductions = deductions;
 }

 public void calculateNetpay() {
  netpay = basicpay + allowances - deductions;
 }

 public String toString() {
  calculateNetpay();

  String rStr = "\nBasic Pay: " + basicpay;
  rStr += "\nAllowances: " + allowances;
  rStr += "\nDeductions: " + deductions;
  rStr += "\nNetpay: " + netpay;
  return rStr;
 }
}
```

```
//File Name: EmployeeApp.java
package com.springdemo;

import org.springframework.context.support.AbstractApplicationContext;
import org.springframework.context.support.ClassPathXmlApplicationContext;

public class EmployeeApp {

 public static void main(String args[]) {
  AbstractApplicationContext context =
                      new ClassPathXmlApplicationContext("beans.xml");
```

```
    Employee employee = (Employee) context.getBean("employee");
    System.out.println(employee);
  }
}
```

Store the following *beans.xml* in the "src" directory of the project.

```
<?xml version="1.0" encoding="UTF-8"?>
<beans xmlns="http://www.springframework.org/schema/beans"
    xmlns:xsi="http://www.w3.org/2001/XMLSchema-instance"
    xmlns:context="http://www.springframework.org/schema/context"
    xsi:schemaLocation="http://www.springframework.org/schema/beans
      http://www.springframework.org/schema/beans/spring-beans-3.0.xsd
        http://www.springframework.org/schema/context
  http://www.springframework.org/schema/context/spring-context-3.0.xsd">

  <context:annotation-config />

  <bean id="employee" class="com.springdemo.Employee" >
   <property name="empNumber" value="1001" />
   <property name="empName" value="Mohamed Ibrahim" />
  </bean>

  <bean id="salary" class="com.springdemo.Salary">
   <constructor-arg index="0" value="10000.0" />
   <constructor-arg index="1" value="3000.0" />
   <constructor-arg index="2" value="2000.0" />
  </bean>

</beans>
```

Note that we did not specify value for property "*salary*" in defining "*employee*". It will be autowired.

```
Emp Number: 1001
Emp Name: Mohamed Ibrahim
Salary:
Basic Pay: 10000.0
Allowances: 3000.0
Deductions: 2000.0
Netpay: 11000.0
```

As said earlier, by default the `@Autowired's required` property is set to true. That is, Spring container will expect the candidate instance that should be available in the container for the @Autowired one. A bean instance can be made available in the container using XML based bean configuration or @Autowired. In the above example, @Autowired is applied for '*salary*' object and a bean named with '*salary*' is defined in *beans.xml* file. Now, remove the bean definition of '*salary*' and run the main program.

Remove the following section in 'beans.xml'.

```
<bean id="salary" class="com.springdemo.Salary">
  <constructor-arg index="0" value="10000.0" />
  <constructor-arg index="1" value="3000.0" />
  <constructor-arg index="2" value="2000.0" />
</bean>
```

Then, exception will be thrown as shown below.

```
Exception in thread "main" org.springframework.beans.factory.
BeanCreationException:
Error creating bean with name 'employee':
Injection of autowired dependencies failed; nested exception is
org.springframework.beans.factory.BeanCreationException:
Could not autowire field: private com.springdemo.Salary
com.springdemo.Employee.salary; nested exception is
org.springframework.beans.factory.NoSuchBeanDefinitionException:
No matching bean of type [com.springdemo.Salary] found for dependency:
expected at least 1 bean which qualifies as autowire candidate for this
dependency.
...
...
Caused by: org.springframework.beans.factory.BeanCreationException:
Could not autowire field: private com.springdemo.Salary com.springdemo.
Employee.salary; nested exception is org.springframework.beans.
factory.NoSuchBeanDefinitionException:
No matching bean of type [com.springdemo.Salary] found for dependency:
expected at least 1 bean which qualifies as autowire candidate for this
dependency.
...
...
```

Now, set the `required` property of `@Autowired` to false and apply it to *salary* field of *Employee* bean.

```
@Autowired(required=false)
private Salary salary;
```

Execute the application; of course *'null'* value will be applied to *salary* field.

```
Emp Number: 1001
Emp Name: Mohamed Ibrahim
Salary: null
```

In XML based bean configuration, we can disable autowiring by setting the value "no" to autowire attribute.

For example,

The following configuration disables autowiring on *Employee* class.

```
<bean id="employee" class="com.springdemo.Employee" autowire="no">
```

However, if `@Autowired` annotation is applied on a bean, then autowiring will be performed even through *autowire* attribute is set to *"no"* in its XML based configuration.

1.13.2.2 Autowiring an arbitrary method

We can instruct Spring container to apply autowiring to arbitrary methods (not setter methods) with one or more arguments.

Change the content of *Employee.java* as below.

```
//File Name: Employee.java
package com.springdemo;

import org.springframework.beans.factory.annotation.Autowired;

public class Employee {
 private int empNumber;
 private String empName;
 private Salary empSalary;

 public void setEmpNumber(int empNumber) {
  this.empNumber = empNumber;
 }

 public void setEmpName(String empName) {
  this.empName = empName;
 }

 @Autowired
 public void displaySalaryDetails(Salary sal) {
  System.out.println("displaySalaryDetails() method is called");
  empSalary = sal;
 }
```

```
  public String toString() {
   String rStr = "Emp Number: " + empNumber + "\nEmp Name: " + empName;
   rStr += empSalary;
   return rStr;
  }
}
```

Change the beans definition (*beans.xml*) as below.

```
<?xml version="1.0" encoding="UTF-8"?>
<beans xmlns="http://www.springframework.org/schema/beans"
  xmlns:xsi="http://www.w3.org/2001/XMLSchema-instance"
     xmlns:context="http://www.springframework.org/schema/context"
  xsi:schemaLocation="http://www.springframework.org/schema/beans
    http://www.springframework.org/schema/beans/spring-beans-3.0.xsd
  http://www.springframework.org/schema/context
  http://www.springframework.org/schema/context/spring-context-3.0.xsd">

  <context:annotation-config />

  <bean id="employee" class="com.springdemo.Employee" >
   <property name="empNumber" value="1001" />
   <property name="empName" value="Mohamed Ibrahim" />
  </bean>

  <bean id="salary" class="com.springdemo.Salary">
   <constructor-arg index="0" value="10000.0" />
   <constructor-arg index="1" value="3000.0" />
   <constructor-arg index="2" value="2000.0" />
  </bean>

</beans>
```

Execute the application, and observe from the result that autowiring is applied for the *salary* object. The result of this application is given below for your reference.

```
displaySalaryDetails() method is called
Emp Number: 1001
Emp Name: Mohamed Ibrahim
Basic Pay: 10000.0
Allowances: 3000.0
Deductions: 2000.0
Netpay: 11000.0
```

1.14 JSR-330 (DEPENDENCY INJECTION FOR JAVA) ANNOTATIONS

JSR-330 is a Java Specification Request, specifies 'Dependency Injection for Java' and this JSR is a part of the Java EE 6 Platform.

Set JSR-330 library jar in CLASSPATH for using these Dependency Injection for Java in your applications. To have JSR 330 library, download the whole Java EE 6 API (javaee-api-6.0.jar) or download only Java Inject API (javax-inject) from the Internet (available in Maven Repository *http://mvnrepository.com* also). If you downloaded the Spring framework with all dependencies option, then you can find this Javax-Inject jar file (com.springsource.javax.inject-1.0.0.jar). To make it available with the project, select the project in Eclipse IDE (in Project Explorer) ⟶ Right Click ⟶ Properties ⟶ Add External JARs... (choose according to your settings) ⟶ Specify the JAR file ⟶ OK.

1.14.1 @Inject –Equivalent to @Autowired

This JSR 330's `@Inject` annotation can be used as an alternative to Spring's `@Autowired` annotation. The difference is that `@Inject` does not have `'required'` attribute, which is available in `@Autowired`. That is, we can not set required as optional with `@Inject`.

Keep the same configuration as in the previous example, and we will change the *Employee.java* as below which uses `@Inject` for constructor based DI. This example also demonstrates how auto-wiring is applied to a constructor. This program can also be written using `@Autowired` annotation instead of `@Inject`.

```
//File Name: Employee.java
package com.springdemo;

import javax.inject.Inject;

public class Employee {
 private int empNumber;
 private String empName;
 private Salary empSalary;

 @Inject
 Employee(Salary sal) {
  System.out.println("Employee(Salary sal) constructor is called");
  empSalary = sal;
 }

 public void setEmpNumber(int empNumber) {
  this.empNumber = empNumber;
 }

 public void setEmpName(String empName) {
```

```
    this.empName = empName;
  }

  public String toString() {
    String rStr = "Emp Number: " + empNumber + "\nEmp Name: " + empName;
    rStr += empSalary;
    return rStr;
  }
}
```

Execute the main application and the result will be as shown below.

```
Employee(Salary sal) constructor is called
Emp Number: 1001
Emp Name: Mohamed Ibrahim
Basic Pay: 10000.0
Allowances: 3000.0
Deductions: 2000.0
Netpay: 11000.0
```

1.14.2 @Qualifier –Specifying specific objects for auto-wiring

Auto-wiring is applied by Spring container when a collaborating (candidate) object is present in the container for the `@Autowired` field (to which auto-wiring is to be applied). When no collaborating object is present, then exception will be raised if 'required' is not set to false. Suppose you want to specify which object is to be auto-wired to which filed, when more than one collaborating objects present in the container.

One way to accomplish this is with Spring's `@Qualifier` annotation. This `@Qualifier` annotation can also be placed on fields, methods, constructors, and parameters.

The following example applies this `@Qualifier` annotation to autowire different objects (but same type) as parameters to a method.

```
//File Name: Complex.java
package com.springdemo;

public class Complex {
  public double real;
  public double img;

  public double getReal() {
    return real;
  }
```

```
  public void setReal(double real) {
   this.real = real;
  }

  public double getImg() {
   return img;
  }

  public void setImg(double img) {
   this.img = img;
  }

  public String toString() {
   return real + " + " + img + "i";
  }
 }
```

```
//File Name: ComplexAddition.java
package com.springdemo;

import org.springframework.beans.factory.annotation.Autowired;
import org.springframework.beans.factory.annotation.Qualifier;

public class ComplexAddition {

 @Autowired
 public void addTwoComplexNumbers(@Qualifier("number1") Complex num1,
                                  @Qualifier("number2") Complex num2) {
  Complex result = new Complex();
  result.setReal(num1.getReal() + num2.getReal());
  result.setImg(num1.getImg() + num2.getImg());

  System.out.println("Complex Number 1: " + num1);
  System.out.println("Complex Number 2: " + num2);
  System.out.println("Result after addition: " + result);
 }
}
```

```
//File Name: ComplexNumbersApp.java
package com.springdemo;

import org.springframework.context.support.AbstractApplicationContext;
import org.springframework.context.support.ClassPathXmlApplicationContext;

public class ComplexNumbersApp {

 public static void main(String args[]) {
  AbstractApplicationContext context =
                    new ClassPathXmlApplicationContext("beans.xml");
  ComplexAddition complexAddition =
               (ComplexAddition) context.getBean("complexAddition");
 }
}
```

Store this *beans.xml* file in the "src" directory of the project.

```
<?xml version="1.0" encoding="UTF-8"?>
<beans xmlns="http://www.springframework.org/schema/beans"
   xmlns:xsi="http://www.w3.org/2001/XMLSchema-instance"
   xmlns:context="http://www.springframework.org/schema/context"
   xsi:schemaLocation="http://www.springframework.org/schema/beans
   http://www.springframework.org/schema/beans/spring-beans-3.0.xsd
   http://www.springframework.org/schema/context
   http://www.springframework.org/schema/context/spring-context-3.0.xsd">

  <context:annotation-config />

  <bean id="complexNumber" class="com.springdemo.Complex">
   <qualifier value="number1"/>
   <property name="real" value="10" />
   <property name="img" value="20" />
  </bean>

  <bean id="complexNumber2" class="com.springdemo.Complex">
   <qualifier value="number2"/>
   <property name="real" value="30" />
   <property name="img" value="40" />
  </bean>

  <bean id="complexAddition" class="com.springdemo.ComplexAddition" />

</beans>
```

Execute *ComplexNumbersApp.java* application and result will be as shown below.

```
Complex Number 1: 10.0 + 20.0i
Complex Number 2: 30.0 + 40.0i
Result after addition: 40.0 + 60.0i
```

1.15 @RESOURCE (JSR-250 ANNOTATION)

This JSR annotation (`javax.annotation.Resource`) declares a bean reference as a resource to an application. This annotation can be applied to a filed, setter method of a filed, and a class (at class level).

This annotation can be used in Java EE applications to refer a JNDI name. This annotation accepts `'name'` and `'type'` attributes and both are optional. The `'name'` attribute specifies a JNDI name of the resource; however in Spring Framework, it refers to any spring-managed bean with that name in the Spring context. The `'type'` attribute specifies the data type (Class/Interface Reference Type) of the resource. These two attributes (`name` and `type`) *must* be specified with `@Resource` if used at class level (Class-based injection). The name of the filed is taken as value for the `'name'` attribute by default if no name is specified at field level (Field-based injection). The corresponding fieldname of the setter method is taken as the value for `'name'` attribute if no name is specified at property-method level (Method-based injection). In both filed and setter property method level, the field data type will be taken as value for `'type'` attribute, if not specified. The setter method must follow the JavaBeans conventions for property names: the method name must begin with `set`, have a `void` return type, and only one parameter. When no name is explicitly specified with `@Resource` and no Spring managed bean is found in the container (for setting default name), the injection mechanism will fallback to a type-match.

This JSR `@Resource` annotation is similar to Spring's `@Autowired` annotation. The difference is, the `@Autowired` can be applied to fields, setter property methods, constructors, and arbitrary methods (with one or more number of arguments), but the `@Resource` should be used at field, and setter property method. `@Autowired` has some limitations while referring resources such as it can not inject beans that they themselves defined as collection.

Note that `@Autowired` wires per type and `@Resource` wires per bean name. However, `@Autowired` in combination with `@Qualifier` also auto-wires by name.

The following example is for illustrating how to apply `@Resource` annotation. Specifically, this annotation should be applied for resources such as database and file handle.

```
//File Name: Employee.java
package com.springdemo;

import javax.annotation.Resource;

public class Employee {
 private int empNumber;
```

```
    private String empName;

    @Resource
    private Salary salary;

    public void setEmpNumber(int empNumber) {
     this.empNumber = empNumber;
    }

    public void setEmpName(String empName) {
     this.empName = empName;
    }

    public String toString() {
     String rStr = "Emp Number: " + empNumber + "\nEmp Name: " + empName;
     rStr += salary;
     return rStr;
    }
   }
```

```
   //File Name: Salary.java
   package com.springdemo;

   public class Salary {
    private double basicpay;
    private double allowances;
    private double deductions;
    private double netpay;

    Salary(double basicpay, double allowances, double deductions) {
     this.basicpay = basicpay;
     this.allowances = allowances;
     this.deductions = deductions;
    }

    public void calculateNetpay() {
     netpay = basicpay + allowances - deductions;
    }

    public String toString() {
     calculateNetpay();
```

```
    String rStr = "\nBasic Pay: " + basicpay;
    rStr += "\nAllowances: " + allowances;
    rStr += "\nDeductions: " + deductions;
    rStr += "\nNetpay: " + netpay;
    return rStr;
  }
}
```

```
//File Name: EmployeeApp.java
package com.springdemo;

import org.springframework.context.support.AbstractApplicationContext;
import org.springframework.context.support.ClassPathXmlApplicationContext;

public class EmployeeApp {

  public static void main(String args[]) {
    AbstractApplicationContext context =
                   new ClassPathXmlApplicationContext("beans.xml");
    Employee employee = (Employee) context.getBean("employee");
    System.out.println(employee);
  }
}
```

Store this *beans.xml* in the "src" directory of the project.

```
<?xml version="1.0" encoding="UTF-8"?>
<beans xmlns="http://www.springframework.org/schema/beans"
   xmlns:xsi="http://www.w3.org/2001/XMLSchema-instance"
   xmlns:context="http://www.springframework.org/schema/context"
   xsi:schemaLocation="http://www.springframework.org/schema/beans
    http://www.springframework.org/schema/beans/spring-beans-3.0.xsd
   http://www.springframework.org/schema/context
   http://www.springframework.org/schema/context/spring-context-3.0.xsd">

  <context:annotation-config />

  <bean id="employee" class="com.springdemo.Employee" >
   <property name="empNumber" value="1001" />
```

```
    <property name="empName" value="Mohamed Ibrahim" />
   </bean>

   <bean id="salary" class="com.springdemo.Salary">
    <constructor-arg index="0" value="10000.0" />
    <constructor-arg index="1" value="3000.0" />
    <constructor-arg index="2" value="2000.0" />
   </bean>

</beans>
```

Execute *EmployeeApp.java* and the result will be as shown below.

```
Emp Number: 1001
Emp Name: Mohamed Ibrahim
Basic Pay: 10000.0
Allowances: 3000.0
Deductions: 2000.0
Netpay: 11000.0
```

In this example, the following annotation will search for instance name of a bean is '*salary*' and it is found in *beans.xml* file. So that the corresponding bean instace is injected.

```
@Resource
private Salary salary;
```

If you change the field-name in to '*empSalary*' as shown below (also change in `toString()` of *Employee.java*), but keeping the same bean definition in *beans.xml* file (the bean instance name as '*salary*').

```
@Resource
private Salary empSalary;
```

We will get the same result. How? First the Spring container search for the bean instance name '*empSalary*' in its context. There is no such '*empSalary*' bean instance name in our case. When it won't find the exact bean instance name match, then it fallback to type (*byType*) and matches the '*salary*' bean instance defined in *beans.xml* file to *empSalary*'s type. Since both type marches, the bean is injected.

We can prevent such kind of fallback to *type* match, and strict with *name* match. To achieve, add the following Spring processor bean before `<context:annotation-config/>` tag in the XML based configuration file.

```
<bean class="org.springframework.context.annotation.Common
                                    AnnotationBeanPostProcessor">
   <property name="fallbackToDefaultTypeMatch" value="false" />
</bean>
```

Note that `fallbackToDefaultTypeMatch` attribute is default to true.

Now, we will create a JDBC application, which uses this `@Resource` annotation for acquiring a database source. This example uses MySQL database, so download MySQL Connector/J (MySQL Driver for Java) from Internet and add it in CLASSPATH of the project. Select project ⟶ Right click ⟶ Properties ⟶ Java Build Path ⟶ Add Jar (mysql-connector-java-5.1.12-bin.jar).

Assumed that a database named '*demodb*' is created for the user '*ibrahim*', whose password is '*pword*'. And a table named '*employee*' with required fields is created in the '*demodb*' database.

Cross Reference: Download MySQL distribution from *http://dev.mysql.com/downloads/* and install it. Give the 'root' user password when prompted. Login as 'root' user, create a user named 'ibrahim' with password 'pword' and grant rights to the user.

Create User - ibrahim

```
C:\Users\Ibrahim> mysql -u root -p<rootpassword>
Welcome to the MySQL monitor.  Commands end with ; or \g.
Server version: 5.5.11 MySQL Community Server (GPL)

mysql> create user 'ibrahim'@'localhost' identified by 'pword';
Query OK, 0 rows affected (0.22 sec)

mysql> grant all privileges on *.* to 'ibrahim'@'localhost'
      with grant option;
Query OK, 0 rows affected (0.00 sec)

Mysql> exit
Bye
```

Create Database - demodb

```
C:\Users\Ibrahim> mysql -u ibrahim -ppword
Welcome to the MySQL monitor. Commands end with ; or \g.
Server version: 5.5.11 MySQL Community Server (GPL)

mysql> create database demodb;
Query OK, 1 row affected (0.05 sec)

mysql> exit
Bye
```

Create Table - employee

```
C:\Users\Ibrahim>mysql -u ibrahim -ppword demodb
welcome to the MySQL monitor. Commands end with ; or \g.
Your MySQL connection id is 5
Server version: 5.1.32-community MySQL Community Server (GPL)
Type 'help;' or '\h' for help. Type '\C' to clear the buffer.
mysql> desc employee;
```

Field	Type	Null	Key	Default	Extra
emp_number	int(11)	YES		NULL	
emp_name	var char (64)	YES		NULL	
basic_pay	double	YES		NULL	
allowances	double	YES		NULL	
deductions	double	YES		NULL	
netpay	double	YES		NULL	

```
6 rows in set (0.05 sec)
```

```
//File Name: Employee.java
package com.springdemo;

import org.springframework.beans.factory.annotation.Autowired;

public class Employee {
 private int empNumber;
 private String empName;

 @Autowired
 private Salary salary;

 public int getEmpNumber() {
  return empNumber;
 }

 public void setEmpNumber(int empNumber) {
  this.empNumber = empNumber;
 }

 public String getEmpName() {
  return empName;
 }

 public void setEmpName(String empName) {
```

```
  this.empName = empName;
 }

 public Salary getSalary() {
  return salary;
 }

 public void setSalary(Salary salary) {
  this.salary = salary;
 }

}
```

```
//File Name: Salary.java
package com.springdemo;

public class Salary {
 private double basicpay;
 private double allowances;
 private double deductions;
 private double netpay;

 Salary(double basicpay, double allowances, double deductions) {
  this.basicpay = basicpay;
  this.allowances = allowances;
  this.deductions = deductions;
 }

 public void calculateNetpay() {
  netpay = basicpay + allowances - deductions;
 }

 public double getBasicpay() {
  return basicpay;
 }

 public void setBasicpay(double basicpay) {
  this.basicpay = basicpay;
 }

 public double getAllowances() {
```

```
    return allowances;
   }

   public void setAllowances(double allowances) {
    this.allowances = allowances;
   }

   public double getDeductions() {
    return deductions;
   }

   public void setDeductions(double deductions) {
    this.deductions = deductions;
   }

   public double getNetpay() {
    return netpay;
   }

   public void setNetpay(double netpay) {
    this.netpay = netpay;
   }
  }
```

```
//File Name: EmployeeDAO.java
package com.springdemo;

public interface EmployeeDAO {

 public void insertEmployee();
}
```

```
//File Name: EmployeeDAOImpl.java
package com.springdemo;

import java.sql.Connection;
import java.sql.PreparedStatement;
import java.sql.SQLException;

import javax.annotation.Resource;
```

```
import org.springframework.beans.factory.annotation.Autowired;
import org.springframework.jdbc.datasource.DriverManagerDataSource;

public class EmployeeDAOImpl implements EmployeeDAO {

 @Resource
 DriverManagerDataSource dataSource;

 @Autowired
 Employee employee;

 @Override
 public void insertEmployee() {
  Connection dbConn = null;
  try {
  dbConn = dataSource.getConnection();
   PreparedStatement ps = dbConn.prepareStatement("INSERT INTO EMPLOYEE
  (EMP_NUMBER, EMP_NAME, BASIC_PAY, ALLOWANCES, DEDUCTIONS, NETPAY) VALUES
   (?, ?, ?, ?, ?, ?)");
   ps.setInt(1, employee.getEmpNumber());
   ps.setString(2, employee.getEmpName());
   ps.setDouble(3, employee.getSalary().getBasicpay());
   ps.setDouble(4, employee.getSalary().getAllowances());
   ps.setDouble(5, employee.getSalary().getDeductions());
   employee.getSalary().calculateNetpay();
   ps.setDouble(6, employee.getSalary().getNetpay());
   int i = ps.executeUpdate();
   if (i == 1) {
    System.out.println("Employee record is inserted successfully");
   }
  }
  catch (SQLException e) {
   System.out.println("Error occurred. Error[" + e.getMessage() + "]");
   e.printStackTrace();
  }
  finally {
   if (dbConn != null) {
    try {
     dbConn.close();
    }
    catch (SQLException e) {
```

```
        e.printStackTrace();
      }
    }
  }
 }
}
```

```
//File Name: EmployeeApp.java
package com.springdemo;

import org.springframework.context.support.AbstractApplicationContext;
import org.springframework.context.support.ClassPathXmlApplicationContext;

public class EmployeeApp {

 public static void main(String args[]) {
  AbstractApplicationContext context =
                    new ClassPathXmlApplicationContext("beans.xml");
 EmployeeDAO employeeDAO = (EmployeeDAO) context.getBean("employeeDAO");
  employeeDAO.insertEmployee();
 }
}
```

Store the following *beans.xml* in the "src" directory of the project.

```
<?xml version="1.0" encoding="UTF-8"?>
<beans xmlns="http://www.springframework.org/schema/beans"
    xmlns:xsi="http://www.w3.org/2001/XMLSchema-instance"
    xmlns:context="http://www.springframework.org/schema/context"
    xsi:schemaLocation="http://www.springframework.org/schema/beans
      http://www.springframework.org/schema/beans/spring-beans-3.0.xsd
    http://www.springframework.org/schema/context
   http://www.springframework.org/schema/context/spring-context-3.0.xsd">

  <context:annotation-config />

  <bean id="employee" class="com.springdemo.Employee" >
   <property name="empNumber" value="1001" />
   <property name="empName" value="Mohamed Ibrahim" />
  </bean>
```

```
    <bean id="salary" class="com.springdemo.Salary">
     <constructor-arg index="0" value="10000.0" />
     <constructor-arg index="1" value="3000.0" />
     <constructor-arg index="2" value="2000.0" />
    </bean>

    <bean id="dataSource"
      class="org.springframework.jdbc.datasource.DriverManagerDataSource">
     <property name="driverClassName" value="com.mysql.jdbc.Driver" />
     <property name="url" value="jdbc:mysql://127.0.0.1:3306/demodb" />
     <property name="username" value="ibrahim" />
     <property name="password" value="pword" />
    </bean>

    <bean id="employeeDAO" class="com.springdemo.EmployeeDAOImpl" />

</beans>
```

Execute the main application (*EmployeeApp.java*) and check with database.

Employee record is inserted successfully

```
mysql> select * from employee;
+------------+-----------------+-------------+------------+------------+--------+
| emp_number | emp_name        | basic_play  | allowances | deductions | netpay |
+------------+-----------------+-------------+------------+------------+--------+
|   1001     | Mohamed Ibrahim |   10000     |    3000    |    2000    | 11000  |
+------------+-----------------+-------------+------------+------------+--------+
1 row in set (0.00 sec)
```

We can rewrite the above application by accessing properties files for JDBC configuration as below.

Store the following *"jdbc.properties"* file in the "src" directory of the project.

```
driver_class_name=com.mysql.jdbc.Driver
url=jdbc:mysql://127.0.0.1:3306/demodb
username=ibrahim
password=pword
```

Change the content of *beans.xml* file as below.

```
<?xml version="1.0" encoding="UTF-8"?>
<beans xmlns="http://www.springframework.org/schema/beans"
    xmlns:xsi="http://www.w3.org/2001/XMLSchema-instance"
     xmlns:context="http://www.springframework.org/schema/context"
```

```
    xsi:schemaLocation="http://www.springframework.org/schema/beans
     http://www.springframework.org/schema/beans/spring-beans-3.0.xsd
    http://www.springframework.org/schema/context
   http://www.springframework.org/schema/context/spring-context-3.0.xsd">

  <context:annotation-config />

  <bean id="employee" class="com.springdemo.Employee" >
   <property name="empNumber" value="1001" />
   <property name="empName" value="Mohamed Ibrahim" />
  </bean>

  <bean id="salary" class="com.springdemo.Salary">
   <constructor-arg index="0" value="10000.0" />
   <constructor-arg index="1" value="3000.0" />
   <constructor-arg index="2" value="2000.0" />
  </bean>

  <context:property-placeholder location="classpath:jdbc.properties"/>

  <bean id="dataSource"
    class="org.springframework.jdbc.datasource.DriverManagerDataSource">
   <property name="driverClassName" value="${driver_class_name}" />
   <property name="url" value="${url}" />
   <property name="username" value="${username}" />
   <property name="password" value="${password}" />
  </bean>

  <bean id="employeeDAO" class="com.springdemo.EmployeeDAOImpl" />

</beans>
```

The following line in *beans.xml* file resolves the *jdbc.properties* files, which is available in CLASSPATH. The value of a key (placeholder) in this properties file can be accessed via `${placeholder}` tokens.

```
<context:property-placeholder location="classpath:jdbc.properties"/>
```

1.16 JSR-250 LIFECYCLE ANNOTATIONS

Recall lifecycle callbacks that we already gone through in the earlier sections. JST-250 specification also provides two annotations: `@PostConstruct` and `@PreDestroy` to trigger Spring initialization and destruction callbacks respectively.

I named *'init'* for post-construct method, and *'destroy'* for pre-destroy method. However, you can use ay allowed method name in Java.

```
package com.springdemo;

import javax.annotation.PostConstruct;
import javax.annotation.PreDestroy;

public class Employee {
 private int empNumber;
 private String empName;

 Employee() {
  System.out.println("Employee() constructor is called");
 }

 Employee(int empNumber) {
  System.out.println("Employee(int empNumber) constructor is called");
  this.empNumber = empNumber;
 }

 public void setEmpName(String empName) {
  System.out.println("setEmpName(String empName) method is called");
  this.empName = empName;
 }

 @PostConstruct
 public void init() {
  System.out.println("init() method is called");
 }

 @PreDestroy
 public void destroy() {
  System.out.println("destroy() method is called");
 }

 public String toString() {
  return "Emp Number: " + empNumber + "\nEmp Name: " + empName;
 }
}
```

```
package com.springdemo;

import org.springframework.context.support.AbstractApplicationContext;
import org.springframework.context.support.ClassPathXmlApplicationContext;

public class EmployeeApp {

 public static void main(String args[]) {
  AbstractApplicationContext context =
                    new ClassPathXmlApplicationContext("beans.xml");
  context.registerShutdownHook();
  Employee employee = (Employee) context.getBean("employee");
  System.out.println(employee);
 }
}
```

Store the following *beans.xml* file in "src" directory of the project.

```
<?xml version="1.0" encoding="UTF-8"?>
<beans xmlns="http://www.springframework.org/schema/beans"
   xmlns:xsi="http://www.w3.org/2001/XMLSchema-instance"
   xmlns:context="http://www.springframework.org/schema/context"
   xsi:schemaLocation="http://www.springframework.org/schema/beans
   http://www.springframework.org/schema/beans/spring-beans-3.0.xsd
   http://www.springframework.org/schema/context
   http://www.springframework.org/schema/context/spring-context-3.0.xsd">

  <context:annotation-config />

  <bean id="employee" class="com.springdemo.Employee" >
   <constructor-arg name="empNumber" value="1001" />
   <property name="empName" value="Mohamed Ibrahim" />
  </bean>

</beans>
```

Execute the main application and the result is shown below.

```
Employee(int empNumber) constructor is called
setEmpName(String empName) method is called
init() method is called
```

```
Emp Number: 1001
Emp Name: Mohamed Ibrahim
destroy() method is called
```

1.17 JAVA-BASED CONTAINER CONFIGURATION

The Spring 3 Framework supports many annotations to configure the container. They define instantiation, configuration and initialization logic for objects to be managed by the Spring container. For example, `@Bean` annotation plays the same role as the <bean> element in XML based configuration.

1.17.1 @Configuration and @Bean

Annotating a class with the `@Configuration` indicates that the class can be used by the Spring container as a source of bean definitions.

Example

```
package com.springdemo;

import org.springframework.context.annotation.Bean;
import org.springframework.context.annotation.Configuration;

@Configuration
public class Employee {

  @Bean
  public Salary salary() {
    return new SalaryImpl();
  }

}
```

The above annotated configuration is equivalent to the following XML based configuration.

```
<beans ...>
  <bean id="salary" class="com.springdemo.SalaryImpl"/>
</beans>
```

The following line in the configuration XML file instructs the Spring container to scan for these container configuration annotation classes (`Component`) from the specified base-package (all of its sub-packages will also be scanned).

```
<context:component-scan base-package="com.springdemo"/>
```

Alternatively, we can use the `scan(String...)` variable argument method provided by `AnnotationConfigApplicationContext` to make the same scan. In this case, you are not required the XML configuration file at all.

Cross Note: The `@Component` annotation is a generic stereotype (generalized) for any Spring-managed component.

The `@Value` creates expression driven dependency injection.

CGLIB is required to process `@Configuration` classes. Copy *com.springsource.net.sf.cglib-2.2.0.jar* file from 'Spring Distribution with All Dependencies' download and add it in CLASSPATH.

```
//File Name: Employee.java
package com.springdemo;

import org.springframework.beans.factory.annotation.Value;

public class Employee {

 @Value(value = "1001")
 private int empNumber;

 @Value(value = "Mohamed Ibrahim")
 private String empName;

 public String toString() {
  return "Emp Number: " + empNumber + "\nEmp Name: " + empName;
 }
}
```

```
package com.springdemo;

import org.springframework.context.annotation.Bean;
import org.springframework.context.annotation.Configuration;

@Configuration
public class EmployeeManipulation {

 public @Bean Employee employeeBean() {
  //This example is for illustration purpose only
  return new Employee();
 }
}
```

```
//File Name: EmployeeApp.java
package com.springdemo;

import
org.springframework.context.annotation.AnnotationConfigApplicationContext;

public class EmployeeApp {

 public static void main(String args[]) {
  AnnotationConfigApplicationContext context =
                     new AnnotationConfigApplicationContext();
  context.scan("com.springdemo");
  context.refresh();

 EmployeeManipulation em = context.getBean(EmployeeManipulation.class);
 Employee employee = em.employeeBean();
 System.out.println(employee);
 }
}
```

Since we are using `AnnotationConfigApplicationContext`, no need to have any XML based configuration file. Execute the main application and the result will be as follows.

```
Emp Number: 1001
Emp Name: Mohamed Ibrahim
```

1.18 USING XML BASED CONFIGURATION IN JAVA BASED CONFIGURATION CONTAINER

We experienced earlier to use XML based configuration in `ClassPathXmlApplicationContext` environment and Java based annotation in `AnnotationConfigApplicationContext` environment. The following example demonstrates how to use XML based configuration in Java based configuration environment. The `@ImportResource` annotation is used to import XML files.

```
//File Name: Employee.java
package com.springdemo;

import org.springframework.beans.factory.annotation.Value;
import org.springframework.context.annotation.Configuration;
import org.springframework.context.annotation.ImportResource;
```

```
@Configuration
@ImportResource("classpath:/beans.xml")
public class Employee {

 @Value("#{employeeProperties['employee_number']}")
 private int empNumber;

 @Value("#{employeeProperties['employee_name']}")
 private String empName;

 public String toString() {
  return "Emp Number: " + empNumber + "\nEmp Name: " + empName;
 }
}
```

```
package com.springdemo;

import org.springframework.context.annotation.Bean;
import org.springframework.context.annotation.Configuration;

@Configuration
public class EmployeeManipulation {

 public @Bean Employee employeeBean() {
  return new Employee();
 }
}
```

```
//File Name: EmployeeApp.java
package com.springdemo;

import
org.springframework.context.annotation.AnnotationConfigApplicationContext;

public class EmployeeApp {

 public static void main(String args[]) {
  AnnotationConfigApplicationContext context =
                      new AnnotationConfigApplicationContext();
  context.scan("com.springdemo");
  context.refresh();
```

```
EmployeeManipulation em = context.getBean(EmployeeManipulation.class);
 Employee employee = em.employeeBean();
 System.out.println(employee);
}
}
```

Store the following *beans.xml* file in the "src' directory of the project (Note that new namespaces are included to support Spring utilities in XML based configuration).

```
<?xml version="1.0" encoding="UTF-8"?>
<beans xmlns="http://www.springframework.org/schema/beans"
   xmlns:xsi="http://www.w3.org/2001/XMLSchema-instance"
   xmlns:util="http://www.springframework.org/schema/util"
   xmlns:context="http://www.springframework.org/schema/context"
   xsi:schemaLocation="http://www.springframework.org/schema/beans
    http://www.springframework.org/schema/beans/spring-beans-3.0.xsd
   http://www.springframework.org/schema/util
   http://www.springframework.org/schema/util/spring-util-3.0.xsd
   http://www.springframework.org/schema/context
  http://www.springframework.org/schema/context/spring-context-3.0.xsd">

    <util:properties id="employeeProperties"
                location="classpath:employee.properties"/>

</beans>
```

Store the following content in "*employee.properties*" files and store it in "src" directory of the project.

```
employee_number=1001
employee_name=Mohamed Ibrahim
```

Execute the main application and the result is produced as shown below.

```
Emp Number: 1001
Emp Name: Mohamed Ibrahim
```

CHAPTER 2

SPRING JDBC SUPPORT

Spring Framework supports and simplifies JDBC programming; it manages the basics to work with JDBC such as opening/closing of database connections, preparation/execution of SQL statements, transaction management, and exception handling. Spring provides an abstract exception layer, which catches all the application server specific exceptions and throws Spring equivalent exceptions (not depend on the underlying database).

2.1 DECLARING DATA SOURCE

A `DataSource` is a JDBC interface that represents an alternative to JDBC's `DriverManager` class. Since it is an interface, any type of implementation can be applied.

The bean configuration file is as shown below, if Apache Commons Basic Data Source is used.

```
Specify the full XML Namespace in the <beans> element
<?xml version="1.0" encoding="UTF-8"?>
<beans xmlns="...">
  <bean id="dataSource" class="org.apache.commons.dbcp.BasicDataSource"
                        destroy-method="close">
     <property name="driverClassName" value="<DRIVER_CLASS_NAME>"/>
     <property name="url" value="<DATABASE_URL>"/>
     <property name="username" value="<DATABASE_USERNAME>"/>
     <property name="password" value="<DATABASE_PASSWORD>"/>
  </bean>
</beans>
```

A sample bean definition for the connection of MySQL database is given below.

```
<bean id="dataSource" class="org.apache.commons.dbcp.BasicDataSource"
                      destroy-method="close">
   <property name="driverClassName" value="com.mysql.jdbc.Driver"/>
   <property name="url" value="jdbc:mysql://127.0.0.1:3306/demodb"/>
   <property name="username" value="ibrahim"/>
   <property name="password" value="pword"/>
</bean>
```

DBCP is database connection pool product by Apache Commons. DBCP 1.4 compiles and runs under JDK 1.6 only (JDBC 4) and DBCP 1.3 compiles and runs under JDK 1.4 and 1.5 (JDBC 3). You can download the DBCP 1.4 jar (commons-dbcp-1.4.jar) file from Maven Repository (http://mvnrepository.com/artifact/commons-dbcp/commons-dbcp/1.4). The jar file "commons-pool-1.5.4.jar" can be downloaded from Apache's download page (http://commons.apache.org/pool/download_pool.cgi). Download MySQL Connector for Java and add it to classpath of the project.

The examples in this section use MySQL database system as data source. Assumed that you already created a database 'demodb' for the user 'ibrahim' with password 'pword', and a table named 'Employee' with adequate fields are created.

Note: Creation of a user and a database in MySQL are given in `@Resource` annotation example in Chapter 1. However, it is repeated here for easy reference.

Create User - ibrahim

```
C:\Users\Ibrahim> mysql -u root -p<rootpassword>
Welcome to the MySQL monitor. Commands end with ; or \g.
Server version: 5.5.11 MySQL Community Server (GPL)

mysql> create user 'ibrahim'@'localhost' identified by 'pword';
Query OK, 0 rows affected (0.22 sec)

mysql> grant all privileges on *.* to 'ibrahim'@'localhost'
 with grant option;
Query OK, 0 rows affected (0.00 sec)

Mysql> exit
Bye
```

Create Database - demodb

```
C:\Users\Ibrahim> mysql -u ibrahim -ppword
Welcome to the MySQL monitor. Commands end with ; or \g.
Server version: 5.5.11 MySQL Community Server (GPL)

mysql> create database demodb;
Query OK, 1 row affected (0.05 sec)

mysql> exit
Bye
```

Login as 'ibrahim' user and create 'employee' table

```
C:\Users\Ibrahim> mysql -u ibrahim -ppword demodb
Welcome to the MySQL monitor. Commands end with ; or \g.
Your MySQL connection id is 24
Server version: 5.1.32-community MySQL Community Server (GPL)

Type 'help;' or '\h' for help. Type '\c' to clear the buffer.

mysql> create table employee (
  -> empnumber int,
  -> empname varchar(32),
  -> basicpay double,
  -> allowances double,
  -> deductions double,
  -> netpay double
  -> );
Query OK, 0 rows affected (0.14 sec)

mysql> desc employee;
```

Field	Type	Null	Key	Default	Extra
empnumber	int(11)	YES		NULL	
empname	varchar(32)	YES		NULL	
basicpay	double	YES		NULL	
allowances	double	YES		NULL	
deductions	double	YES		NULL	
netpay	double	YES		NULL	

```
6 rows in set (0.00 sec)
```

2.2 JDBC TEMPLATE CLASS

The `JdbcTemplate` simplifies to work directly with instances of the `Statement`, `PreparedStatement`, and `CallableStatement` to execute SQL queries, DDL/DML SQL statements and stored procedure calls. It uses many callback interfaces to achieve the required operations with database.

A typical flow of the execution of `JdbcTemplate` is shown as below.

(a) The `JdbcTemplate` uses the `DataSource` to obtain a database connection.

(b) It calls the `StatementCreator` instance to create the SQL statement to be executed.

(c) It calls the `StatementCallback` to perform SQL statement execution and returns the result.

(d) It closes the database connection.

If StatementCreator/StatementCallback throw exceptions, then the JdbcTemplate class catches them and translates them into Spring based data access exceptions.

The PreparedStatementCreator callback interface creates a PreparedStatement and the CallableStatementCreator interface creates a CallableStatement. The RowCallbackHandler interface extracts values from each row of a ResultSet.

2.2.1 JdbcTemplate.execute

This *execute* method is to execute any DDL (create, alter, drop ...) and DML (select, insert, update, delete, call ...) SQL commands.

ConnectionCallback execute method syntax

```
Object  execute(ConnectionCallback  obj)
```

This executes the code in ConnectionCallback.doInConnection() method and returns the value returned from that callback.

```
doInConnection(Connection  connection)
```

This method is called by JdbcTemplate.execute() method with an active database connection as parameter. The programmer does not need to care about opening and closing the database connection and this will be done by Spring. We can create any number of Statement or PreparedStatement with the available Connection object.

Example

```
// File Name: JDBCOperations.java
package com.springdemo;

import java.sql.Connection;
import java.sql.PreparedStatement;
import java.sql.SQLException;
import java.sql.Statement;

import org.springframework.beans.factory.annotation.Autowired;
import org.springframework.dao.DataAccessException;
import org.springframework.jdbc.core.ConnectionCallback;
import org.springframework.jdbc.core.JdbcTemplate;


public class JDBCOperations {

  @Autowired
  private JdbcTemplate jdbcTemplate;

  private static class MyConnectionCallback
          implements ConnectionCallback {
```

```
@Override
public Object doInConnection(Connection connection)
                        throws SQLException,
                             DataAccessException {

    String sqlInsert = "insert into employee
              (empnumber, empname, basicpay,
              allowances, deductions)
              values (?, ?, ?, ?, ?)";
  PreparedStatement psInsert = connection.prepareStatement(sqlInsert);
    psInsert.setInt(1, 1001);
    psInsert.setString(2, "Mohamed Ibrahim");
    psInsert.setDouble(3, 10000.0);
    psInsert.setDouble(4, 3000.0);
    psInsert.setDouble(5, 2000.0);
    psInsert.execute();

    String sqlUpdate = "update employee set netpay =
              (basicpay + allowances - deductions)";
    Statement stUpdate = connection.createStatement();
    stUpdate.execute(sqlUpdate);

    return null;
  }
 }

 public void doDatabaseOperations() {
    jdbcTemplate.execute(new MyConnectionCallback());
 }
}
```

```
// File Name: JdbcTemplateExecuteDemo.java
package com.springdemo;

import org.springframework.context.support.AbstractApplicationContext;
import org.springframework.context.support.ClassPathXmlApplication
Context;

public class JdbcTemplateExecuteDemo {
```

```
  public static void main(String[] args) {
     AbstractApplicationContext context =
                    new ClassPathXmlApplicationContext("beans.xml");
     JDBCOperations jdbcOperations =
                    (JDBCOperations) context.getBean("jdbcOperations");
     jdbcOperations.doDatabaseOperations();
     System.out.println("Operation performed successfully.");
   }
}
```

Store the following "beans.xml" file in the "src" directory of the project. Change the values of the data source properties according to your database settings.

```
<?xml version="1.0" encoding="UTF-8"?>
<beans xmlns="http://www.springframework.org/schema/beans"
    xmlns:xsi="http://www.w3.org/2001/XMLSchema-instance"
    xmlns:context="http://www.springframework.org/schema/context"
    xsi:schemaLocation="http://www.springframework.org/schema/beans
    http://www.springframework.org/schema/beans/spring-beans-3.0.xsd
    http://www.springframework.org/schema/context
 http://www.springframework.org/schema/context/spring-context-3.0.xsd">

<context:annotation-config />

  <bean id="dataSource" class="org.apache.commons.dbcp.BasicDataSource"
                     destroy-method="close">
    <property name="driverClassName" value="com.mysql.jdbc.Driver"/>
    <property name="url" value="jdbc:mysql://127.0.0.1:3306/demodb"/>
    <property name="username" value="ibrahim"/>
    <property name="password" value="pword"/>
 </bean>

 <bean id="jdbcTemplate"
        class="org.springframework.jdbc.core.JdbcTemplate">
    <property name="dataSource" ref="dataSource"/>
 </bean>

 <bean id="jdbcOperations" class="com.springdemo.JDBCOperations"/>

 </beans>
```

Execute the main application and observe from the database that one record is inserted.

```
mysql> select * from employee;
```

empnumber	empname	basicpay	allowances	deductions	netpay
1001	Mohamed Ibrahim	10000	3000	2000	11000

```
1 row in set (0.00 sec)
```

The above *JDBCOperations.java* can be written as below using anonymous inner class.

```
// File Name: JDBCOperations.java
package com.springdemo;

import java.sql.Connection;
import java.sql.PreparedStatement;
import java.sql.SQLException;

import org.springframework.beans.factory.annotation.Autowired;
import org.springframework.dao.DataAccessException;
import org.springframework.jdbc.core.ConnectionCallback;
import org.springframework.jdbc.core.JdbcTemplate;


public class JDBCOperations {

 @Autowired
 private JdbcTemplate jdbcTemplate;

 public void doDatabaseOperations() {

   jdbcTemplate.execute(new ConnectionCallback() {
     @Override
     public Object doInConnection(Connection connection)
                   throws SQLException, DataAccessException {
       String sqlInsert = "insert into employee
                         (empnumber, empname, basicpay,
                          allowances, deductions)
                          values (?, ?, ?, ?, ?)";
      PreparedStatement psInsert =
                    connection.prepareStatement(sqlInsert);
```

```
            psInsert.setInt(1, 1001);
            psInsert.setString(2, "Mohamed Ibrahim");
            psInsert.setDouble(3, 10000.0);
            psInsert.setDouble(4, 3000.0);
            psInsert.setDouble(5, 2000.0);
            psInsert.execute();

            String sqlUpdate = "update employee set netpay =
                             (basicpay + allowances - deductions)";
            Statement stUpdate = connection.createStatement();
            stUpdate.execute(sqlUpdate);

            return null;
          }
        });
      }
    }
```

StatementCallback execute method syntax

`Object   execute(StatementCallback   obj)`

This executes the code in `StatementCallback.doInStatement()` and returns the value returned from the callback. We can execute multiple SQL statements, but with the single `Statement` object.

`doInStatement(Statement   statement)`

This method is called by `JdbcTemplate.execute()` method with an active JDBC Statement as parameter.

Example

```
// File Name: JDBCOperations.java
package com.springdemo;

import java.sql.ResultSet;
import java.sql.SQLException;
import java.sql.Statement;

import org.springframework.beans.factory.annotation.Autowired;
import org.springframework.dao.DataAccessException;
import org.springframework.jdbc.core.JdbcTemplate;
import org.springframework.jdbc.core.StatementCallback;


public class JDBCOperations {
```

```
    @Autowired
    private JdbcTemplate jdbcTemplate;

  private static class MyStatementCallback implements StatementCallback{

      @Override
      public Object doInStatement(Statement statement)
                              throws SQLException, DataAccessException {
        String sqlInsert = "insert into employee
                             (empnumber, empname, basicpay,
                             allowances, deductions)
                             values (1002, 'Kumar',
                             12000.0, 3000.0, 1500.0)";
        statement.executeUpdate(sqlInsert);

        statement.executeUpdate("update employee set netpay =
                                (basicpay + allowances - deductions)");

        boolean isRecordAvailable = statement.execute(
                                      "select * from employee");
        if (isRecordAvailable) {
          ResultSet rs = statement.getResultSet();
          while (rs.next()){
             int empnumber = rs.getInt(1);
             String empname = rs.getString(2);
             double basicpay = rs.getDouble(3);
             double allowances = rs.getDouble(4);
             double deductions = rs.getDouble(5);
             double netpay = rs.getDouble(6);
             System.out.printf("%6s | %-20s | %8.2f | %8.2f |
                                %8.2f | %8.2f \n",
                                empnumber, empname, basicpay,
                                allowances, deductions, netpay);
          }
        }

      return null;
    }
  }

    public void doDatabaseOperations() {
      jdbcTemplate.execute(new MyStatementCallback());
    }
  }
```

execute method with String parameter syntx

`void   execute(String)`

It executes the specified SQL statement as String parameter. If you want to obtain the result of the SQL statement, then it method is not suitable.

Example

```
// File Name: JDBCOperations.java
package com.springdemo;

import org.springframework.beans.factory.annotation.Autowired;
import org.springframework.jdbc.core.JdbcTemplate;

public class JDBCOperations {

  @Autowired
  private JdbcTemplate jdbcTemplate;

  public void doDatabaseOperations() {
     String sqlDelete = "delete from employee where empnumber = 1001";
     jdbcTemplate.execute(sqlDelete);
  }
}
```

PreparedStatementCreator/PreparedStatementCallback execute method syntax

`Object execute(PreparedStatementCreator obj1, PreparedStatementCallback obj2)`

It executes the code in

`PreparedStatementCallback.doInPreparedStatement()` method. The argument for the `doInPreparedStatement()` method is the

`PreparedStatement` returned by the

`PreparedStatementCreator.createPreparedStatement()` method.

The first parameter creates and returns a `PreparedStatment` and the second parameter takes that resultant `PreaparedStatement` for its method.

Example

```
// File Name: JDBCOperations.java
package com.springdemo;

import java.sql.Connection;
import java.sql.PreparedStatement;
import java.sql.SQLException;
```

```
import org.springframework.beans.factory.annotation.Autowired;
import org.springframework.dao.DataAccessException;
import org.springframework.jdbc.core.JdbcTemplate;
import org.springframework.jdbc.core.PreparedStatementCallback;
import org.springframework.jdbc.core.PreparedStatementCreator;


public class JDBCOperations {

   @Autowired
   private JdbcTemplate jdbcTemplate;

   private static class MyPreparedStatementCreator
                  implements PreparedStatementCreator {

  @Override
  public PreparedStatement createPreparedStatement(Connection connection)
                                                   throws SQLException {
    String sqlInsert = "insert into employee
                        (empnumber, empname, basicpay,
                        allowances, deductions)
                        values (?, ?, ?, ?, ?)";
    PreparedStatement ps = connection.prepareStatement(sqlInsert);
    return ps;
   }
  }

  private static class MyPreparedStatementCallback
                  implements PreparedStatementCallback {

   @Override
   public Object doInPreparedStatement(PreparedStatement ps)
                             throws SQLException, DataAccessException {
     ps.setInt(1, 1001);
     ps.setString(2, "Mohamed Ibrahim");
     ps.setDouble(3, 10000.0);
     ps.setDouble(4, 3000.0);
     ps.setDouble(5, 2000.0);
     ps.execute();
     return ps.getUpdateCount();
   }
  }
```

```
  public void doDatabaseOperations() {
    //Autoboxing convertes Integer object into int datatype
    int recordsAffected = (Integer) jdbcTemplate.execute(
                                   new MyPreparedStatementCreator(),
                                   new MyPreparedStatementCallback());
     System.out.println(recordsAffected + " record is inserted.");
  }
}
```

Check with database:

```
mysql>  select*from  employee;
```

empnumber	empname	basicpay	allowances	deductions	netpay
1001	Mohamed Ibrahim	10000	3000	2000	NULL

```
1  row  in  set  (0.00  sec)
```

execute method with String SQL parameter and PreparedStatementCallback

`Object execute(String s, PreparedStatementCallback obj)`

This method is similar to the previous one, except it creates the `PreparedStatement` from the String argument. It executes the `PreparedStatementCallback.doInPreparedStatement` when the `PreparedStatement` is created.

```
// File Name: JDBCOperations.java
package com.springdemo;

import java.sql.PreparedStatement;
import java.sql.SQLException;

import org.springframework.beans.factory.annotation.Autowired;
import org.springframework.dao.DataAccessException;
import org.springframework.jdbc.core.JdbcTemplate;
import org.springframework.jdbc.core.PreparedStatementCallback;

public class JDBCOperations {

  @Autowired
  private JdbcTemplate jdbcTemplate;
```

```
private static class MyPreparedStatementCallback
                implements PreparedStatementCallback {

    @Override
    public Object doInPreparedStatement(PreparedStatement ps)
                    throws SQLException, DataAccessException {
        ps.setInt(1, 1001);
        ps.setString(2, "Mohamed Ibrahim");
        ps.setDouble(3, 10000.0);
        ps.setDouble(4, 3000.0);
        ps.setDouble(5, 2000.0);
        ps.execute();
        return ps.getUpdateCount();
    }
}

public void doDatabaseOperations() {
    String sqlInsert = "insert into employee
                    (empnumber, empname, basicpay,
                     allowances, deductions)
                     values (?, ?, ?, ?, ?)";

    int recordsAffected =
        (Integer) jdbcTemplate.execute(sqlInsert,
        new MyPreparedStatementCallback());
         System.out.println(recordsAffected + " record is inserted.");
    }
}
```

`Object execute(CallableStatementCreator obj1, CallableStatementCallback obj2)`

This method is similar to the `execute(PreparedStatementCreator, PreparedStatementCallback)` method, but operates on Callable Statement.

Example

Create a function in MySQL.

```
mysql> delimiter //
mysql> CREATE FUNCTION AreaOfRectangle(l BIGINT, b BIGINT) RETURNS BIGINT
    -> BEGIN
    -> RETURN l * b;
    -> END
    -> //
```

```
Query OK, 0 rows affected (0.00 sec)

mysql> delimiter ;
mysql> select AreaOfRectangle(10,20);
              +------------------------+
              | AreaOfRectangle(10,20) |
              +------------------------+
              |                    200 |
              +------------------------+
1 row in set (0.01 sec)
```

```
// File Name: JDBCOperations.java
package com.springdemo;

import java.sql.CallableStatement;
import java.sql.Connection;
import java.sql.SQLException;
import java.sql.Types;

import org.springframework.beans.factory.annotation.Autowired;
import org.springframework.dao.DataAccessException;
import org.springframework.jdbc.core.CallableStatementCallback;
import org.springframework.jdbc.core.CallableStatementCreator;
import org.springframework.jdbc.core.JdbcTemplate;


public class JDBCOperations {

  @Autowired
  private JdbcTemplate jdbcTemplate;

  private static class MyCallableStatementCreator
                  implements CallableStatementCreator {

    @Override
    public CallableStatement createCallableStatement
                              (Connection connection)
                              throws SQLException {
    CallableStatement cs =
       connection.prepareCall("{? = call AreaOfRectangle(?,?)}");
    cs.registerOutParameter(1, Types.INTEGER);
```

```
        return cs;
    }
  }

  private static class MyCallableStatementCallback
                    implements CallableStatementCallback {
    @Override
    public Object doInCallableStatement(CallableStatement cs)
                                        throws SQLException,
                                            DataAccessException {
    cs.setInt(2, 10);
    cs.setInt(3, 20);
    cs.execute();
    return cs.getInt(1);
   }
  }

  public void doDatabaseOperations() {
     System.out.println("Area of Rectangle (Length = 10
                          and breadth = 20) is " +
       jdbcTemplate.execute(new MyCallableStatementCreator(),
                     new MyCallableStatementCallback()));
    }
  }
```

Output

```
Area of Rectangle (Length = 10 and breadth = 20) is 200
Operation performed successfully.
```

2.2.2 JdbcTemplate.query

Assume that the employee table contains the following data.

```
mysql> select * from employee;
```

empnumber	empname	basicpay	allowances	deductions	netpay
1001	Mohamed Ibrahim	10000	3000	2000	11000
1002	Kumar	12000	4000	2500	13500
1003	Ajay	8000	1500	800	8700

```
3 rows in set (0.00 sec)
```

Many query methods provided by this class, however the following of them simplifies the query operations.

`int queryForInt(String sql)`

Executes the specified SQL statement. The result is only one row with one column, whose value will be converted to `int` type and returned.

`long queryForLong(String sql)`

Executes the specified SQL statement and returns a single value in `long` data type as the result.

`Object queryForObject(String sql, Class requiredType)`

Executes the specified SQL statement. This SQL statement should return a single row with one column or null value. The returned value will be converted into `"requiredType"` (such as Integer, Long, String, etc.) object and returned.

`List queryForList(String sql)`

Executes the specified SQL statement. The column values of each row will be stored in a `Map` (column-name as the key and its value as value). All the `Maps` (one per row) will be added to a `List` and this `List` will be returned.

`Map queryForMap(String sql)`

Executes the specified SQL statement and only one is expected as result. The row is mapped to a `Map` (column-name as the key and its value as value) and this `Map` is returned.

`SqlRowSet queryForRowSet(String sql)`

Executes the specified SQL statement and returns the resultant row(s) in `SqlRowSet` representation.

Example

```
// File Name: JDBCOperations.java
package com.springdemo;

import java.util.List;
import java.util.Map;

import org.springframework.beans.factory.annotation.Autowired;
import org.springframework.jdbc.core.JdbcTemplate;
import org.springframework.jdbc.support.rowset.SqlRowSet;

public class JDBCOperations {

  @Autowired
  private JdbcTemplate jdbcTemplate;

  public void doDatabaseOperations() {
```

```
    //Single int value
     System.out.println("queryForInt(String sql)");
     int numOfRecords = jdbcTemplate
                        .queryForInt("select count(*) from employee");
     System.out.println("Total number of records in employee table [" +
                        numOfRecords + "]");

  //Single value in the specified type
  System.out.println("\nT queryForObject(String sql,
                     Object[] args, Class<T> requiredType)");
  double netpayOfEmployee = jdbcTemplate
                            .queryForObject("select netpay from
                            employee where empnumber = ?",
                            new Object[] { 1001 }, Double.class);
  System.out.println("Netpay of employee number 1001 is " +
                            netpayOfEmployee);

  //Multiple columns, but single row
  System.out.println("\nMap queryForMap(String sql, Object[] args)");
  Map<String, Object> employeeMap = jdbcTemplate.queryForMap(
            "select * from employee where empnumber = ?",
            new Object[] { 1001 });
  System.out.println("employeeMap " + employeeMap);

  for (Object item : employeeMap.entrySet()) {
    Map.Entry<String, Object> entry = (Map.Entry<String, Object>) item;
   System.out.println(entry.getKey() + " = " + entry.getValue());
   }

   //Multiple rows, but single column
   System.out.println("\nList queryForList(String sql)");
   List<Map<String, Object>> employeeNumberList =
                    jdbcTemplate.queryForList
                    ("select empnumber from employee");
   System.out.println("employeeMap " + employeeNumberList);
   for (Map<String, Object> item : employeeNumberList){
      System.out.println(item.get("empnumber"));
   }

   System.out.println("\nSqlRowSet queryForRowSet(String sql)");
   SqlRowSet rs = jdbcTemplate.queryForRowSet
                              ("select * from employee");
```

```
while (rs.next()) {
    int empnumber = rs.getInt("empnumber");
    String empname = rs.getString("empname");
    Double basicpay = rs.getDouble("basicpay");
    Double allowances = rs.getDouble("allowances");
    Double deductions = rs.getDouble("deductions");
    Double netpay = rs.getDouble("netpay");
    System.out.printf("%6s | %-20s | %8.2f | %8.2f |
                      %8.2f | %8.2f \n",
                      empnumber, empname, basicpay,
                      allowances, deductions, netpay);
    }
    if (rs != null) {
      rs = null;
     }
   }

}
```

Output:

```
queryForInt(String sql)
Total number of records in employee table [3]

T queryForObject(String sql, Object[] args, Class<T> requiredType)
Netpay of employee number 1001 is 11000.0

Map queryForMap(String sql, Object[] args)
employeeMap {empnumber=1001, empname=Mohamed Ibrahim, basicpay=10000.0,
allowances=3000.0, deductions=2000.0, netpay=11000.0}
empnumber = 1001
empname = Mohamed Ibrahim
basicpay = 10000.0
allowances = 3000.0
deductions = 2000.0
netpay = 11000.0

List queryForList(String sql)
employeeMap [{empnumber=1001}, {empnumber=1002}, {empnumber=1003}]
1001
1002
1003
```

```
SqlRowSet queryForRowSet(String sql)
```

1001	Mohamed Ibrahim	10000.00	3000.00	2000.00	11000.00
1002	Kumar	12000.00	4000.00	2500.00	13500.00
1003	Ajay	8000.00	1500.00	800.00	8700.00

```
Operation performed successfully.
```

2.2.3 JdbcTemplate.update

`int update(String sql)`

Executes the specified SQL statement and returns the total number of affected rows.

`int update(PreparedStatementCreator obj)`

Executes the statement returned from the `PreparedStatementCreator` and returns the number of rows affected.

`int update(String sql, Object[] args, int[] argTypes)`

Executes the specified SQL PreparedStatement (first argument) with argument values bind to the positional parameters in that PreparedStatement (second argument) and the data type of these positional parameter values are specified in the third argument.

The `data type` for the values of the `positional parameters` can be represented with `java.sql.Types` class.

Constant	SQL Type
Types.CHAR	CHAR
Types.VARCHAR	VARCHAR
Types.INTEGER	INTEGER
Types.DECIMAL	DECIMAL
Types.FLOAT	FLOAT
Types.DOUBLE	DOUBLE
Types.BIGINT	BIGINT
Types.BINARY	BINARY
Types.BIT	BIT
Types.BLOB	BLOB
Types.CLOB	CLOB
Types.DATE	DATE
Types.TIME	TIME
Types.TIMESTAMP	TIMESTAMP
Types.NULL	NULL

Example

Assumed that the "employee" table has the following values.

```
mysql> select * from employee;
```

empnumber	empname	basicpay	allowances	deductions	netpay
1001	Mohamed Ibrahim	10000	3000	2000	11000
1002	Kumar	12000	4000	2500	13500
1003	Ajay	8000	1500	800	8700

```
3 rows in set (0.16 sec)
```

```
// File Name: JDBCOperations.java
package com.springdemo;

import java.sql.Connection;
import java.sql.PreparedStatement;
import java.sql.SQLException;
import java.sql.Types;

import org.springframework.beans.factory.annotation.Autowired;
import org.springframework.jdbc.core.JdbcTemplate;
import org.springframework.jdbc.core.PreparedStatementCreator;

public class JDBCOperations {

  @Autowired
  private JdbcTemplate jdbcTemplate;

  public void doDatabaseOperations() {

     jdbcTemplate.update(new PreparedStatementCreator() {

     @Override
      public PreparedStatement createPreparedStatement(
                                     Connection connection)
                                     throws SQLException {

        PreparedStatement ps = connection
             .prepareStatement("update employee
             set allowances = (allowances + 500) where empnumber = ?");
        ps.setInt(1, 1001);
       return ps;
```

```
        }
    });

    jdbcTemplate.update("update employee set allowances =
               (allowances + 700)
               where empnumber = ?", new Object[] {1002},
               new int[] {Types.INTEGER});

      jdbcTemplate.update("update employee set netpay =
                        (basicpay + allowances - deductions)");
    }

  }
```

Check with database.

```
mysql> select * from employee;
```

empnumber	empname	basicpay	allowances	deductions	netpay
1001	Mohamed Ibrahim	10000	3500	2000	11500
1002	Kumar	12000	4700	2500	14200
1003	Ajay	8000	1500	800	8700

```
3 rows in set (0.00 sec)
```

2.3 SimpleJdbcInsert

A `SimpleJdbcInsert` provides easy insert capabilities for a database table.

SimpleJdbcInsert: Inserting values for all the columns

```
// File Name: Employee.java
package com.springdemo;

public class Employee {

  private int empNumber;
  private String empName;
  private double basicpay;
  private double allowances;
  private double deductions;
```

```
private double netpay;

public int getEmpNumber() {
  return empNumber;
}

public void setEmpNumber(int empNumber) {
 this.empNumber = empNumber;
}

public String getEmpName() {
  return empName;
}

public void setEmpName(String empName) {
  this.empName = empName;
}

public double getBasicpay() {
  return basicpay;
}

public void setBasicpay(double basicpay) {
  this.basicpay = basicpay;
}

public double getAllowances() {
  return allowances;
}

public void setAllowances(double allowances) {
  this.allowances = allowances;
}

public double getDeductions() {
  return deductions;
}

public void setDeductions(double deductions) {
  this.deductions = deductions;
}
```

```
    public double getNetpay() {
        return netpay;
    }

    public void setNetpay(double netpay) {
        this.netpay = netpay;
    }

}
```

```
// File Name: JDBCOperations.java
package com.springdemo;

import javax.sql.DataSource;

import org.springframework.beans.factory.annotation.Autowired;
import org.springframework.jdbc.core.namedparam
                                .BeanPropertySqlParameterSource;
import org.springframework.jdbc.core.simple.SimpleJdbcInsert;

public class JDBCOperations {

    private SimpleJdbcInsert simpleJdbcInsert;

    @Autowired
    JDBCOperations(DataSource dataSource) {
        simpleJdbcInsert = new SimpleJdbcInsert(dataSource);
    }

    public void doDatabaseOperations() {
        Employee employee = new Employee();
        employee.setEmpNumber(5001);
        employee.setEmpName("Arun Prakash");
        employee.setBasicpay(6000.0);
        employee.setAllowances(1500.0);
        employee.setDeductions(1000.0);
        employee.setNetpay(employee.getBasicpay() +
                        employee.getAllowances() -
                        employee.getDeductions());
```

```
simpleJdbcInsert.withTableName("employee")
                        .usingColumns("empnumber", "empname", "basicpay",
                                      "allowances", "deductions", "netpay")
                .execute(new BeanPropertySqlParameterSource(employee));

    }

}
```

Store the following "beans.xml" in the "src" directory of the project.

```
<?xml version="1.0" encoding="UTF-8"?>
<beans xmlns="http://www.springframework.org/schema/beans"
    xmlns:xsi="http://www.w3.org/2001/XMLSchema-instance"
    xmlns:context="http://www.springframework.org/schema/context"
    xsi:schemaLocation="http://www.springframework.org/schema/beans
    http://www.springframework.org/schema/beans/spring-beans-3.0.xsd
    http://www.springframework.org/schema/context
 http://www.springframework.org/schema/context/spring-context-3.0.xsd">

 <context:annotation-config />

 <bean id="dataSource" class="org.apache.commons.dbcp.BasicDataSource"
                        destroy-method="close">
    <property name="driverClassName" value="com.mysql.jdbc.Driver"/>
    <property name="url" value="jdbc:mysql://127.0.0.1:3306/demodb"/>
    <property name="username" value="ibrahim"/>
    <property name="password" value="pword"/>
  </bean>

  <bean id="jdbcOperations" class="com.springdemo.JDBCOperations"/>

</beans>
```

Check with database.

```
mysql>  select  *  from  employee;
```

empnumber	empname	basicpay	allowances	deductions	netpay
5001	Arun Prakash	6000	1500	1000	6500

```
1  row  in  set  (0.02  sec)
```

SimpleJdbcInsert: Inserting values for some of the columns

```
// File Name: JDBCOperations.java
package com.springdemo;

import javax.sql.DataSource;

import org.springframework.beans.factory.annotation.Autowired;
import
org.springframework.jdbc.core.namedparam.BeanPropertySqlParameterSource;
import org.springframework.jdbc.core.simple.SimpleJdbcInsert;

public class JDBCOperations {

    private SimpleJdbcInsert simpleJdbcInsert;

    @Autowired
    JDBCOperations(DataSource dataSource) {
      simpleJdbcInsert = new SimpleJdbcInsert(dataSource);
    }

    public void doDatabaseOperations() {
      Employee employee = new Employee();
      employee.setEmpNumber(5002);
      employee.setEmpName("Ajay");
      simpleJdbcInsert.withTableName("employee")
                      .usingColumns("empnumber", "empname")
               .execute(new BeanPropertySqlParameterSource(employee));

    }

}
```

Check with database.

```
mysql> select * from employee;
```

empnumber	empname	basicpay	allowances	deductions	netpay
5001	Arun Prakash	6000	1500	1000	6500
5002	Ajay	NULL	NULL	NULL	NULL

```
2 rows in set (0.00 sec)
```

SimpleJdbcInsert: Inserting values for some of the columns (Bean Property names and Database Table Field names are different)

```
// File Name: Employee.java
package com.springdemo;

public class Employee {

    private int employeeNumber;
    private String employeeName;
    private double basicpay;
    private double allowances;
    private double deductions;
    private double netpay;

    public int getEmployeeNumber() {
        return employeeNumber;
    }

    public void setEmployeeNumber(int employeeNumber) {
        this.employeeNumber = employeeNumber;
    }

    public String getEmployeeName() {
        return employeeName;
    }

    public void setEmployeeName(String employeeName) {
        this.employeeName = employeeName;
    }

    public double getBasicpay() {
        return basicpay;
    }

    public void setBasicpay(double basicpay) {
        this.basicpay = basicpay;
    }

    public double getAllowances() {
        return allowances;
    }
```

```
    public void setAllowances(double allowances) {
      this.allowances = allowances;
    }

    public double getDeductions() {
      return deductions;
    }

    public void setDeductions(double deductions) {
      this.deductions = deductions;
    }

    public double getNetpay() {
      return netpay;
    }

    public void setNetpay(double netpay) {
      this.netpay = netpay;
    }

}
```

```
// File Name: JDBCOperations.java
package com.springdemo;

import java.util.HashMap;
import java.util.Map;

import javax.sql.DataSource;

import org.springframework.beans.factory.annotation.Autowired;
import org.springframework.jdbc.core.simple.SimpleJdbcInsert;

public class JDBCOperations {

    private SimpleJdbcInsert simpleJdbcInsert;

    @Autowired
    JDBCOperations(DataSource dataSource) {
      simpleJdbcInsert = new SimpleJdbcInsert(dataSource);
    }
```

```
public void doDatabaseOperations() {
    Employee employee = new Employee();
    employee.setEmployeeNumber(6001);
    employee.setEmployeeName("Kumar");

    Map<String, Object> parameters = new HashMap<String, Object>(2);
    parameters.put("empnumber", employee.getEmployeeNumber());
    parameters.put("empname", employee.getEmployeeName());
    simpleJdbcInsert.withTableName("employee").execute(parameters);
  }

}
```

Check with database.

```
mysql> select * from employee;
```

empnumber	empname	basicpay	allowances	deductions	netpay
6001	Kumar	NULL	NULL	NULL	NULL

```
1 row in set (0.00 sec)
```

2.4 BATCH UPDATE

Batch Update feature provides the ability to submit multiple update statements to the database for processing as a single unit. This batch updating is significantly more efficient and fast for processing bulk updates, rather than executing each update (insert, update, delete ...) statements separately.

```
// File Name: JDBCOperations.java
package com.springdemo;

import java.util.ArrayList;

import javax.sql.DataSource;

import org.springframework.beans.factory.annotation.Autowired;
import org.springframework.jdbc.core.namedparam.SqlParameterSource;
import org.springframework.jdbc.core.namedparam.SqlParameterSourceUtils;
import org.springframework.jdbc.core.simple.SimpleJdbcTemplate;
```

```
public class JDBCOperations {

   private SimpleJdbcTemplate simpleJdbcTemplate;

   @Autowired
   JDBCOperations(DataSource dataSource) {
      simpleJdbcTemplate = new SimpleJdbcTemplate(dataSource);
   }

   public void doDatabaseOperations() {
      Employee emp[] = new Employee[3];
      for (int i = 0; i < 3; i++){
         emp[i] = new Employee();
      }

      ArrayList<Employee> empList = new ArrayList<Employee>();

      Employee emp1 = new Employee();
      emp1.setEmpNumber(1001);
      emp1.setEmpName("Ibrahim");
      empList.add(emp1);

      Employee emp2 = new Employee();
      emp2.setEmpNumber(1002);
      emp2.setEmpName("Ajay");
      empList.add(emp2);

      Employee emp3 = new Employee();
      emp3.setEmpNumber(1003);
      emp3.setEmpName("Kumar");
      empList.add(emp3);

      SqlParameterSource[] batchData =
       SqlParameterSourceUtils.createBatch(empList.toArray());

   // Specify fields names in the Employee bean
   // prefixed with colon (:)
   simpleJdbcTemplate.batchUpdate
                ("insert into employee(empnumber, empname)
                 values (:empNumber, :empName)", batchData);
   }

}
```

Check with database.

```
mysql> select * from employee;
```

empnumber	empname	basicpay	allowances	deductions	netpay
1001	Ibrahim	NULL	NULL	NULL	NULL
1002	Ajay	NULL	NULL	NULL	NULL
1003	Kumar	NULL	NULL	NULL	NULL

```
3 rows in set (0.00 sec)
```

CHAPTER 3

DAO AND TRANSACTION MANAGEMENT

The **Data Access Object (DAO)** is a design pattern, provides abstract interface to a database (any persistence storage). DAO separates a data resource's client interface from its data access mechanisms, so it is easy to handle code while switching to other database systems. The **Object Relational Mapping (ORM)** is technique to map (convert) data represented in Object Oriented Programming Languages into Relational database and vice versa. Spring provides support to DAO and popular ORM frameworks such as Hibernate and iBATIS. Hibernate is an open source Java based ORM framework.

3.1 @ Repository

This annotation can be applied to any DAO, which uses any persistence technique such as Hiberante, JPA and JDBC.

This `@Repository` annotation is to translate technology specific (native) exceptions into more meaningful Spring Framework specific exceptions. For example, `HibernateException` (or sub-classes of it) will be thrown by the DAO if an exception is thrown in Hibernate environment, subclass of a `PersistenceException` and subclass of `JDOException` will be thrown in case of JPA and JDO environment respectively. All these kind of exceptions are run-time exception and cannot be caught. In such cases, this `@Repository` annotation is handy in converting these kinds of technology specific exceptions into Spring Framework specific exceptions.

The `@Component` is a generic stereotype for any Spring-managed component. The `@Repository`, `@Service`, and `@Controller` are specializations of `@Component` for more specific functionalities, for example, in the persistence, service, and presentation layers, respectively; the `@Repository` is a marker annotation for a class that fulfils the role or stereotype (also known as Data Access Object) of a repository.

This kind of annotation based configuration, instead of XML based configuration, provides automatic component scanning support to find all DAO classes (which are annotated with `@Repository`).

Spring Framework can automatically detect stereotyped classes (`@Component`, `@Repository`, `@Service`, and `@Controller`) and register their corresponding Bean Definitions with the *ApplicationContext*. To do, include `"context:component-scan"` element.

To auto-detect these classes and register the corresponding beans, you need to include the following element in XML, where the base-package element is a common parent package for the classes (Alternatively, you can specify a comma-separated list that includes the parent package of each class).

The following definition will scan and detect all stereotyped classes under com.springdemo package.

```
<?xml version="1.0" encoding="UTF-8"?>
<beans xmlns="http://www.springframework.org/schema/beans"
    xmlns:xsi="http://www.w3.org/2001/XMLSchema-instance"
    xmlns:context="http://www.springframework.org/schema/context"
    xsi:schemaLocation="http://www.springframework.org/schema/beans
    http://www.springframework.org/schema/beans/spring-beans-3.0.xsd
    http://www.springframework.org/schema/context
  http://www.springframework.org/schema/context/spring-context-3.0.xsd">

<context:component-scan base-package="com.springdemo"/>

</beans>
```

Example,

```
@Repository
public class EmployeeDAOImpl implements EmployeeDAO {

}
```

We will take Hibernate 3 as ORM for our example programs.

Hibernate SessionFactory is used to create Sessions through which interaction with database is performed. One can inject SessionFactory as shown in the following code segment.

```
@Repository
public class EmployeeDAOImpl implements EmployeeDAO {

    @Autowired
    SessionFactory sessionFactory;

}
```

The bean object sessionFactory should be defined in the Spring application context. The following code sets up a JDBC data source (in our case, the demodb database in MySQL database system) and a Hibernate SessionFactory on top of it.

```
<beans ...>

   <bean id="dataSource" class="org.apache.commons.dbcp.BasicDataSource"
                                destroy-method="close">
      <property name="driverClassName" value="com.mysql.jdbc.Driver"/>
      <property name="url" value="jdbc:mysql://127.0.0.1:3306/demodb"/>
      <property name="username" value="ibrahim"/>
      <property name="password" value="pword"/>
   </bean>

   <bean id="sessionFactory"
   class=" org.springframework.orm.hibernate4.LocalSessionFactoryBean">
         <property name="dataSource" ref="dataSource"/>
   ...
   </bean>
```

3.2 TRANSACTION

Transaction is a sequence of operations which are considered as a single unit. The core idea behind a transaction is that all the operations in a transaction should be executed successfully or none of them should be executed.

If any one of the operations in a transaction fails, then all the already executed operations in the transaction should not be applied (This is called **'rollback',** which brings the operations to their previous state) and remaining operations in that transaction, if any, will not be executed.

If all the operations in a transaction became successful, then the transaction can be declared as permanent (This is called **'commit'**).

Spring supports both Declarative and Programmatic transaction management. You can write your transaction using Java code directly in Programmatic Transaction Management. Declarative Transaction Management is a non-programmatic demarcation of transaction boundaries, achieved by configuring the beans to be transactional (without writing any transaction management code at all).

3.2.1 Declarative Transaction Management

Spring supports both XML based and Annotation based approach of declaring declarative transactions. We will use annotation based configuration in our example.

The following configuration in the beans declaration XML enables the annotation based transaction behaviour.

```
<tx:annotation-driven />
```

A Transaction Manager should also be specified in the beans configuration XML file. The following code is for specifying Hibernate based Transaction Manager.

```
<bean id="transactionManager"
      class=" org.springframework.orm.hibernate4
              .HibernateTransactionManager">
    <property name="sessionFactory" ref="sessionFactory"/>
</bean>
```

Note that the name of the transaction manager bean (id) should be "transactionManager". If you want to use different name, then you must specify that name in `<tx:annotation-driven />` using `transaction-manager` attribute.

@Transactional

This annotation is used to indicate that a class, a method in a class, interface, or a method in an interface should have transaction semantics. When this annotation is applied to a method in a class, then that method should have 'public' visibility. It is recommended to apply this annotation on classes and methods in classes, but not with interfaces and methods in interfaces as applying on interfaces have some limitations. The `@Transactional` setting at class level applies to all the methods in that class, however the `@Transactional` setting at the method level takes precedence over the setting at class level.

General Format of @Transactional

```
@Transactional
 (propagation = [Propagation.REQUIRED |
                 Propagation.REQUIRES_NEW],
 Isolation  =   [Isolation.DEFAULT |
                 Isolation.READ_COMMITTED |
                 Isolation.READ_UNCOMMTTED |
                 Isolation.REPEATABLE_READ |
                 Isolation.SERIALIZABLE],
 readOnly = [true | false],
 timeout=seconds,
 rollbackFor = [array of class objects],
 rollbackForClassname = [array of String class names],
 noRollbackFor = [array of class objects],
 noRollbackForClassname = [array of String class names])
```

All the attributes of `@Transactional` annotation are optional.

propagation: This attribute defines the transaction boundary, where does the transaction start and where does it end?. When a method in a transaction scope calls another method, then what level of transaction scope that should be applied for the called method?

There are few transaction types available, two of the frequently used types are listed below.

`Propagation.REQUIRED`: It is the default value. It supports a current transaction, creates a new one if none exists.

`Propogation.REQUIRES_NEW`: It always starts a new transaction when the method is started, whether or not an existing transaction is present and suspends the current transaction if one exists.

`isolation`: Isolation property specifies which version of data should be taken at concurrent transaction environment (When simultaneous transaction are running with a database table(s), then the data at table(s) are dirty at the middle of the transactions). Some possible values for this attribute are listed below.

`Isolation.DEFAULT`: Uses the default isolation level of the underlying data-source.

`Isolation.READ_COMMITTED`: Non-Repeatable Read/Phantom read are allowed.

`Isolation.READ_UNCOMMTTED`: Dirty Read/Non-Repeatable Read/Phantom read are allowed.

`Isolation.REPEATABLE_READ`: Phantom read is allowed.

`Isolation.SERIALIZABLE`: Dirty Read/Non-Repeatable Read/Phantom read are not allowed.

`readOnly`: Default to false. Set to 'true' for read-only transaction and 'false' for read/write transaction.

`timeout`: Raises timeout if the transaction is not completed within the specified interval of time.

`rollbackFor`: By default, any `RuntimeException` triggers rollback, and any checked `Exception` does not. This attribute accepts an array of exception class (must be derived from `Throwable`) objects which should cause rollback.

> Cross Reference: A checked exception is any subclass of Exception (or Exception itself), excluding class RuntimeException and its subclasses. Checked exceptions must be caught (using try...catch or throws) at compile time, Runtime exceptions do not need to be.

`rollbackForClassname`: This attribute accepts an array of exception class (must be derived from `Throwable`) names that must cause rollback.

`noRollbackFor`: This attribute accepts an array of exception class (must be derived from `Throwable`) objects which should not cause rollback.

`noRollbackForClassname`: This attribute accepts an array of exception class (must be derived from `Throwable`) names that must not cause rollback.

Example Application,

Here is the application for Employee payroll. This application uses JPA (Java Persistence API) with Hibernate to access employee data stored in MySQL database system.

Assumed that you are following the same setting as described in the first chapter (1.1 Setting up the Environment section). The examples in this chapter use MySQL database system as data source. Assumed that you had already created a database 'demodb' for the user 'ibrahim' with password 'pword'. Refer first chapter for creating user/database in MySQL.

Download latest Hibernate distribution from *hibernate.org/sourceforce.net* (Hibernate version 4.1.10 is used in executing the following example). Unzip the downloaded file (hibernate-release-4.1.10.Final.zip) and copy all the jar files under "\lib\required" directory to our projects "lib" directory.

Download the following required jar files from Maven repository (you can download from their own distribution sites) and place them on our project's "lib" directory.

aopalliance-1.0.jar (AOP Alliance API)

commons-dbcp-1.4.jar (Apache Database Connection Pool)

commons-pool-1.6.jar (Apache Pool)

mysql-connector-java-5.1.23.jar (MySQL Connector for Java)

commons-logging-1.1.1.jar (Logging)

Then include all the jar files under this "lib" directory into classpath of the project.

It will be easier if you use Maven, a project management tool, for developing Spring based applications that no need to manually find and download all dependent library jars and Maven will do for you.

Create a package `com.springdemo.entity`. Store the following file in this package.

```
//File Name: Employee.java
package com.springdemo.entity;

import javax.persistence.Column;
import javax.persistence.Entity;
import javax.persistence.GeneratedValue;
import javax.persistence.Id;
import javax.persistence.Table;

import org.hibernate.annotations.GenericGenerator;

@Entity
@Table(name = "EMPLOYEE")
public class Employee {

   @Id
   @GeneratedValue(generator = "idGen")
   @GenericGenerator(name = "idGen", strategy="assigned")
   @Column(name="EMPNUMBER")
   private int empNumber;
```

```
    @Column(name="EMPNAME")
    private String empName;

    @Column(name="BASICPAY")
    private double basicpay;

    @Column(name="ALLOWANCES")
    private double allowances;

    @Column(name="DEDUCTIONS")
    private double deductions;

    @Column(name="NETPAY")
    private double netpay;

    public Employee() {}

    public Employee(int empNumber, String empName, double basicpay,
                    double allowances, double deductions){
        this.empNumber = empNumber;
        this.empName = empName;
        this.basicpay = basicpay;
        this.allowances = allowances;
        this.deductions = deductions;

        netpay = basicpay + allowances - deductions;
    }

    public int getEmpNumber() {
        return empNumber;
    }

  public void setEmpNumber(int empNumber) {
  this.empNumber = empNumber;
  }

  public String getEmpName() {
    return empName;
  }

   public void setEmpName(String empName) {
     this.empName = empName;
```

```
}

public double getBasicpay() {
  return basicpay;
}

public void setBasicpay(double basicpay) {
  this.basicpay = basicpay;
}

public double getAllowances() {
  return allowances;
}

public void setAllowances(double allowances) {
  this.allowances = allowances;
}

public double getDeductions() {
  return deductions;
}

public void setDeductions(double deductions) {
  this.deductions = deductions;
}

public double getNetpay() {
  return netpay;
}

public void setNetpay(double netpay) {
  this.netpay = netpay;
}

public String toString() {
  String rStr = "\nEmp Number: " + empNumber +
                "\nEmp Name:   " + empName +
                "\nBasicpay:   " + basicpay +
                "\nAllowances: " + allowances +
                "\nDeductions: " + deductions +
                "\nNetpay :    " + netpay;
 return rStr;
 }
}
```

Create a package `com.springdemo.dao`. Store the following file in this package.

```
//File Name: EmployeeDAO.java
package com.springdemo.dao;

import java.util.List;

import com.springdemo.entity.Employee;

public interface EmployeeDAO
{
  void addEmployee(Employee employee);
  Employee getEmployee(int empNumber);
  List<Employee> getAllEmployees();
  void deleteEmployee(int empNumber) throws Exception;
  void updateEmployee(Employee employee);
}
```

Create a package `com.springdemo.daoimpl`. Store the following file in this package.

```
//File Name: EmployeeDAOImpl.java
package com.springdemo.daoimpl;

import java.util.List;

import org.hibernate.Criteria;
import org.hibernate.SessionFactory;
import org.hibernate.criterion.Restrictions;
import org.springframework.beans.factory.annotation.Autowired;
import org.springframework.stereotype.Repository;
import org.springframework.transaction.annotation.Transactional;

import com.springdemo.dao.EmployeeDAO;
import com.springdemo.entity.Employee;

@Repository
@Transactional
public class EmployeeDAOImpl implements EmployeeDAO {

   @Autowired
   SessionFactory sessionFactory;
```

```
@Override
public void addEmployee(Employee employee) {
    sessionFactory.getCurrentSession().save(employee);
}

@Override
public void deleteEmployee(int empNumber) throws Exception {
   Employee employee = getEmployee(empNumber);
   if (employee == null)
          throw new Exception("Employee record not found");
    sessionFactory.getCurrentSession().delete(employee);
}

@Override
@Transactional(readOnly = true)
public Employee getEmployee(int empNumber) {
   Criteria criteria = sessionFactory.getCurrentSession()
                                     .createCriteria(Employee.class)
                        .add(Restrictions.eq("empNumber", empNumber));
  List<Employee> list = criteria.list();
  if (!list.isEmpty())
    return list.get(0);
  return null;
}

@Override
@Transactional(readOnly = true)
public List<Employee> getAllEmployees() {
   Criteria criteria = sessionFactory.getCurrentSession()
                                    .createCriteria(Employee.class);
   List<Employee> list = criteria.list();
   return list;
 }

 @Override
 public void updateEmployee(Employee employee) {
  sessionFactory.getCurrentSession().update(employee);
}

}
```

In com.springdemo package, add the following files.

```
//File Name: DAOOperations.java
package com.springdemo;

import java.util.List;

import org.springframework.beans.factory.annotation.Autowired;

import com.springdemo.dao.EmployeeDAO;
import com.springdemo.entity.Employee;

public class DAOOperations {

   @Autowired
   EmployeeDAO employeeDAO;

   void doOperations() {
      Employee employeeIbrahim =
                 new Employee(1001, "Ibrahim", 10000.0, 3000.0, 1000.0);
      Employee employeeKumar =
                    new Employee(1002, "Kumar", 8000.0, 2000.0, 500.0);
      employeeDAO.addEmployee(employeeIbrahim);
      employeeDAO.addEmployee(employeeKumar);

  System.out.println("Retrieving data from database for Employee Number
      1001");
   Employee employee1 = employeeDAO.getEmployee(1001);
   System.out.println(employee1);

   System.out.println("Updating the retrieved record");
   employee1.setEmpName("Mr. " + employee1.getEmpName());
   employeeDAO.updateEmployee(employee1);

   System.out.println("Retrieving data after update");
   Employee employee2 = employeeDAO.getEmployee(1001);
   System.out.println(employee2);

   System.out.println("Getting all the employees");
   List<Employee> empList = employeeDAO.getAllEmployees();
   for (Employee emp : empList) {
      System.out.println(emp);
   }
```

```
System.out.println("Deleting employee record with employee number 1002");
try {
   employeeDAO.deleteEmployee(1002);
}
catch (Exception e) {
   System.out.println("Error occurred [" + e.getMessage() +"]");
   e.printStackTrace();
}

System.out.println("Getting all the employees after the deletion");
empList = employeeDAO.getAllEmployees();
for (Employee emp : empList) {
   System.out.println(emp);
  }

 }
}
```

```
//File Name: HibernateDAODemo.java
package com.springdemo;

import org.springframework.context.support.AbstractApplicationContext;
import org.springframework.context.support.ClassPathXmlApplicationContext;

public class HibernateDAODemo {

   public static void main(String[] args) {
      AbstractApplicationContext context =
                  new ClassPathXmlApplicationContext("beans.xml");
      DAOOperations daoOperations =
                 (DAOOperations) context.getBean("daoOperations");
      daoOperations.doOperations();
      System.out.println("Operation performed successfully.");
   }
}
```

Store the following “beans.xml” file in the “src” directory of the project.

```
<?xml version="1.0" encoding="UTF-8"?>
<beans xmlns="http://www.springframework.org/schema/beans"
   xmlns:xsi="http://www.w3.org/2001/XMLSchema-instance"
   xmlns:context="http://www.springframework.org/schema/context"
   xmlns:tx="http://www.springframework.org/schema/tx"
   xsi:schemaLocation="http://www.springframework.org/schema/beans
    http://www.springframework.org/schema/beans/spring-beans-3.0.xsd
   http://www.springframework.org/schema/context
   http://www.springframework.org/schema/context/spring-context-3.0.xsd
    http://www.springframework.org/schema/tx
    http://www.springframework.org/schema/tx/spring-tx-2.5.xsd">

 <context:annotation-config/>
 <context:component-scan base-package="com.springdemo"/>

 <tx:annotation-driven/>

 <bean id="dataSource" class="org.apache.commons.dbcp.BasicDataSource"
                         destroy-method="close">
    <property name="driverClassName" value="com.mysql.jdbc Driver"/>
    <property name="url" value="jdbc:mysql://127.0.0.1:3306/demodb"/>
    <property name="username" value="ibrahim"/>
    <property name="password" value="pword"/>
</bean>

<!-- Hibernate Annotated SessionFactory -->
<bean id="sessionFactory"
       class=" org.springframework.orm.hibernate4
                 .LocalSessionFactoryBean">
     <property name="dataSource" ref="dataSource"/>

     <!-- All Hiberated annotated classes @Entity -->
     <property name="annotatedClasses">
        <list>
           <value>com.springdemo.entity.Employee</value>
       </list>
    </property>

    <!-- Hibernate configuration properties -->
```

```
    <property name="hibernateProperties">
        <props>
            <prop key="hibernate.hbm2ddl.auto">create</prop>
            <prop key="hibernate.dialect">
                org.hibernate.dialect.MySQLDialect
            </prop>
            <prop key="hibernate.show_sql">true</prop>
            <prop key="hibernate.c3p0.minPoolSize">5</prop>
            <prop key="hibernate.c3p0.maxPoolSize">20</prop>
            <prop key="hibernate.c3p0.timeout">600</prop>
            <prop key="hibernate.c3p0.max_statement">50</prop>
        </props>
    </property>
  </bean>

  <bean id="transactionManager"
        class=" org.springframework.orm.hibernate4
                .HibernateTransactionManager">
        <property name="sessionFactory" ref="sessionFactory"/>
    </bean>

     <bean id="daoOperations" class="com.springdemo.DAOOperations"/>

</beans>
```

The following is the output while executing HibernateDAODemo.java program.

```
Hibernate: drop table if exists EMPLOYEE
Hibernate: create table EMPLOYEE (EMPNUMBER integer not null, ALLOWANCES
double precision, BASICPAY double precision, DEDUCTIONS double precision,
EMPNAME varchar(255), NETPAY double precision, primary key (EMPNUMBER))
INFO: HHH000230: Schema export complete
org.springframework.orm.hibernate4.HibernateTransactionManager
afterPropertiesSet
INFO: Using DataSource [org.apache.commons.dbcp.BasicDataSource@42f352]
of Hibernate SessionFactory for HibernateTransactionManager
Hibernate: insert into EMPLOYEE (ALLOWANCES, BASICPAY, DEDUCTIONS, EMPNAME,
NETPAY, EMPNUMBER) values (?, ?, ?, ?, ?, ?)
Hibernate: insert into EMPLOYEE (ALLOWANCES, BASICPAY, DEDUCTIONS, EMPNAME,
NETPAY, EMPNUMBER) values (?, ?, ?, ?, ?, ?)
Retrieving data from database for Employee Number 1001
```

```
Hibernate: select this_.EMPNUMBER as EMPNUMBER0_0_, this_.ALLOWANCES as
ALLOWANCES0_0_, this_.BASICPAY as BASICPAY0_0_, this_.DEDUCTIONS as
DEDUCTIONS0_0_, this_.EMPNAME as EMPNAME0_0_, this_.NETPAY as NETPAY0_0_
from EMPLOYEE this_ where this_.EMPNUMBER=?

Emp Number: 1001
Emp Name:   Ibrahim
Basicpay:   10000.0
Allowances: 3000.0
Deductions: 1000.0
Netpay :    12000.0
Updating the retrieved record
Hibernate: update EMPLOYEE set ALLOWANCES=?, BASICPAY=?, DEDUCTIONS=?,
EMPNAME=?, NETPAY=? where EMPNUMBER=?
Retrieving data after update
Hibernate: select this_.EMPNUMBER as EMPNUMBER0_0_, this_.ALLOWANCES as
ALLOWANCES0_0_, this_.BASICPAY as BASICPAY0_0_, this_.DEDUCTIONS as
DEDUCTIONS0_0_, this_.EMPNAME as EMPNAME0_0_, this_.NETPAY as NETPAY0_0_
from EMPLOYEE this_ where this_.EMPNUMBER=?

Emp Number: 1001
Emp Name: Mr. Ibrahim
Basicpay:   10000.0
Allowances: 3000.0
Deductions: 1000.0
Netpay :    12000.0
Getting all the employees
Hibernate: select this_.EMPNUMBER as EMPNUMBER0_0_, this_.ALLOWANCES as
ALLOWANCES0_0_, this_.BASICPAY as BASICPAY0_0_, this_.DEDUCTIONS as
DEDUCTIONS0_0_, this_.EMPNAME as EMPNAME0_0_, this_.NETPAY as NETPAY0_0_
from EMPLOYEE this_

Emp Number: 1001
Emp Name: Mr. Ibrahim
Basicpay:   10000.0
Allowances: 3000.0
Deductions: 1000.0
Netpay :    12000.0

Emp Number: 1002
Emp Name: Kumar
Basicpay: 8000.0
Allowances: 2000.0
```

```
Deductions: 500.0
Netpay :    9500.0
Deleting employee record with employee number 1002
Hibernate: select this_.EMPNUMBER as EMPNUMBER0_0_, this_.ALLOWANCES as
ALLOWANCES0_0_, this_.BASICPAY as BASICPAY0_0_, this_.DEDUCTIONS as
DEDUCTIONS0_0_, this_.EMPNAME as EMPNAME0_0_, this_.NETPAY as NETPAY0_0_
from EMPLOYEE this_ where this_.EMPNUMBER=?
Hibernate: delete from EMPLOYEE where EMPNUMBER=?
Getting all the employees after the deletion
Hibernate: select this_.EMPNUMBER as EMPNUMBER0_0_, this_.ALLOWANCES as
ALLOWANCES0_0_, this_.BASICPAY as BASICPAY0_0_, this_.DEDUCTIONS as
DEDUCTIONS0_0_, this_.EMPNAME as EMPNAME0_0_, this_.NETPAY as NETPAY0_0_
from EMPLOYEE this_

Emp Number: 1001
Emp Name: Mr. Ibrahim
Basicpay:   10000.0
Allowances: 3000.0
Deductions: 1000.0
Netpay :    12000.0
Operation performed successfully.
```

Check with database.

```
mysql> desc employee;
```

Field	Type	Null	Key	Default	Extra
EMPNUMBER	int(11)	NO	PRI	NULL	
ALLOWANCES	double	YES		NULL	
BASICPAY	double	YES		NULL	
DEDUCTIONS	double	YES		NULL	
EMPNAME	varchar(255)	YES		NULL	
NETPAY	double	YES		NULL	

```
6 rows in set (0.06 sec)

mysql> select * from employee;
```

EMPNUMBER	ALLOWANCES	BASICPAY	DEDUCTIONS	EMPNAME	NETPAY
1001	3000	10000	1000	Mr. Ibrahim	12000

```
1 row in set (0.00 sec)
```

3.2.2 Programmatic Transaction Management

In this programmatic transaction management case, the programmer has more control over transactions. The programmer uses external methods to invoke commit or rollback operations.

The following example demonstrates how to use programmatic transaction in a JDBC based application.

Create a table named "account" and insert two records as shown below.

```
C:\>mysql -u ibrahim -ppword demodb
Welcome to the MySQL monitor. Commands end with ; or \g.
Server version: 5.5.11 MySQL Community Server (GPL)

mysql> create table account (
     -> acc_num int not null,
     -> amount double unsigned not null default '0' );
Query OK, 0 rows affected (0.48 sec)

mysql> desc account;
```

Field	Type	Null	Key	Default	Extra
acc_num	int(11)	NO		NULL	
amount	double unsigned	NO		0	

```
2 rows in set (0.17 sec)

mysql> insert into account(acc_num, amount) values
      -> (1001, 5000.0);
Query OK, 1 row affected (0.05 sec)

mysql> insert into account(acc_num, amount) values
      -> (1002, 6000.0);
Query OK, 1 row affected (0.01 sec)

mysql> select * from account;
```

acc_num	amount
1001	5000
1002	6000

```
2 rows in set (0.00 sec)
```

Store the following file named "ProgrammaticTxn.java" in the "com.springdemo" package.

```
//File Name: ProgrammaticTxn.java

package com.springdemo;

import javax.sql.DataSource;

import org.springframework.beans.factory.annotation.Autowired;
import org.springframework.jdbc.core.simple.SimpleJdbcTemplate;
import org.springframework.transaction.PlatformTransactionManager;
import org.springframework.transaction.TransactionDefinition;
import org.springframework.transaction.TransactionStatus;
import org.springframework.transaction.support
                            .DefaultTransactionDefinition;

public class ProgrammaticTxn {

      private SimpleJdbcTemplate simpleJdbcTemplate;
      private PlatformTransactionManager transactionManager;

      @Autowired
      ProgrammaticTxn(DataSource dataSource) {
            simpleJdbcTemplate = new SimpleJdbcTemplate(dataSource);
            System.out.println("simpleJdbcTemplate is set");
      }

      @Autowired
      public void setTransactionManager
           (PlatformTransactionManager transactionManager) {
           this.transactionManager = transactionManager;
           System.out.println("transactionManager is set");
      }

      public void doTransaction(int fromAccount, int toAccount,
                                double transferAmount) {
           String debitSQL = "update account set amount = amount - " +
                             transferAmount +
                             " where acc_num = " + fromAccount;
```

```
        String creditSQL = "update account set amount = amount + " +
                           transferAmount +
                           " where acc_num = " + toAccount;

        TransactionDefinition txnDefinition =
                             new DefaultTransactionDefinition();
        TransactionStatus txnStatus =
              transactionManager.getTransaction(txnDefinition);
        System.out.println("Start of Transaction");

        try {
              simpleJdbcTemplate.update(debitSQL);
              simpleJdbcTemplate.update(creditSQL);

              transactionManager.commit(txnStatus);
              System.out.println("Transaction is committed");
        }
        catch (Exception e) {
              e.printStackTrace();
              transactionManager.rollback(txnStatus);
              System.out.println("Transaction is rolled back");
        }
        System.out.println("End of Transaction");
    }
}
```

Store the following file named "ProgramaticTxnDemo.java" in the "com.springdemo" package.

```
//File Name: ProgramaticTxnDemo.java

package com.springdemo;

import org.springframework.context.support.AbstractApplicationContext;
import org.springframework.context.support.ClassPathXmlApplicationContext;

public class ProgramaticTxnDemo {

  public static void main(String[] args) {
```

```
        AbstractApplicationContext context =
                       new ClassPathXmlApplicationContext("beans.xml");
        ProgrammaticTxn programmaticTxn = (ProgrammaticTxn)
                                 context.getBean("programmaticTxn");
        programmaticTxn.doTransaction(1001, 1002, 500.0);
    }
}
```

Store the following "beans.xml" file in the "src" directory of the project.

```
<?xml version="1.0" encoding="UTF-8"?>
<beans xmlns="http://www.springframework.org/schema/beans"
   xmlns:xsi="http://www.w3.org/2001/XMLSchema-instance"
   xmlns:context="http://www.springframework.org/schema/context"
   xmlns:tx="http://www.springframework.org/schema/tx"
   xsi:schemaLocation="http://www.springframework.org/schema/beans
   http://www.springframework.org/schema/beans/spring-beans-3.0.xsd
   http://www.springframework.org/schema/context
  http://www.springframework.org/schema/context/spring-context-3.0.xsd
   http://www.springframework.org/schema/tx
   http://www.springframework.org/schema/tx/spring-tx-2.5.xsd">

 <context:annotation-config/>
 <context:component-scan base-package="com.springdemo"/>

 <tx:annotation-driven/>

 <bean id="dataSource" class="org.apache.commons.dbcp.BasicDataSource"
                    destroy-method="close">
   <property name="driverClassName" value="com.mysql.jdbc.Driver"/>
   <property name="url" value="jdbc:mysql://127.0.0.1:3306/demodb"/>
   <property name="username" value="ibrahim"/>
   <property name="password" value="pword"/>
 </bean>

 <bean id="transactionManager"
       class="org.springframework.jdbc.datasource
               .DataSourceTransactionManager">
    <property name="dataSource" ref="dataSource"/>
 </bean>

 <bean id="programmaticTxn" class="com.springdemo.ProgrammaticTxn"/>

</beans>
```

The following will be the output when executing the "ProgramaticTxnDemo.java" application.

```
simpleJdbcTemplate is set
transactionManager is set
Start of Transaction
Transaction is committed
End of Transaction
```

A check on database:

```
mysql> select * from account;
```

acc_num	amount
1001	4500
1002	6500

```
2 rows in set (0.00 sec)
```

Change the code to transfer amount 6000.0 from account 1001 to account 1001 and observe the result.

```
programmaticTxn.doTransaction(1001, 1002, 6000.0);
```

CHAPTER 4

XML MARSHALLING

The **Object-XML Mapping** (O/X Mapping) is a process of converting an object (Java object...) into XML and vice versa. This is also called as **'XML Marshalling'**, **'XML Serialization'** or **'XML Binding'.** In technical terms, marshalling is the process of serializing an object into XML and unmarshalling is the process of deserializing the XML into object.

4.1 SPRING SUPPORTED MARSHALLING/UNMARSHALLING

Spring provides an interface named `Marshaller`, which contains the following method syntax.

```
void marshal(Object graph, Result result)
```

The first argument accepts the object that is to be converted into XML. The resultant XML is represented in the second argument. The result implementation may be DOM, SAX or data stream as given below.

```
DOMResult       org.w3c.dom.Node,
                javax.xml.transform.dom.DOMResult
SAXResult       org.xml.sax.ContentHandler,
                javax.xml.transform.sax.SAXResult
StreamResult    javax.xml.transform.stream.StreamResult,
                java.io.File,
                java.io.Writer,
                java.io.OutputStream, ...
```

Spring provides an interface named `Unmarshaller`, which contains the following method syntax.

```
Object unmarshal(Source source)
```

This method accepts a XML representation as its argument and converts it into corresponding object and returns it. The input XML data can be represented in the following implementations.

```
DOMSource       org.w3c.dom.Node,
                javax.xml.transform.dom.DOMSource
SAXSource       org.xml.sax.InputSource,
                org.xml.sax.XMLReader,
                javax.xml.transform.sax.SAXSource
StreamSource    javax.xml.transform.stream.StreamSource,
                java.io.File,
                java.io.InputStream,
                java.io.Reader, ...
```

The following example use Castor XML mapping. It is an open source XML binding framework.

Download and add com.springsource.org.castor-1.2.0.jar and com.springsource.org.apache.xerces-2.8.1.jar into the project `classpath`.

Store the following files in `"com.springdemo"` package.

```
//File Name: Employee.java
package com.springdemo;

public class Employee {

   private int empNumber;
   private String empName;
   private double basicpay;
   private double allowances;
   private double deductions;
   private double netpay;

   //Castor requires no-argument constructor
   public Employee() {}

  public Employee(int empNumber, String empName, double basicpay,
                  double allowances, double deductions){
      this.empNumber = empNumber;
      this.empName = empName;
      this.basicpay = basicpay;
      this.allowances = allowances;
      this.deductions = deductions;
```

```
    netpay = basicpay + allowances - deductions;
  }

  public int getEmpNumber() {
    return empNumber;
  }

  public void setEmpNumber(int empNumber) {
    this.empNumber = empNumber;
  }

  public String getEmpName() {
    return empName;
  }

  public void setEmpName(String empName) {
    this.empName = empName;
  }

  public double getBasicpay() {
    return basicpay;
  }

  public void setBasicpay(double basicpay) {
    this.basicpay = basicpay;
  }

  public double getAllowances() {
    return allowances;
  }

  public void setAllowances(double allowances) {
    this.allowances = allowances;
  }

  public double getDeductions() {
    return deductions;
  }

  public void setDeductions(double deductions) {
    this.deductions = deductions;
```

```
    }

    public double getNetpay() {
        return netpay;
    }

    public void setNetpay(double netpay) {
        this.netpay = netpay;
    }

    public String toString() {
        String rStr = "\nEmp Number: " + empNumber +
                      "\nEmp Name:   " + empName +
                      "\nBasicpay:   " + basicpay +
                      "\nAllowances: " + allowances +
                      "\nDeductions: " + deductions +
                      "\nNetpay     : " + netpay;
        return rStr;
    }
}
```

```
//File Name: XMLMarshallingOperations.java
package com.springdemo;

import java.io.FileInputStream;
import java.io.FileOutputStream;

import javax.xml.transform.stream.StreamResult;
import javax.xml.transform.stream.StreamSource;

import org.springframework.oxm.Marshaller;
import org.springframework.oxm.Unmarshaller;

public class XMLMarshallingOperations {

    private Marshaller marshaller;
    private Unmarshaller unmarshaller;

    public void setMarshaller(Marshaller marshaller) {
        this.marshaller = marshaller;
    }
```

```
    public void setUnmarshaller(Unmarshaller unmarshaller) {
        this.unmarshaller = unmarshaller;
    }

    void doOperations() throws Exception {
      Employee employee =
              new Employee(1001, "Ibrahim", 10000.0, 3000.0, 1000.0);

      System.out.println("Marshalling employee object
                                  into employee.xml file");
      FileOutputStream fos = new FileOutputStream("C:/employee.xml");
      marshaller.marshal(employee, new StreamResult(fos));
      fos.close();
      System.out.println("Object marshalled into employee.xml file");

      System.out.println("Unmarshalling employee object from
                                     employee.xml file");
      FileInputStream fis = new FileInputStream("C:/employee.xml");
      Employee deserialisedObject =
              (Employee) unmarshaller.unmarshal(new StreamSource(fis));
      System.out.println(deserialisedObject);
    }
}
```

```
//File Name: XMLMarshallingDemo.java
package com.springdemo;

import org.springframework.context.support.AbstractApplicationContext;
import org.springframework.context.support.ClassPathXmlApplicationContext;

public class XMLMarshallingDemo {

  public static void main(String[] args) {
    AbstractApplicationContext context =
                new ClassPathXmlApplicationContext("beans.xml");
    XMLMarshallingOperations marshallingOperations =
     (XMLMarshallingOperations) context.getBean("marshallingOperations");
     try {
```

```
        marshallingOperations.doOperations();
      }
      catch (Exception e) {
        System.out.println("Error [" + e + "]");
        e.printStackTrace();
      }
      System.out.println("Operation performed successfully.");
    }
  }
```

Store the following "beans.xml" file in the "src" directory of the project.

```
<?xml version="1.0" encoding="UTF-8"?>
<beans xmlns="http://www.springframework.org/schema/beans"
    xmlns:xsi="http://www.w3.org/2001/XMLSchema-instance"
    xsi:schemaLocation="http://www.springframework.org/schema/beans
     http://www.springframework.org/schema/beans/spring-beans-3.0.xsd" >

  <bean id="castorMarshaller"
        class="org.springframework.oxm.castor.CastorMarshaller"/>

  <bean id="marshallingOperations"
        class="com.springdemo.XMLMarshallingOperations">
   <property name="marshaller" ref="castorMarshaller"/>
   <property name="unmarshaller" ref="castorMarshaller"/>
  </bean>

</beans>
```

Execute the application (XMLMarshallingDemo.java), and the result will be as follows.

```
Marshalling employee object into employee.xml file
Object marshalled into employee.xml file
Unmarshalling employee object from employee.xml file

Emp Number: 1001
Emp Name:   Ibrahim
Basicpay:   10000.0
```

```
Allowances: 3000.0
Deductions: 1000.0
Netpay     : 12000.0
Operation performed successfully.
```

The content of employee.xml at `C:` drive.

```
<?xml version="1.0" encoding="UTF-8"?>
<employee emp-number="1001" netpay="12000.0" allowances="3000.0"
basicpay="10000.0" deductions="1000.0"><emp-name>Ibrahim</emp-name></
employee>
```

4.2 XStream

XStream is a simple library to serialize objects to XML and back again. It is an XML serialization library, not a data binding library. Therefore, it has limited namespace support.

Cross Reference:

Java-XML Binding vs' **Java-XML Serialization:** Both the techniques are used to convert Java objects to XML and vice versa. In Binding process, Java source code file is generated from an XML Schema/DTD. Sun's JAXB and Apache's XMLBeans are examples for Java-XML Binding. In Serialization process, Java reflection API is used to convert a Java object to XML and vice versa. It is a runtime conversion approach. It is a fast when compared to Binding, but cannot be ensured that the source XML will correctly de-serialize to an instance of the target Java class. One of the popular Java-XML serialization API is XStream from Codehaus.The serialized form of an object may not be suitable for using outside of a Java environment as it may be embedded Java class names in it. As such, it is rather unsuitable for usage within Web services.

Download and add the following jars into the project `classpath`.

- `com.springsource.com.thoughtworks.xstream-1.3.0.jar,`
- `com.springsource.org.xmlpull-1.1.4.jar`
- `smack.jar`

Store the following files in `"com.springdemo"` package.

```
// File Name: Employee.java
package com.springdemo;

public class Employee {
```

```
    private int empNumber;
    private String empName;
    private double basicpay;
    private double allowances;
    private double deductions;
    private double netpay;

    public Employee() {}

    public Employee(int empNumber, String empName, double basicpay,
                double allowances, double deductions){
      this.empNumber = empNumber;
      this.empName = empName;
      this.basicpay = basicpay;
      this.allowances = allowances;
      this.deductions = deductions;

      netpay = basicpay + allowances - deductions;
    }

    public int getEmpNumber() {
      return empNumber;
    }

    public void setEmpNumber(int empNumber) {
      this.empNumber = empNumber;
    }

    public String getEmpName() {
      return empName;
    }

    public void setEmpName(String empName) {
      this.empName = empName;
    }

    public double getBasicpay() {
      return basicpay;
    }

    public void setBasicpay(double basicpay) {
      this.basicpay = basicpay;
    }
```

```
  public double getAllowances() {
    return allowances;
  }

  public void setAllowances(double allowances) {
    this.allowances = allowances;
  }

  public double getDeductions() {
    return deductions;
  }

  public void setDeductions(double deductions) {
    this.deductions = deductions;
  }

  public double getNetpay() {
    return netpay;
  }

  public void setNetpay(double netpay) {
    this.netpay = netpay;
  }

  public String toString() {
    String rStr = "\nEmp Number:   " + empNumber +
                  "\nEmp Name:     " + empName +
                  "\nBasicpay:     " + basicpay +
                  "\nAllowances:   " + allowances +
                  "\nDeductions:   " + deductions +
                  "\nNetpay     :  " + netpay;
    return rStr;
  }
}
```

```
// File Name: XMLMarshallingOperations.java
package com.springdemo;

import java.io.FileInputStream;
import java.io.FileOutputStream;
```

```
import javax.xml.transform.stream.StreamResult;
import javax.xml.transform.stream.StreamSource;

import org.springframework.oxm.Marshaller;
import org.springframework.oxm.Unmarshaller;

public class XMLMarshallingOperations {

  private Marshaller marshaller;
  private Unmarshaller unmarshaller;

  public void setMarshaller(Marshaller marshaller) {
    this.marshaller = marshaller;
  }

  public void setUnmarshaller(Unmarshaller unmarshaller) {
    this.unmarshaller = unmarshaller;
  }

  void doOperations() throws Exception {
    Employee employee =
           new Employee(1001, "Ibrahim", 10000.0, 3000.0, 1000.0);

    System.out.println("Marshalling employee object
                                   into employee.xml file");
    FileOutputStream fos = new FileOutputStream("C:/employee.xml");
    marshaller.marshal(employee, new StreamResult(fos));
    fos.close();
    System.out.println("Object marshalled into employee.xml file");

    System.out.println("Unmarshalling employee object
                                 from employee.xml file");
    FileInputStream fis = new FileInputStream("C:/employee.xml");
    Employee deserialisedObject =
           (Employee) unmarshaller.unmarshal(new StreamSource(fis));
    System.out.println(deserialisedObject);
  }
}
```

```
// File Name: XMLMarshallingDemo.java
package com.springdemo;

import org.springframework.context.support.AbstractApplicationContext;
import
  org.springframework.context.support.ClassPathXmlApplicationContext;

public class XMLMarshallingDemo {

  public static void main(String[] args) {
    AbstractApplicationContext context =
                  new ClassPathXmlApplicationContext("beans.xml");
    XMLMarshallingOperations marshallingOperations =
   (XMLMarshallingOperations) context.getBean("marshallingOperations");
    try {
      marshallingOperations.doOperations();
    }
    catch (Exception e) {
      System.out.println("Error [" + e + "]");
      e.printStackTrace();
    }
    System.out.println("Operation performed successfully.");
  }
}
```

Store the following "beans.xml" file into the "src" directory of the project.

```
<?xml version="1.0" encoding="UTF-8"?>
<beans xmlns="http://www.springframework.org/schema/beans"
  xmlns:xsi="http://www.w3.org/2001/XMLSchema-instance"
  xsi:schemaLocation="http://www.springframework.org/schema/beans
  http://www.springframework.org/schema/beans/spring-beans-3.0.xsd" >

  <bean id="xstreamMarshaller"
        class="org.springframework.oxm.xstream.XStreamMarshaller" />

  <bean id="marshallingOperations"
        class="com.springdemo.XMLMarshallingOperations">
   <property name="marshaller" ref="xstreamMarshaller"/>
   <property name="unmarshaller" ref="xstreamMarshaller"/>
  </bean>

</beans>
```

Execute the main application (XMLMarshallingDemo.java) and the output will be as shown below.

```
Marshalling employee object into employee.xml file
Object marshalled into employee.xml file
Unmarshalling employee object from employee.xml file

Emp Number:  1001
Emp Name:    Ibrahim
Basicpay:    10000.0
Allowances:  3000.0
Deductions:  1000.0
Netpay     : 12000.0
Operation performed successfully.
```

The content of the file C:\employee.xml

```
<com.springdemo.Employee>
  <empNumber>1001</empNumber>
  <empName>Ibrahim</empName>
  <basicpay>10000.0</basicpay>
  <allowances>3000.0</allowances>
  <deductions>1000.0</deductions>
  <netpay>12000.0</netpay>
</com.springdemo.Employee>
```

4.3 JAXB

The Java Architecture for XML Binding (JAXB) provides API for marshalling and unmarshalling Java objects. The Jaxb2Marshaller class implements both the Spring supported Marshaller and Unmarshaller interface. The list of classes that are to be supported by the JAXB marshaller should be specified in classesToBound property.

We can apply the following annotations on POJOs to customize XML marshalling.

Example Applications:

Download and add the "jaxb-api-2.1.jar" file into classpath of the project.

4.3.1 @XmlAccessorType and @XmlRootElement Annotations

JAXB serializes public fields (data member) and properties (setter methods) by default. We can change the accessor type by using the @XmlAccessorType annotation. The following are the values to this annotation.

`XmlAccessType.NONE`	Do not apply serialization. Only annotated fields / properties should be serialized.
`XmlAccessType.FIELD`	All the fields (private/public) should be serialised.
`XmlAccessType.PROPERTY`	All the properties (private/public) should be serialized.
`XmlAccessType.PUBLIC_MEMBER`	All public fields and properties (default)

`@XmlRootElement` marks a class as a top-level XML node.

Store the following files in `"com.springdemo"` package.

```
//File Name: Employee.java
package com.springdemo;

import javax.xml.bind.annotation.XmlAccessType;
import javax.xml.bind.annotation.XmlAccessorType;
import javax.xml.bind.annotation.XmlRootElement;

@XmlAccessorType(XmlAccessType.FIELD)
@XmlRootElement
public class Employee {
  private int empNumber;
  private String empName;
  private double basicpay;
  private double allowances;
  private double deductions;
  private double netpay;

  public Employee() {
  }

  public Employee(int empNumber, String empName, double basicpay,
                  double allowances, double deductions) {
    this.empNumber = empNumber;
    this.empName = empName;
    this.basicpay = basicpay;
    this.allowances = allowances;
    this.deductions = deductions;

    netpay = basicpay + allowances - deductions;
  }

  public int getEmpNumber() {
    return empNumber;
  }
```

```
public void setEmpNumber(int empNumber) {
  this.empNumber = empNumber;
}

public String getEmpName() {
  return empName;
}

public void setEmpName(String empName) {
  this.empName = empName;
}

public double getBasicpay() {
  return basicpay;
}

public void setBasicpay(double basicpay) {
  this.basicpay = basicpay;
}

public double getAllowances() {
  return allowances;
}

public void setAllowances(double allowances) {
  this.allowances = allowances;
}

public double getDeductions() {
  return deductions;
}

public void setDeductions(double deductions) {
  this.deductions = deductions;
}

public double getNetpay() {
  return netpay;
}

public void setNetpay(double netpay) {
  this.netpay = netpay;
}
```

```
  public String toString() {
    String rStr = "\nEmp Number:   " + empNumber +
                  "\nEmp Name:     " + empName +
                  "\nBasicpay:     " + basicpay +
                  "\nAllowances:   " + allowances +
                  "\nDeductions:   " + deductions +
                  "\nNetpay      : " + netpay;
    return rStr;
  }

}
```

```
//File Name: XMLMarshallingOperations.java
package com.springdemo;

import java.io.FileInputStream;
import java.io.FileOutputStream;

import javax.xml.transform.stream.StreamResult;
import javax.xml.transform.stream.StreamSource;

import org.springframework.oxm.Marshaller;
import org.springframework.oxm.Unmarshaller;

public class XMLMarshallingOperations {

  private Marshaller marshaller;
  private Unmarshaller unmarshaller;

  public void setMarshaller(Marshaller marshaller) {
    this.marshaller = marshaller;
  }

  public void setUnmarshaller(Unmarshaller unmarshaller) {
    this.unmarshaller = unmarshaller;
  }

  void doOperations() throws Exception {
    Employee employee = new Employee(1001, "Ibrahim", 10000.0,
                                     3000.0, 1000.0);
```

```
    System.out.println("Marshalling employee object
                        into employee.xml file");
    FileOutputStream fos = new FileOutputStream("C:/employee.xml");
    marshaller.marshal(employee, new StreamResult(fos));
    fos.close();
    System.out.println("Object marshalled into employee.xml file");

    System.out.println("Unmarshalling employee object
                        from employee.xml file");
    FileInputStream fis = new FileInputStream("C:/employee.xml");
    Employee deserialisedObject =
        (Employee) unmarshaller.unmarshal(new StreamSource(fis));
    System.out.println(deserialisedObject);
  }
}
```

```
//File Name: XMLMarshallingDemo.java
package com.springdemo;

import org.springframework.context.support.AbstractApplicationContext;
import org.springframework.context.support.ClassPathXmlApplicationContext;

public class XMLMarshallingDemo {

  public static void main(String[] args) {
    AbstractApplicationContext context =
            new ClassPathXmlApplicationContext("beans.xml");
    XMLMarshallingOperations marshallingOperations =
                (XMLMarshallingOperations)
                 context.getBean("marshallingOperations");
    try {
      marshallingOperations.doOperations();
    }
    catch (Exception e) {
      System.out.println("Error [" + e + "]");
      e.printStackTrace();
    }
    System.out.println("Operation performed successfully.");
  }
}
```

Store the following "beans.xml" file in the "src" directory of the project.

```
<?xml version="1.0" encoding="UTF-8"?>
<beans xmlns="http://www.springframework.org/schema/beans"
  xmlns:xsi="http://www.w3.org/2001/XMLSchema-instance"
  xsi:schemaLocation="http://www.springframework.org/schema/beans
  http://www.springframework.org/schema/beans/spring-beans-3.0.xsd" >

  <bean id="marshallingOperations"
       class="com.springdemo.XMLMarshallingOperations">
   <property name="marshaller" ref="jaxb2Marshaller"/>
   <property name="unmarshaller" ref="jaxb2Marshaller"/>
  </bean>

  <bean id="jaxb2Marshaller"
       class="org.springframework.oxm.jaxb.Jaxb2Marshaller">
   <property name="classesToBeBound">
     <list>
         <value>com.springdemo.Employee</value>
     </list>
   </property>
  </bean>

</beans>
```

Execute the main program (XMLMarshallingDemo.java) and the output is expected as below.

```
Marshalling employee object into employee.xml file
Object marshalled into employee.xml file
Unmarshalling employee object from employee.xml file

Emp Number: 1001
Emp Name:   Ibrahim
Basicpay:   10000.0
Allowances: 3000.0
Deductions: 1000.0
Netpay     : 12000.0
Operation performed successfully.
```

The content of the file employee.xml at `C:` drive is shown below.

```
<?xml version="1.0" encoding="UTF-8" standalone="yes" ?>
<employee>
   <empNumber>1001</empNumber>
   <empName>Ibrahim</empName>
   <basicpay>10000.0</basicpay>
   <allowances>3000.0</allowances>
   <deductions>1000.0</deductions>
   <netpay>12000.0<netpay>
  </employee>
```

4.3.2 @XmlTransient Annotation

`@XmlTransient` prevents serialization, overriding the `@XmlAccessorType`.

Change the above `Employee.java` file as below and execute the main program.

```
//File Name: Employee.java
package com.springdemo;

import javax.xml.bind.annotation.XmlAccessType;
import javax.xml.bind.annotation.XmlAccessorType;
import javax.xml.bind.annotation.XmlRootElement;
import javax.xml.bind.annotation.XmlTransient;

@XmlAccessorType(XmlAccessType.FIELD)
@XmlRootElement
public class Employee {
  private int empNumber;
  private String empName;

  @XmlTransient
  private double basicpay;

  @XmlTransient
  private double allowances;

  @XmlTransient
  private double deductions;

  private double netpay;

  //Setter and Getter methods, Constructors, toString methods
}
```

The output will be as shown below. Observe that the values for basic-pay, allowances and deductions became 0.

```
Marshalling employee object into employee.xml file
Object marshalled into employee.xml file
Unmarshalling employee object from employee.xml file

Emp Number: 1001
Emp Name:   Ibrahim
Basicpay:   0.0
Allowances: 0.0
Deductions: 0.0
Netpay    : 12000.0
Operation performed successfully.
```

The content of the file employee.xml at `C:` drive is shown below.

```
<?xml version ="1.0" encoding="UTF-8" standalone="yes" ?>
<employee>
   <empNumber>10001<empNumber>
   <empName>Ibrahim</empName>
   <netpay>12000.0<netpay>
</employee>
```

4.3.3 @XmlAttribute Annotation

`@XmlAttribute` marks a field or property as serialized to an XML attribute, not as an element. `@XmlAttribute` can also customize the XML attribute name. By default, the field name will be taken as attribute name.

Change the above `Employee.java` file as below and execute the main program.

```
//File Name: Employee.java
package com.springdemo;

import javax.xml.bind.annotation.XmlAccessType;
import javax.xml.bind.annotation.XmlAccessorType;
import javax.xml.bind.annotation.XmlAttribute;
import javax.xml.bind.annotation.XmlRootElement;

@XmlAccessorType(XmlAccessType.FIELD)
@XmlRootElement
public class Employee {
  private int empNumber;
  private String empName;
```

```
    @XmlAttribute
    private double basicpay;

    @XmlAttribute
    private double allowances;

    @XmlAttribute(name="salary_deductions")
    private double deductions;

    private double netpay;

    //Setter and Getter methods, Constructors, toString methods
}
```

The output will be as shown below.

```
Marshalling employee object into employee.xml file
Object marshalled into employee.xml file
Unmarshalling employee object from employee.xml file

Emp Number: 1001
Emp Name:   Ibrahim
Basicpay:   10000.0
Allowances: 3000.0
Deductions: 1000.0
Netpay     : 12000.0
Operation performed successfully.
```

The content of the file employee.xml at `C:` drive is shown below. Observe that the fields: basicpay, allowances and deductions are defined in attributes.

```
<?xml version="1.0" encoding="UTF-8" standalone="yes" ?>
<employee salary_deductions="1000.0" allowances="3000.0"
        basicpay="10000.0">
   <empNumber>1001</empNumber>
   <empName>Ibrahim</empName>
   <netpay>12000.0</netpay>
</employee>
```

4.3.4 @XmlElement Annotation

`@XmlElement` marks a field or property as serialized to an XML element. `@XmlElement` can also customize the XML element name. By default, the field name will be taken as attribute name.

Change the above `Employee.java` file as below and execute the main program.

```
//File Name: Employee.java
package com.springdemo;

import javax.xml.bind.annotation.XmlAccessType;
import javax.xml.bind.annotation.XmlAccessorType;
import javax.xml.bind.annotation.XmlElement;
import javax.xml.bind.annotation.XmlRootElement;

@XmlAccessorType(XmlAccessType.FIELD)
@XmlRootElement
public class Employee {
  @XmlElement(name="employee_number")
  private int empNumber;

  @XmlElement(name="employee_name")
  private String empName;

  private double basicpay;
  private double allowances;
  private double deductions;
  private double netpay;

  //Setter and Getter methods, Constructors, toString methods
}
```

The output will be as shown below.

```
Marshalling employee object into employee.xml file
Object marshalled into employee.xml file
Unmarshalling employee object from employee.xml file

Emp Number:  1001
Emp Name:    Ibrahim
Basicpay:    10000.0
Allowances:  3000.0
Deductions:  1000.0
Netpay     : 12000.0
Operation performed successfully.
```

The content of the file employee.xml at C: drive is shown below. Observe that the fields: empNumber and empName are defined with the specified names.

```
<?xml version="1.0" encoding="UTF-8" standalone="yes" ?>
<employee?
  <employee_number>1001</employee_number>
  <employee_name>Ibrahim</employee_name>
  <basicpay>10000.0</basicpay>
  <allowances>3000.0</allowances>
  <deductions>1000.0</deductions>
  <netpay>12000.0<netpay>
</employee>
```

4.3.5 @XmlElementWrapper Annotation

@XmlElementWrapper adds a wrapper XML tag for list values.

Change the above Employee.java file as below.

```
//File Name: Employee.java
package com.springdemo;

import java.util.List;

import javax.xml.bind.annotation.XmlAccessType;
import javax.xml.bind.annotation.XmlAccessorType;
import javax.xml.bind.annotation.XmlElementWrapper;
import javax.xml.bind.annotation.XmlRootElement;

@XmlAccessorType(XmlAccessType.FIELD)
@XmlRootElement
public class Employee {
  private int empNumber;
  private String empName;

   @XmlElementWrapper(name="employee_skills")
  private List<String> skills;

  private double basicpay;
  private double allowances;
  private double deductions;
  private double netpay;

  public Employee() {}
```

```
public Employee(int empNumber, String empName,
            double basicpay, double allowances,
            double deductions, List<String> skills){
  this.empNumber = empNumber;
  this.empName = empName;
  this.basicpay = basicpay;
  this.allowances = allowances;
  this.deductions = deductions;

  netpay = basicpay + allowances - deductions;
  this.skills = skills;
}

public int getEmpNumber() {
  return empNumber;
}

public void setEmpNumber(int empNumber) {
  this.empNumber = empNumber;
}

public String getEmpName() {
  return empName;
}

public void setEmpName(String empName) {
  this.empName = empName;
}

public List<String> getSkills() {
  return skills;
}

public void setSkills(List<String> skills) {
  this.skills = skills;
}

public double getBasicpay() {
  return basicpay;
}

public void setBasicpay(double basicpay) {
```

```
    this.basicpay = basicpay;
  }

  public double getAllowances() {
    return allowances;
  }

  public void setAllowances(double allowances) {
    this.allowances = allowances;
  }

  public double getDeductions() {
    return deductions;
  }

  public void setDeductions(double deductions) {
    this.deductions = deductions;
  }

  public double getNetpay() {
    return netpay;
  }

  public void setNetpay(double netpay) {
    this.netpay = netpay;
  }

  public String toString() {
    String rStr = "\nEmp Number:     " + empNumber +
                  "\nEmp Name:       " + empName +
                  "\nSkills:         " + skills +
                  "\nBasicpay:       " + basicpay +
                  "\nAllowances:     " + allowances +
                  "\nDeductions:     " + deductions +
                  "\nNetpay :        " + netpay;
    return rStr;
  }
}
```

Change the XMLMarshallingOperations.java as below.

```
package com.springdemo;

import java.io.FileInputStream;
import java.io.FileOutputStream;
import java.util.ArrayList;
import java.util.List;

import javax.xml.transform.stream.StreamResult;
import javax.xml.transform.stream.StreamSource;

import org.springframework.oxm.Marshaller;
import org.springframework.oxm.Unmarshaller;

public class XMLMarshallingOperations {

  private Marshaller marshaller;
  private Unmarshaller unmarshaller;

  public void setMarshaller(Marshaller marshaller) {
    this.marshaller = marshaller;
  }

  public void setUnmarshaller(Unmarshaller unmarshaller) {
    this.unmarshaller = unmarshaller;
  }

  void doOperations() throws Exception {
    List<String> skills = new ArrayList<String>();
    skills.add("C");
    skills.add("Java");
    skills.add("Oracle");
    Employee employee = new Employee(1001, "Ibrahim",
                          10000.0, 3000.0, 1000.0, skills);

    System.out.println("Marshalling employee object
                          into employee.xml file");
    FileOutputStream fos = new FileOutputStream("C:/employee.xml");
    marshaller.marshal(employee, new StreamResult(fos));
    fos.close();
    System.out.println("Object marshalled into employee.xml file");
```

```
    System.out.println("Unmarshalling employee object
                                   from employee.xml file");
    FileInputStream fis = new FileInputStream("C:/employee.xml");
    Employee deserialisedObject = (Employee)
                   unmarshaller.unmarshal(new StreamSource(fis));
    System.out.println(deserialisedObject);
  }
}
```

The output will be as shown below.

```
Marshalling employee object into employee.xml file
Object marshalled into employee.xml file
Unmarshalling employee object from employee.xml file

Emp Number: 1001
Emp Name:   Ibrahim
Skills:     [C, Java, Oracle]
Basicpay:   10000.0
Allowances: 3000.0
Deductions: 1000.0
Netpay     : 12000.0
Operation performed successfully.
```

The content of the file employee.xml at C: drive is shown below. Observe that a wrapper "employee_skills" is added to the lists of "skills" tags.

```
<?xml version="1.0" encoding="UTF-8" standalone="yes" ?>
<employee>
   <empNumber>1001</empNumber>
   <empName>Ibrahim</empName>
   <employee_skills>
      <skills>C</skills>
      <skills>Java</skills>
      <skills>Oracle</skills>
   </employee_skills>
   <basicpay>10000.0</basicpay>
   <allowances>3000.0</allowances>
   <deductions>1000.0<deductions>
   <netpay>12000.0</netpay>
</employee>
```

CHAPTER 5

SPRING AOP

The word 'Aspect' in Software development refers to the 'unit of modularity' of any cross-cutting concerns within the applications such as logging, transaction management, locking, event handling, and applying security on the applications. We can separate the logging related code in an application to a separate entity (module), this is one 'Aspect' and concern is logging. Likewise, we can separate the concern on transaction based activities in the entire application, this is another aspect. Thus aspects are derived bases on concerns, cohesive areas of functionality.

Aspect-oriented Programming (AOP) is modularity based application development programming technique, where the modules are aspects. AOP is distinguished from Object-oriented Programming (OOP) as OOP is based on classes where AOP is based on aspects.

5.1 BASIC AOP CONCEPTS

AOP is a concept; there are many AOP implementation frameworks on the market, the following three AOP frameworks are dominant among them.

- AspectJ
- JBoss AOP
- Spring AOP

In this book, we will look into only Spring AOP. Before that, we will go through some basic AOP concepts.

Join Point: A Join Point is a point in the execution of the application where an aspect can be plugged in. It refers to a location in the code where the advice should be executed. For example, 'execution of a particular method' is a join point. There will be several join points in an application. Spring supports only method invocation join points. There are many other join points that are supported in AOP concept, such as field access, constructor invocation, etc.

Advice: It is the action taken by an aspect on a join point. It refers to the code that is fulfilling the aspect logic, and will be invoked at a particular join point. The following are the types of advices.

- *Before Advice:* Advice that executes before a join point. For example, if a join point is a method invocation, then this advice will be executed before the method is invoked.
- *After Returning Advice:* Advice that executes after a join point completes normally. For example, if a join point is a method invocation, then this advice will be executed after the method returns without throwing any exception.
- *After Throwing Advice:* Advice that executes after the join point throws an exception. For example, if a join point is a method invocation, then this advice will be executed after the method exits by throwing an exception.
- *After Advice:* Advice that executes after the join point irrespective of the join point throws exception or not.
- *Around Advice:* Advice that executes before and after the join point.

Pointcut: An advice can be applied to several join points. A pointcut is a set of join points where an advice should be executed.

Target/Target Object/Adviced Object: The object that one or more aspects are applied on.

5.2 ANNOTATION BASED SPRING AOP

Spring AOP supports both XML based and annotation based configuration. In the XML based approach, you are required to define all the AOP configuration in a single (usually) XML file in a particular place. Java 5 and the later versions support annotation based configuration (`@AspectJ support`), it is a simple and easy way of defining configuration over XML based approach. In this book, annotation based approach is chosen in explaining AOP concepts.

The following element in the bean configuration XML enables `@AspectJ` support. This enables Spring to automatically create proxies for any of the beans, which are matched by `AspectJ aspects`.

```
<aop:aspectj-autoproxy/>
```

And add the `aop` schema definition to the `<beans>` root element. Then, the bean configuration XML file looks below.

```
<beans xmlns="http://www.springframework.org/schema/beans"
       xmlns:xsi="http://www.w3.org/2001/XMLSchema-instance"
       xmlns:aop="http://www.springframework.org/schema/aop"
       xsi:schemaLocation="http://www.springframework.org/schema/beans
          http://www.springframework.org/schema/beans/spring-beans-
            3.0.xsd
          http://www.springframework.org/schema/aop
          http://www.springframework.org/schema/aop/spring-aop-
            3.0.xsd">

  <aop:aspectj-autoproxy />

  Bean definitions

</beans>
```

Add 'aspectjrt' and 'aspectjweaver' library jars (aspectjrt-1.6.8.jar, aspectjweaver-1.6.8.jar) into the *classpath* of the application. The jars can be downloaded from Maven repository or get them from AspectJ distribution.

5.2.1 @Aspect—Declaring an Aspect

This annotation declares a class as Aspect.

Example:

```
@Aspect
public class ArithmeticOperations {
}
```

5.2.2 @Pointcut—Declaring a Pointcut

This annotation declares a pointcut (set of interested join points). As already mentioned, Spring AOP only supports method execution join points. A pointcut-declared method in an aspect class should have 'void' return type. A pointcut can also be directly embedded with an advice.

General format:

```
@Pointcut(pointcut_expression)
```

A `pointcut_expression` is a regular expression, made up of AspectJ Pointcut Designators (PCD). The following are some of the Spring AOP supported pointcut designators.

`execution`: It matches method execution join point.

General format:

```
execution(modifiers-pattern return-type-pattern
method-name-pattern(parameter-pattern) throws-pattern)
```

All patterns are optional except return-type-pattern. The parameter-pattern, `()` matches method with no parameters; `(..)` matches method with zero or more parameters; `(*)` matches method with one parameter of any type; `(data_type)` matches method with one parameter of the specified type.

`within`: It matches join points within certain types.

General format:

```
within(TypePattern)
```

`args(type)`: It matches to join points where the arguments are instances of the specified data types. The wildcard character '*' matches any argument, and '..' matches any number of arguments.

`bean(beanid)`: It is a Spring-specific extension to the standard AspectJ BCDs. It limits the matching of join points to a particular named Spring bean(s).

Examples:

Expression	Description
execution(* * *(..))	Matches all the methods
execution(public * *(..))	Matches all the public methods
execution(public * set*(..))	Matches all the public methods whose method name starts with 'set'
execution(* set*(..))	Matches all the methods whose method name starts with 'set'
execution(* com.springdemo.*.*(..))	Matches any method (in the classes) in com.springdemo package, not in its sub-packages
execution(* com.springdemo..*.*(..)	Matches any method (in the classes) in com.springdemo package and its sub-packages
execution(* com.springdemo.Arithmetic.*(..)	Matches any method defined in the com.springdemo.Arithmetic class/interface.
execution(* com.springdemo.Arithmetic.subtract(..)	Matches any method named 'subtract' in com.sprindemo.Arithmetic class/interface.
execution(double com.springdemo.Arithmetic.	Matches the method named subtract in com.springdemo.Arithmetic class/interface and the method accepts an integer type parameter and its return type is double
execution(int com.springdemo.Arithmetic.subtract (*, int)	Matches the method name subtract in com.springdemo.Arithmetic and the method's first parameter of any type, second parameter of type int and returns integer value
within(com.springdemo.*)	Matches any join point within the com.springdemo package, does not include sub-packages. Note that only method execution join points are allowed in Spring AOP.
within(com.springdemo..*)	Matches any join point within the com.springdemo packages and its sub-packages.
within(com.springdemo.Arithmetic)	Matches any join point belongs to the execution of class com.springdemo.Arithmetic.
args(int)	Joint point whose argument type is 'int'
args(int, .., String)	Matches join points where the first argument is an int, and the last argument is String. It may have none or many parameters in between.

Pointcut expressions can be combined using '&&', '||' and '!'. We can also use 'and', 'or' and 'not' instead of symbols. For example,

```
execution(* com.springdemo.substract(..)) and bean(arithmetic)
```

It applies aspect advice to the execution of subtract method, but limited to the bean whose bean-id is `'arithmetic'`.

Declaring an Advice

An advice is associated with a pointcut expression. Spring AOP supports only method execution joint-points, so advice runs before, after, or around those method executions. The following are annotations for different types of advices.

`@Before`	Before Advice
`@After`	After Advice
`@AfterReturning`	After Returning Advice
`@AfterThrowing`	After Throwing Advice
`@Around`	Around Advice

5.3 DEVELOPING A SAMPLE APPLICATION USING SPRING AOP

I am using the same `'SpringDemo'` project, which we created earlier (refer previous chapters). Create a package named `'com.springdemo.arithmetic'` and add the following two files.

```
//File Name: Arithmetic.java
package com.springdemo.arithmetic;

public interface Arithmetic {
    int addition(int a, int b);
    int subtract(int a, int b);
    double multiply(double a, double b);
    double divide(double a, double b) throws Exception;
}
```

```
//File Name: ArithmeticOperations.java
package com.springdemo.arithmetic;

public class ArithmeticOperations implements Arithmetic {
  public int addition(int a, int b) {
    int c = a + b;
    System.out.println("\nIn addition method. a[" + a +
                        "] b[" + b + "] c[" + c + "]\n");
    return c;
  }
```

```
    public int subtract(int a, int b) {
      int c = a - b;
      System.out.println("\nIn subtract method. a[" + a +
                                  "] b[" + b + "] c[" + c + "]\n");
      return c;
    }

    public double multiply(double a, double b) {
      double c = a * b;
      System.out.println("\nIn multiply method. a[" + a +
                        "] b[" + b + "] c[" + c + "]\n");
      return c;
    }

    public double divide(double a, double b) throws Exception {
      if (b == 0)
        throw new Exception("Dividing a number by zero");
      double c;
      c = a / b;
      System.out.println("\nIn divide method. a[" + a +
                                  "] b[" + b + "] c[" + c + "]\n");
      return c;
    }
  }
```

Place the following LogAspect.java file in the `com.springdemo` package.

```
package com.springdemo;

import java.util.Arrays;

import org.aspectj.lang.JoinPoint;
import org.aspectj.lang.ProceedingJoinPoint;
import org.aspectj.lang.annotation.After;
import org.aspectj.lang.annotation.AfterReturning;
import org.aspectj.lang.annotation.AfterThrowing;
import org.aspectj.lang.annotation.Aspect;
import org.aspectj.lang.annotation.Before;
import org.springframework.stereotype.Component;

@Component
@Aspect
public class LogAspect {
```

```
@Before("execution(* com.springdemo.arithmetic.Arithmetic.*(..))")
public void beforeLog(JoinPoint joinPoint) {
  System.out.println("Before calling " +
                     joinPoint.getSignature().getName());
  System.out.print("Arguments to the method: " +
                   Arrays.toString(joinPoint.getArgs()));
  System.out.println();
}

@After("execution(* com.springdemo.arithmetic.Arithmetic.*(..))")
public void afterLog(JoinPoint joinPoint) {
  System.out.println("After calling " +
                     joinPoint.getSignature().getName());
  System.out.print("Arguments to the method: " +
                   Arrays.toString(joinPoint.getArgs()));
  System.out.println();
}

@AfterReturning(
  pointcut = "execution(* com.springdemo.arithmetic.Arithmetic.*(..))",
  returning="result")
public void afterReturningLog(JoinPoint joinPoint, Object result) {
  System.out.println("\nAfter Returning (No Exception) from " +
                     joinPoint.getSignature().getName());
  System.out.print("Arguments to the method: " +
                   Arrays.toString(joinPoint.getArgs()));
  System.out.println("\nReturned Value: " + result + "\n");
}

@AfterThrowing(
pointcut = "execution(* com.springdemo.arithmetic.Arithmetic.*(..))",
throwing= "error")
public void afterThrowingLog(JoinPoint joinPoint, Throwable error) {
System.out.println("After Returning (Throwing Exception) calling " +
                   joinPoint.getSignature().getName());
   System.out.print("Arguments to the method: " +
                    Arrays.toString(joinPoint.getArgs()));
   System.out.println("\n Exception [" + error.getMessage() + "]\n");
}

//Use Around, when Before or After point-cut is not used.
//@Around("execution(* com.springdemo.arithmetic.Arithmetic.*(..))")
```

```
public void aroundLog(ProceedingJoinPoint joinPoint) throws Throwable {
    System.out.println("Around calling " +
                    joinPoint.getSignature().getName());
    System.out.print("Arguments to the method: " +
                Arrays.toString(joinPoint.getArgs()));
    System.out.println("\nBefore method call");
    //We can even change the parameter values, while calling proceed()
    joinPoint.proceed(new Object[]{50,60});
    System.out.println("After method call");

  }
}
```

The @Around annotation line is intentionally commented in the above code, as we are using @Before and @After advices for the same pointcut. Later on, try this same application with uncommenting @Around advice and commenting all other advices.

In this application, the pointcut expressions are directly embedded with advices. Otherwise, you can also declare pointcuts using @Pointcut in one Aspect and refer that method name in advices.

Observe that this class is marked as @Component for auto-detection from the classpath by Spring container.

Add the following bean configuration XML (beans.xml) under 'src' directory of the project.

```
<?xml version="1.0" encoding="UTF-8"?>
<beans xmlns="http://www.springframework.org/schema/beans"
      xmlns:xsi="http://www.w3.org/2001/XMLSchema-instance"
      xmlns:context="http://www.springframework.org/schema/context"
      xmlns:aop="http://www.springframework.org/schema/aop"
      xsi:schemaLocation="http://www.springframework.org/schema/beans
      http://www.springframework.org/schema/beans/spring-beans-3.0.xsd
      http://www.springframework.org/schema/context
      http://www.springframework.org/schema/context/spring-context
      3.0.xsd
      http://www.springframework.org/schema/aop
      http://www.springframework.org/schema/aop/spring-aop-3.0.xsd">

  <context:annotation-config/>
  <context:component-scan base-package="com.springdemo"/>
  <aop:aspectj-autoproxy/>

  <bean id="arithmeticOperations"
        class="com.springdemo.arithmetic.ArithmeticOperations"/>

</beans>
```

The following two lines are added for annotation based component scanning.

```
<context:annotation-config/>
<context:component-scan base-package="com.springdemo"/>
```

The configuration `<aop:aspectj-autoproxy/>` enables `@AspectJ` annotation support such as `@Aspect`, `@Before`, `@After` ...

Do not forget to add 'aspectjrt' and `'aspectjweaver'` library jars (aspectjrt-1.6.8.jar, aspectjweaver-1.6.8.jar) into the *classpath* of the application.

Add the main application (`AOPDemo.java`) in the `com.springdemo` package.

```
//File Name: AOPDemo.java
package com.springdemo;

import org.springframework.context.support.AbstractApplicationContext;
import org.springframework.context.support.ClassPathXmlApplicationContext;

import com.springdemo.arithmetic.Arithmetic;

public class AOPDemo {

  public static void main(String[] args) throws Exception {
    AbstractApplicationContext context =
                 new ClassPathXmlApplicationContext("beans.xml");
    Arithmetic arithmeticOperations =
             (Arithmetic) context.getBean("arithmeticOperations");

    int addValue = arithmeticOperations.addition(5, 2);
    System.out.println("5 + 2 = " + addValue);

    int subValue = arithmeticOperations.subtract(5, 2);
    System.out.println("5 - 2 = " + subValue);

    double mulValue = arithmeticOperations.multiply(5.0, 2.0);
    System.out.println("5.0 * 2.0 = " + mulValue);

    try {
      double divValue = arithmeticOperations.divide(5.0, 0);
      System.out.println("5.0 / 0 = " + divValue);
    }
    catch (Exception e) {
      System.out.println("Error " + e.getMessage());
    }
```

```
        System.out.println("\nOperation performed successfully.");
    }
}
```

Execute this application (Choose File → Right Click → Run As → Java Application). Here is the output.

```
Before calling addition
Arguments to the method: [5, 2]

In addition method. a[5] b[2] c[7]

After calling addition
Arguments to the method: [5, 2]

After Returning (No Exception) from addition
Arguments to the method: [5, 2]
Returned Value: 7

5 + 2 = 7
Before calling subtract
Arguments to the method: [5, 2]

In subtract method. a[5] b[2] c[3]

After calling subtract
Arguments to the method: [5, 2]

After Returning (No Exception) from subtract
Arguments to the method: [5, 2]
Returned Value: 3

5 - 2 = 3
Before calling multiply
Arguments to the method: [5.0, 2.0]

In multiply method. a[5.0] b[2.0] c[10.0]

After calling multiply
```

```
Arguments to the method: [5.0, 2.0]

After Returning (No Exception) from multiply
Arguments to the method: [5.0, 2.0]
Returned Value: 10.0

5.0 * 2.0 = 10.0
Before calling divide
Arguments to the method: [5.0, 0.0]
After calling divide
Arguments to the method: [5.0, 0.0]
After Returning (Throwing Exception) calling divide
Arguments to the method: [5.0, 0.0]
 Exception [Dividing a number by zero]

Error Dividing a number by zero

Operation performed successfully.
```

CHAPTER 6

JOB SCHEDULING USING QUARTZ

In many applications, it is required to execute certain jobs and tasks (specific functionalities – batch works) at an specified time or at regular intervals of time; at once or repeatedly. Even though, many Operating Systems provide support for scheduling functionality, they are not control over through code. There are also a plenty of job scheduling techniques and libraries are available for cross-platforms. Among all, Quartz scheduler is one of the popular and efficient job scheduling tools in Java.

6.1 QUARTZ SCHEDULER

Quartz Enterprise Job Scheduler is an open source job scheduling service that can be integrated with Java. Quartz can be used to create simple to complex scheduled jobs. Spring provides API and support to use Quartz in the stand-alone or web-based applications.

6.1.1 Cron Expressions

Before we go to write a demo application, let us learn a bit about "cron" expression which is used to specify what time the specified job is to be scheduled for its execution.

Each cron expression consists of seven segments separated by spaces, the seventh segment is optional and all others are mandatory. The seven segments in a cron expression are positioned as below.

```
Second Minute Hour DayOfMonth Month DayOfWeek Year
```

The value ranges for these positions are given below.

```
Second          0 - 59
Minute          0 - 59
Hour            0 - 23
DayOfMonth      1 - 31
Month           1 - 12 (or) JAN - DEC
DayOfWeek       1 - 7 (or) SUN - SAT
Year            1970 - 2099; Default to current year
```

Each position can be assigned to a specific value (eg. 5), a range of values (eg. 3–12), a list of values separated by comma (eg. 2, 5, 8, 12), a wildcard character * (matches all values), or a question mark (matches any value, means no specific value). The question mark should be assigned in either for `DayOfMonth` or `DayOfWeek` for matching any value in the corresponding position, but cannot be applied for both. The character `'/'` specifies increments, so 0/10 represents every 10 i.e. 0, 10, 20, 30 so on...

Example Cron Expressions:

Expression	Description
`0 30 20 * * ?`	Fires 20:30 every day
`* 30 20 ? * *`	Fires 20:30 every day
`0 0 11 * * ?`	Fires 11 AM every day
`0 0 11 * * ? *`	Fires 11 AM every day
`0 0 11 * * ? * 2014`	Fires 11 AM every day during the year 2014
`0 * 11 * * ?`	Fires every minute from 11:00 AM to 11:59 AM
`0 0/10 11 * * ?`	Fires every ten minutes from 11:00 AM to 11:59 AM (i.e. the last fire is at 11:50 AM)
`0 0/10 11,15 * * ?`	Fires every ten minutes from 11:00 AM to 11:59 AM (i.e. up to 11:50 AM) and every ten minutes from 3 PM to 3:59 PM (i.e. up to 3:50 PM)
`0 0/10 11 ? * MON`	Fires every ten minutes from 11:00 AM to 11:59 AM (i.e. the last fire is at 11:50 AM) every Monday
`0 0/10 11 1 * ?`	Fires every ten minutes from 11:00 AM to 11:59 AM (i.e. the last fire is at 11:50 AM) every 1st day of every month
`0 0 2,4,6,20,22`	Fires every day at 2 AM, 4 AM, 6 AM, 8 PM, and 10 PM
`0 0,10,20,50 * * ?`	Fires every first, 10th, 20th, and 50th minutes on every hour

6.2 DEFINING JOBS

Spring provides the following two bean classes to declare Quartz jobs.

- MethodInvokingJobDetailFactoryBean
- JobDetailBean

6.2.1 MethodInvokingJobDetailFactoryBean

This is the simplest method of defining jobs and well suitable for simple jobs; just specify the object of job class and the scheduled business method name in the job class. By default, jobs in this MethodInvokingJobDetailFactoryBean run concurrently. To set to run non-concurrently, set the 'concurrent' property to 'false'.

Example:

The class 'DisplayTimeJob' is the job class, it contains the schedule business method named 'displayTime'.

```
<!— Instance of Job class —>
<bean id="displayTimeJob" class="com.springdemo.job.DisplayTimeJob"/>

<!— Define Job —>
<bean id="displayTimeJobDetail" class="org.springframework.
                    scheduling.quartz.MethodInvokingJobDetailFactoryBean">
  <property name="targetObject" ref="displayTimeJob"/>
  <property name="targetMethod" value="displayTime"/>
  <property name="concurrent" value="false"/>
</bean>
```

6.2.2 JobDetailBean

This method is more flexible and suited for complex scheduling jobs. The job class should extend the Spring provided `QuartzJobBean`, and define the job scheduling operation in the overridden `executeInternal()` method.

Example:

```
public class DisplayTimeJob extends QuartzJobBean {

 protected void executeInternal(JobExecutionContext context)
                                   throws JobExecutionException {
   ...
 }
}
```

In the Spring bean configuration:

```
<bean name="displayTimeJob"
      class="org.springframework.scheduling.quartz.JobDetailBean">
<property name="jobClass" value="com.springdemo.job.DisplayTimeJob"/>
  <property name="jobDataAsMap">
  <map>
    <entry key="displayTimeTask" value-ref="displayTimeTask"/>
  </map>
  </property>
</bean>
```

6.3 DEFINING TRIGGERS

Triggers refer to actions to invoke the jobs, for scheduling. They define when will run the scheduler jobs.

The following two types of triggers are supported by Quartz (Spring's support to Quartz).

- SimpleTrigger
- CronTrigger

6.3.1 SimpleTrigger

This trigger is suitable for simple and straightforward jobs; requires the bean instance of the job, repeat interval and delay for the first time in executing jobs.

Example:

```
<bean id="simpleTrigger"
      class="org.springframework.scheduling.quartz.SimpleTriggerBean">
  <property name="jobDetail" ref="displayTimeJobDetail"/>
  <property name="repeatInterval" value="10000"/>
  <property name="startDelay" value="1000"/>
</bean>
```

6.3.2 CronTrigger

This trigger is more flexible and suited for defining complex scheduling. It supports the efficient UNIX like 'cron' expressions to specify the date and time for running jobs.

Example:

```
<bean id="cronTrigger"
      class="org.springframework.scheduling.quartz.CronTriggerBean">
  <property name="jobDetail" ref="displayTimeJob"/>
  <property name="cronExpression" value="0/5 * * * * ?"/>
</bean>
```

6.4 SchedulerFactoryBean

Spring provides a bean class `'SchedulerFactoryBean'` to integrate the job details and triggers together.

General format of bean declaration:

```
<bean class="org.springframework.scheduling.quartz.SchedulerFactoryBean">
  <property name="jobDetails">
   <list>
     Job References
   </list>
  </property>
```

```
    <property name="triggers">
      <list>
        Trigger References
      </list>
    </property>
  </bean>
```

Example Code using MethodInvokingJobDetailFactoryBean and SimpleTriggerBean

We will use the same "SpringDemo" project, which is created and used in earlier chapters.

Download and add the quartz library jar and put it on the classpath of the project. The quartz library jar can be downloaded from Maven repository; the quartz 1.5.2 version is used in our demonstration application.

Create a package named `'com.springdemo.job'` under `"src"` directory of the project, and place the following file.

```
//File Name: DisplayTimeJob.java
package com.springdemo.job;

import java.util.Date;

public class DisplayTimeJob {

 public void displayTime() {
  System.out.println(new Date());
 }

}
```

Place the following Spring bean configuration file `'beans.xml'` under `"src"` directory of the project.

```
<?xml version="1.0" encoding="UTF-8"?>
<beans xmlns="http://www.springframework.org/schema/beans"
  xmlns:xsi="http://www.w3.org/2001/XMLSchema-instance"
  xsi:schemaLocation="http://www.springframework.org/schema/beans
  http://www.springframework.org/schema/beans/spring-beans-3.0.xsd">

<bean id="displayTimeJob" class="com.springdemo.job.DisplayTimeJob"/>

 <!— Define Job —>
 <bean id="displayTimeJobDetail" class="org.springframework.
                scheduling.quartz.MethodInvokingJobDetailFactoryBean">
```

```
  <property name="targetObject" ref="displayTimeJob"/>
  <property name="targetMethod" value="displayTime"/>
  <property name="concurrent" value="false"/>
 </bean>

 <!– Define Trigger (Simple Trigger); Every 10 seconds,
     initially 1 second delay –>
 <bean id="simpleTrigger" class="org.springframework.scheduling.
                          quartz.SimpleTriggerBean">
  <property name="jobDetail" ref="displayTimeJobDetail"/>
  <property name="repeatInterval" value="10000"/>
  <property name="startDelay" value="1000"/>
 </bean>

  <!– Schedule Job –>
 <bean class="org.springframework.scheduling.quartz.SchedulerFactoryBean">
  <property name="triggers" ref="simpleTrigger"/>
 </bean>

</beans>
```

Place the following main application 'QuartzJobSchedulingDemo.java' under "com.springdemo" package and execute it.

```
//File Name: QuartzJobSchedulingDemo.java
package com.springdemo;

import org.springframework.context.support.ClassPathXmlApplicationContext;

public class QuartzJobSchedulingDemo {

 public static void main(String args[]) {
  new ClassPathXmlApplicationContext("beans.xml");
 }

}
```

The execution of the above main application results as below.

```
Tue Mar 12 10:52:35 SGT 2013
Tue Mar 12 10:52:45 SGT 2013
Tue Mar 12 10:52:55 SGT 2013
Tue Mar 12 10:53:05 SGT 2013
Tue Mar 12 10:53:15 SGT 2013
```

Example Code using JobDetailBean and CronTriggerBean

Now we will write a job scheduling application using Spring's `JobDetailBean` and `CronTriggerBean`. It is not mandatory that the `MethodInvokingJobDetailFactoryBean` should use `SimpleTriggerBean` and `JobDetailBean` should use `CronTriggerBean` as their pairs. Either of `MethodInvokingJobDetailFactoryBean` and `JobDetailBean` can use either of `SimpleTriggerBean` and `CronTriggerBean` as its trigger for executing jobs.

Place the following `'DisplayTimeTask.java'` file under `"com.springdemo.job"` package.

```
//File Name: DisplayTimeTask.java
package com.springdemo.job;

import java.util.Date;

public class DisplayTimeTask {

 public void displayTime() {
  System.out.println(new Date());
 }

}
```

Place the following `'DisplayTimeJob.java'` file under `"com.springdemo.job"` package.

```
package com.springdemo.job;

import org.quartz.JobExecutionContext;
import org.quartz.JobExecutionException;
import org.springframework.scheduling.quartz.QuartzJobBean;

public class DisplayTimeJob extends QuartzJobBean {
 private DisplayTimeTask displayTimeTask;

 public void setDisplayTimeTask(DisplayTimeTask displayTimeTask) {
  this.displayTimeTask = displayTimeTask;
 }

 protected void executeInternal(JobExecutionContext context)
                          throws JobExecutionException {
  displayTimeTask.displayTime();
 }
}
```

Store the following Spring configuration file 'beans.xml' under "src" directory of the project.

```
<?xml version="1.0" encoding="UTF-8"?>
<beans xmlns="http://www.springframework.org/schema/beans"
  xmlns:xsi="http://www.w3.org/2001/XMLSchema-instance"
  xsi:schemaLocation="http://www.springframework.org/schema/beans
  http://www.springframework.org/schema/beans/spring-beans-3.0.xsd">

 <!-- Tasks -->
 <bean id="displayTimeTask" class="com.springdemo.job.DisplayTime
                                                            Task"/>

 <!-- Define Job -->
 <bean name="displayTimeJob"
      class="org.springframework.scheduling.quartz.JobDetailBean">
  <property name="jobClass" value="com.springdemo.job.DisplayTimeJob"/>
  <property name="jobDataAsMap">
  <map>
   <entry key="displayTimeTask" value-ref="displayTimeTask"/>
  </map>
  </property>
 </bean>

 <!-- Define Trigger (Cron Trigger); Every 10 seconds -->
 <bean id="cronTrigger"
      class="org.springframework.scheduling.quartz.CronTriggerBean">
  <property name="jobDetail" ref="displayTimeJob"/>
  <property name="cronExpression" value="0/5 * * * * ?"/>
 </bean>

 <!-- Schedule Job -->
<bean class="org.springframework.scheduling.quartz.SchedulerFactoryBean">
  <property name="triggers">
  <list>
  <ref bean="cronTrigger"/>
  </list>
  </property>
 </bean>
</beans>
```

Place the following main application under "com.springdemo" and execute it.

```
//File Name: QuartzJobSchedulingDemo.java
package com.springdemo;
import org.springframework.context.support.ClassPathXmlApplicationContext;

public class QuartzJobSchedulingDemo {

 public static void main(String[] args) {
  new ClassPathXmlApplicationContext("beans.xml");
 }

}
```

The execution of the above main application results as below.

```
Tue Mar 12 11:02:00 SGT 2013
Tue Mar 12 11:02:05 SGT 2013
Tue Mar 12 11:02:10 SGT 2013
Tue Mar 12 11:02:15 SGT 2013
Tue Mar 12 11:02:20 SGT 2013
Tue Mar 12 11:02:25 SGT 2013
Tue Mar 12 11:02:30 SGT 2013
Tue Mar 12 11:02:35 SGT 2013
```

CHAPTER 7

JAVA MESSAGE SERVICE (JMS)

The Java Message Service (JMS) is a Java support for Message Oriented Middleware (MOM) solution; provides asynchronous communication between client and server on client-server applications. In asynchronous communication mode, the client is not needed to wait until the server responses for its request; the client can proceed its operation and consume the response of the server through message queues. JMS is the concept by Sun Microsystems, where many vendors implemented it; those implementations are known as "JMC Provider" (aka Message Broker), Apache Active MQ is one of the most popular message brokers for Java and it is also an open-source.

7.1 SOME JMS KEY TERMS

Some of the key terms in regard to JMS:

- **JMS Message:** Message that carries data between JMS Clients.
- **JMS Producer:** An application that creates and sends the JMS messages.
- **JMS Consumer:** An application that receives and processes the JMS messages.
- **JMS Client:** Java application to send and receive the JMS messages.
- **JMS Message Delivery Modes (JMS Domains):** Defines how the JMS messages are delivered from JMS Producer to JMS Consumer.

Two types of delivery modes: (i) **Point-to-Point** (in short **'PTP'**–One to One), and (ii) **Publish/Subscribe** (in short 'pub/sub'–One to Many). In Point-to-Point communication, the messages are sent and received from a destination called **"Queue"**, each message from the message producer will be delivered to ONLY ONE consumer, and the message delivery is guaranteed. In the case of Publish/Subscribe communication, the messages are sent and received from a destination called **"Topic"**, the message producers (known as Publishers) send the messages to the topic, where ALL the message consumers (known as Subscribers) who registered with that topic are eligible to receive the message. In this communication, the message delivery is not guaranteed to all the subscribers as some of them may not be 'online' at that time of message and the message might be timeout when the subscribers become online. However, a 'durable subscription' is possible and it makes the subscribers to receive those messages that are arrived on the topic when the subscribers were on offline.

7.2 JMS MESSAGE STRUCTURE

Each JMS Message consists of three important parts: (i) Message Header contain information of JMS destination, deliver mode... (ii) Message Properties, contains additional information based on the JMS Provider, and (iii) Message Payload, the body of the message. In general, all the JMS Providers supports the following types of data as message payload.

`TextMessage` : Message whose message body contains text (String data type) data. Used to transfer Alert text, XML text ...

`BytesMessage` : Message whose message body contains sequence of bytes.

`StreamMessage` : Message whose message body contains stream of Primitive data (data of Java primitive data types such as int, double ... including String).

`MapMessage` : Message whose message body contains a set of name-value pairs (Map) data.

`ObjectMessage` : Message whose message body contains an object (The object of the Java Class should be Serialized).

7.3 APACHE ActiveMQ

ActiveMQ is one of the most popular JMS providers from Apache Software Foundation and it is also an open-source. We can download the latest version from ActiveMQ download page (http://activemq.apache.org/download.html). The ActiveMQ version 5.5.1 (apache-activemq-5.5.1-bin.zip) is used for the demonstration applications in the following sections.

7.3.1 Setting up ActiveMQ

The sub-directories under ActiveMQ home directory (extracted directory of the activemq distribution): The `"bin"` directory contains start-up scripts, the `"conf"` directory contains all configuration details, the `"data"` directory contains the log files and Message Persistence data (default for `kahadb`), the `"webapps"` directory contains ActiveMQ web console, the `"lib"` directory contains all the library files that are needed for ActiveMQ, any additional lib files (such as JDBC Connector) can be included in `"optional"` directory under this `"lib"` directory (`lib/optional`). The jar file (activemq-all-5.5.1.jar) in the home directory should be included in `CLASSPATH` of our Java Project in order to use the API of `ActiveMQ`.

The `"conf"` directory contains many XML files, carrying default configurations and we can modify them according to our needs. The parent file is `"activemq.xml"`.

Open activemq.xml file and you can update the Broker Name, which is default to 'localhost'.

```
<broker xmlns="http://activemq.apache.org/schema/core"
       brokerName="localhost"
       dataDirectory="${activemq.base}/data"
       destroyApplicationContextOnStop="true">
```

To enable to persist the messages (for the Queues and Topics) in a database, we have to configure `'persistenceAdapter'`. In our demonstration, we are using MySQL database system to persist the message. If you want to use some other RDBMS, specify the database URL in correct format.

Install MySQL database and login as 'root' user. Create a database named 'activemq' and create a user, named 'activemquser' with password 'activemqpword' (username and password are up to you) and grant all the privileges on 'activemq' database to this user 'activemquser'

```
mysql> create database activemq;
Query OK, 1 row affected (0.06 sec)

mysql> grant all privileges on activemq.* to activemquser@localhost
    ->        identified by 'activemqpword';
Query OK, 0 rows affected (0.13 sec)
```

Open activemq.xml file, and configure as shown below.

Delete the default `kahaDB` configuration

Delete the following segment in the <persistenceAdapter> element.

```
<kahaDB directory="${activemq.base}/data/kahadb"/>
```

Change the default persistence data store from 'derby' to 'mysql'

```
<persistenceAdapter>
  <jdbcPersistenceAdapter dataDirectory="${activemq.base}/data"
                          dataSource="#mysql-ds"/>
</persistenceAdapter>
```

And include the following segment within the <beans> root element.

```
<bean id="mysql-ds" class="org.apache.commons.dbcp.BasicDataSource"
    destroy-method="close">
  <property name="driverClassName" value="com.mysql.jdbc.Driver"/>
  <property name="url"
      value="jdbc:mysql://localhost/activemq?relaxAutoCommit=true"/>
  <property name="username" value="activemquser"/>
  <property name="password" value="activemqpword"/>
  <property name="maxActive" value="200"/>
  <property name="poolPreparedStatements" value="true"/>
</bean>
```

A partial content of activemq.xml file in editor is as shown below.

```
            </policyEntries>
        </policyMap>
    </destinationPolicy>

    <persistenceAdapter>
        <jdbcPersistenceAdapter dataDirectory="${activemq.base}/data" dataSource="#mysql-ds"/>
    </persistenceAdapter>

    <transportConnectors>
        <transportConnector name="openwire" uri="tcp://0.0.0.0:61616"/>
    </transportConnectors>

</broker>

<import resource="jetty.xml"/>

<bean id="mysql-ds" class="org.apache.commons.dbcp.BasicDataSource" destroy-method="close">
    <property name="driverClassName" value="com.mysql.jdbc.Driver"/>
    <property name="url" value="jdbc:mysql://localhost/activemq?relaxAutoCommit=true"/>
    <property name="username" value="activemquser"/>
    <property name="password" value="activemqpword"/>
    <property name="maxActive" value="200"/>
    <property name="poolPreparedStatements" value="true"/>
</bean>

</beans>
```

Include MySQL Connector/J library file in 'conf' directory

Download JDBC Driver for MySQL (Connector/J) from MySQL web site (http://www.mysql.com/products/connector/) in .zip format and extract it. I downloaded Connector/J version 5.1.18 (mysql-connector-java-5.1.17.zip).

Copy the jar file (mysql-connector-java-5.1.18-bin.jar) from the extracted one, and paste it in `ActiveMQ_Home/lib/optional` directory.

Follow the same procedure to include database connector library jar files, if you are using different RDBMS.

Create `ACTIVEMQ_HOME` Environment Variable

Select My Computer → Right Click → Properties → Advanced system settings → Environment Variables → Add a new System variable `"ACTIVEMQ_HOME"` with the value "C:\Install\apache-activemq-5.5.1" (Home directory of ActiveMQ).

7.3.2 Running ActiveMQ

Go to `"bin"` directory of ActiveMQ Home directory in a DOS window (in MS Windows OS environment). And invoke `"activemq.bat"`.

Press `Ctrl+C` (`^C`) to stop ActiveMQ execution in DOS window.

Now check with underlying MySQL database (`activemq`), necessary tables are created automatically by ActiveMQ.

```
mysql> show tables;
```

Tables_in_activemq
activemq_acks
activemq_lock
activemq_msgs

```
3 rows in set (0.00 sec)
```

Invoke ActiveMQ Web Console with the URL: `http://localhost:8161/admin/`

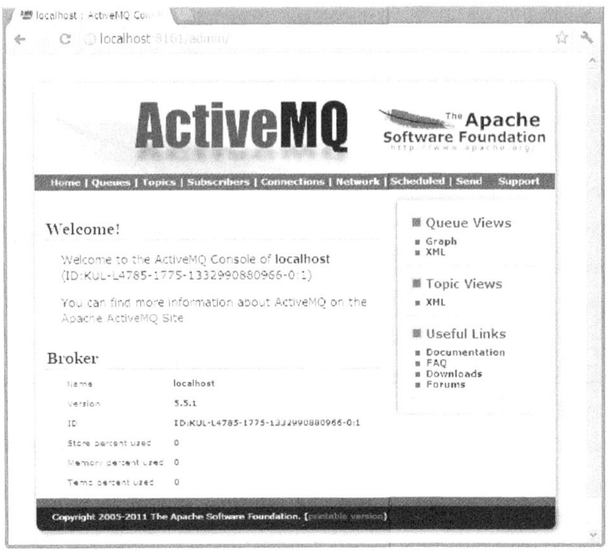

Creating Queue and Topic for our demo applications: Create a Queue named "DemoQueue", and create a Topic named "DemoTopic" in ActiveMQ.

To do, start the ActiveMQ (invoke activemq.bat at `bin` directory of ActiveMQ installation. Click on "Queues", type "DemoQueue" as Queue Name and click on "Create". Then, the specified queue will be created.

Click on "Topics", type "DemoTopic" as Topic Name and click on "Create". Then, the specified topic will be created.

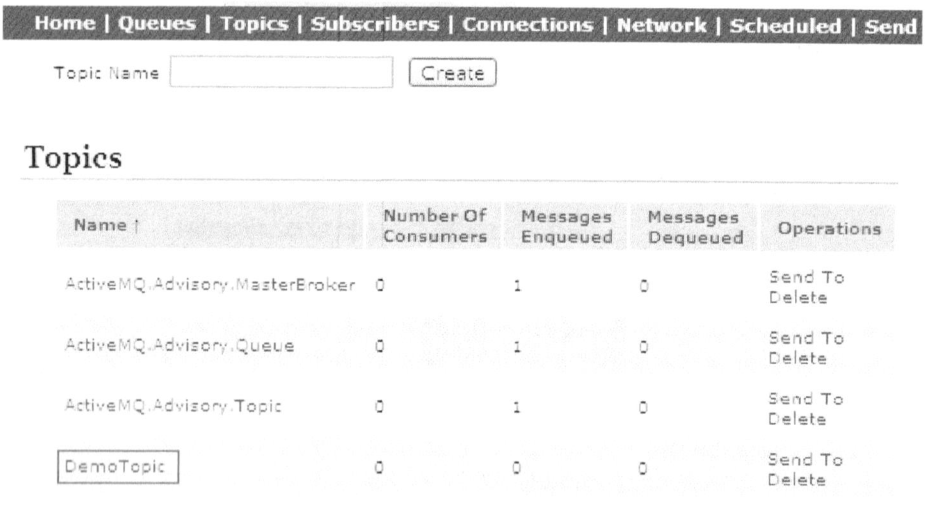

7.4 SPRING API FOR JMS

Spring provides API which simplifies the use of JMS. The core class `'JmsTemplate'` does not expect the programmers to open/close the connection/resources, it will do for them.

The following are core API classes/interfaces to access JMS (since JMS 1.2).

`MessageCreator`	Creates a JMS message for a specified session	
`MessageConverter`	It is a converter between Java data types and JMS messages. Spring provides a class `'SimpleMessageConverter'` which implements this interface `'MessageConverter'` and it converts data as below.	
	<u>Java Data Type</u>	<u>JMS Message Type</u>
	`String`	`TextMessage`
	`byte array (byte[])`	`BytesMessage`
	`Map`	`MapMessage`
	Java Serializable Java class object	`ObjectMessage`
`JmsException`	Base class for JMS exception	

7.5 EXAMPLE: POINT-TO-POINT MESSAGING

We will use the same "SpringDemo" Java project to demonstrate JMS operations. Add the following jars into the class path of the project; add them to the 'lib' directory under the project, Select the project, right click, properties → Java Build Path → Libraries → Add JARs.

- activemq-all-5.5.1.jar (found at HOME directory of Active-MQ installation)
- All the jar files under ACTIVEMQ_HOME\lib\optional

Create a package named 'com.springdemo.jms' and place the following program.

```
//File Name: QueueMsgProducer.java
package com.springdemo.jms;

import org.springframework.beans.factory.annotation.Autowired;
import org.springframework.jms.core.JmsTemplate;
import org.springframework.stereotype.Component;

@Component
public class QueueMsgProducer
{
  @Autowired
  private JmsTemplate jmsTemplate;

  private String queueName;

  public void setQueueName(String queueName) {
    this.queueName = queueName;
  }

  public void send(String message) {
```

```
    jmsTemplate.convertAndSend(queueName, message );
  }
}
```

Store the following "beans.xml" in the "src" directory of the project.

```
<?xml version="1.0" encoding="UTF-8"?>
<beans xmlns="http://www.springframework.org/schema/beans"
     xmlns:amq="http://activemq.apache.org/schema/core"
     xmlns:jms="http://www.springframework.org/schema/jms"
     xmlns:context="http://www.springframework.org/schema/context"
     xmlns:xsi="http://www.w3.org/2001/XMLSchema-instance"
     xsi:schemaLocation="http://www.springframework.org/schema/beans
     http://www.springframework.org/schema/beans/spring-beans 2.5.xsd
     http://activemq.apache.org/schema/core
     http://activemq.apache.org/schema/core/activemq-core-5.2.0.xsd
     http://www.springframework.org/schema/context
    http://www.springframework.org/schema/context/spring-context
       2.5.xsd
     http://www.springframework.org/schema/jms
     http://www.springframework.org/schema/jms/spring-jms-2.5.xsd">

  <context:annotation-config/>
  <context:component-scan base-package="com.springdemo"/>

  <!-- creates an ActiveMQ Connection Factory using the amq namespace -->
  <amq:connectionFactory id="amqConnectionFactory"
                         brokerURL="tcp://localhost:61616"/>

  <!-- JmsTemplate Definition -->
 <bean id="jmsTemplate" class="org.springframework.jms.core.JmsTemplate">
     <constructor-arg ref="amqConnectionFactory"/>
  </bean>

 <bean id="queueMsgProducer" class="com.springdemo.jms.QueueMsgProducer">
    <property name="queueName" value="DemoQueue"/>
  </bean>

 </beans>
```

Store the following main application in "com.springdemo" package and then execute.

```
//File Name: JMSSendMessage.java
package com.springdemo;

import org.springframework.context.support.AbstractApplicationContext;
import org.springframework.context.support.ClassPathXmlApplicationContext;

import com.springdemo.jms.QueueMsgProducer;

public class JMSSendMessage {

  public static void main(String[] args) {
    AbstractApplicationContext context =
              new ClassPathXmlApplicationContext("beans.xml");
    QueueMsgProducer queueMsgProducer =
             (QueueMsgProducer) context.getBean("queueMsgProducer");
    queueMsgProducer.send("This is a message");
    System.out.println("Operation performed successfully.");
  }
}
```

Check the ActiveMQ queue (http://localhost:8161/admin/queues.jsp).

You can observe that one (1) message in pending in the queue for consumption.

Our setting is to persist the messages in MySQL database. A database query using MySQL Workbench,

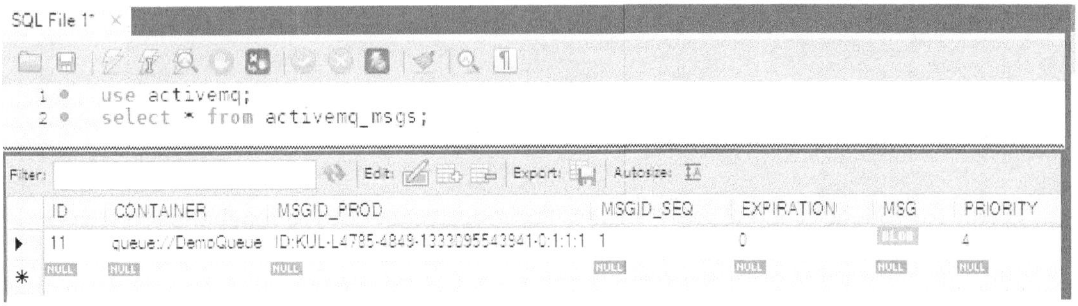

Now, we will write an application to consume the message(s) in the queue.

```
//File Name: QueueMsgConsumer.java
package com.springdemo.jms;

import org.springframework.beans.factory.annotation.Autowired;
import org.springframework.jms.JmsException;
import org.springframework.jms.core.JmsTemplate;
import org.springframework.stereotype.Component;

@Component
public class QueueMsgConsumer {
  @Autowired
  private JmsTemplate jmsTemplate;

  private String queueName;

  public void setQueueName(String queueName) {
    this.queueName = queueName;
  }

  public String receive() {
    String msg = "";
    try {
      jmsTemplate.setReceiveTimeout(10000); // Ten Seconds
      msg = (String) jmsTemplate.receiveAndConvert(queueName);

    }
    catch (JmsException e) {
     msg = "Error occurred while receiving message. Error ["
          + e.getMessage() + "]";
      e.printStackTrace();
    }
    return msg;
  }
}
```

Add the following lines in the “beans.xml” file.

```
<bean id="queueMsgConsumer" class="com.springdemo.jms.QueueMsgConsumer">
      <property name="queueName" value="DemoQueue"/>
</bean>
```

Write the following main application and execute it.

```
//File Name: JMSReceiveMessage.java
package com.springdemo;

import org.springframework.context.support.AbstractApplicationContext;
import org.springframework.context.support.ClassPathXmlApplicationContext;

import com.springdemo.jms.QueueMsgConsumer;

public class JMSReceiveMessage {

  public static void main(String[] args) {
    AbstractApplicationContext context =
            new ClassPathXmlApplicationContext("beans.xml");
    QueueMsgConsumer queueMsgConsumer =
            (QueueMsgConsumer) context.getBean("queueMsgConsumer");
    String msg = queueMsgConsumer.receive();
    System.out.println("Message: " + msg);
    System.out.println("Operation performed successfully.");
  }
}
```

Output:

```
Message: This is a message
Operation performed successfully.
```

Now check the queue status.

Queues

Name	Number Of Pending Messages	Number Of Consumers	Messages Enqueued	Messages Dequeued	Views	Operations
DemoQueue	0	0	1	1	Browse Active Consumers atom rss	Send To Purge Delete

Observe that the pending message (1) is consumed by our application. So number of pending messages became zero.

A message producer may send many messages to a queue; where a message consumer can receive them. The above given application (JMSReceiveMessage.java) is not a professional way of getting messages from the queue. The following application uses message-driven listener approach, which will automatically receive the messages as soon as they enter to the queue.

```
//File Name: QueueListener.java
package com.springdemo;

import javax.jms.JMSException;
import javax.jms.Message;
import javax.jms.MessageListener;
import javax.jms.TextMessage;

import org.springframework.stereotype.Component;

@Component
public class QueueListener implements MessageListener {

  public void onMessage(final Message message) {
    System.out.println("Listening for message...");
    if (message instanceof TextMessage) {
      final TextMessage textMessage = (TextMessage) message;
      try {
      System.out.println("Received Message: " + textMessage.getText());
      }
      catch (final JMSException e) {
        e.printStackTrace();
      }
    }
    else {
      System.out.println("Received message is not a text message");
    }
  }
}
```

Add the following segment in the Spring configuration file 'beans.xml'.

```
<context:annotation-config />
<context:component-scan base-package="com.springdemo"/>

<!-- creates an ActiveMQ Connection Factory using the amq namespace -->
<amq:connectionFactory id="connectionFactory"
                    brokerURL="tcp://localhost:61616" />
```

```
<!-- JmsTemplate Definition -->
<bean id="jmsTemplate" class="org.springframework.jms.core.JmsTemplate">
    <constructor-arg ref="connectionFactory"/>
</bean>

<bean id="queueMsgProducer" class="com.springdemo.jms.QueueMsgProducer">
    <property name="queueName" value="DemoQueue"/>
</bean>

<bean id="queueListener" class="com.springdemo.QueueListener"/>

<!-- concurrency defines the max number of concurrent listeners
     that can be started -->
<jms:listener-container concurrency="5" >
    <jms:listener id="jmsQueueListener" destination="DemoQueue"
                                     ref="queueListener"/>
</jms:listener-container>
```

Execute the JMSSendMessage.java to send a message, our application receives the message as shown below.

Listening for message...

Received Message: This is a message

Operation performed successfully.

Immediately message is consumed by the `QueueListener` and note that the application is not terminated and still running.

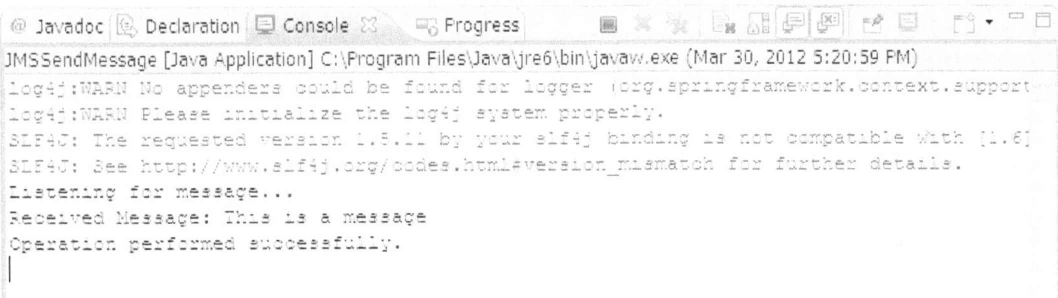

Now try to send some more messages to the queue, and you can see that all the messages will be consumed by the listener. At end, press the End button (in case of Eclipse) or Ctrl+C (in command shell) to terminate the application.

Now we try to send messages using ActiveMQ GUI. Click on "Send To" link of the 'Queues" page.

Type some text in the message body and click on "Send" button. Repeat for sending some more messages.

The following are the output of the listener (application).

```
Listening for message...
Received Message: This is a message
Operation performed successfully.
Listening for message...
Received Message: This is 1.
Listening for message...
Received Message: This is 2
Listening for message...
Received Message: This is 3
```

You can also write a small simulation application to send multiple messages.

```
//File Name: JMSSendMessage.java
package com.springdemo;

import org.springframework.context.support.AbstractApplicationContext;
import org.springframework.context.support.ClassPathXmlApplicationContext;
import com.springdemo.jms.QueueMsgProducer;

public class JMSSendMessage {
 public static void main(String[] args) {
  AbstractApplicationContext context =
                   new ClassPathXmlApplicationContext("beans.xml");
  QueueMsgProducer queueMsgProducer =
             (QueueMsgProducer) context.getBean("queueMsgProducer");
  for (int i=1; i <= 10; i++) {
    queueMsgProducer.send("This is a message " + i);
  }
   System.out.println("Operation performed successfully.");
 }
}
```

Output:

```
Listening for message...
Received Message: This is a message 1
Listening for message...
Received Message: This is a message 2
Listening for message...
Received Message: This is a message 3
Listening for message...
Received Message: This is a message 4
Listening for message...
Received Message: This is a message 5
Listening for message...
Received Message: This is a message 6
Listening for message...
Received Message: This is a message 7
Listening for message...
Received Message: This is a message 8
Listening for message...
Received Message: This is a message 9
Listening for message...
Received Message: This is a message 10
```

In the above example, we send and receive text messages. Now we will write code to send and receive Map message. Then, follow the same procedure for sending and receiving other types of messages such as Byte Messages, Object Messages, and Stream Messages.

The following application sends one Text message and one Map message together to the queue.

```
//File Name: JMSSendMessage.java
package com.springdemo;

import java.util.HashMap;
import java.util.Map;
import org.springframework.context.support.AbstractApplicationContext;
import org.springframework.context.support.ClassPathXmlApplicationContext;
import com.springdemo.jms.QueueMsgProducer;

public class JMSSendMessage {
public static void main(String[] args) {
  AbstractApplicationContext context =
                     new ClassPathXmlApplicationContext("beans.xml");
  QueueMsgProducer queueMsgProducer =
               (QueueMsgProducer) context.getBean("queueMsgProducer");

  queueMsgProducer.send("This is a text message");

  Map<String, String> mapMessage = new HashMap<String, String>();
  mapMessage.put("empid", "EMP1001");
  mapMessage.put("empname", "Ibrahim");
  mapMessage.put("salary", "50000");
  queueMsgProducer.send(mapMessage);

  System.out.println("Operation performed successfully.");
 }
}
```

The following class contains the core logic to communicate with queue to send the messages.

```
//File Name: QueueMsgProducer.java
package com.springdemo.jms;

import org.springframework.beans.factory.annotation.Autowired;
```

```
import org.springframework.jms.core.JmsTemplate;
import org.springframework.stereotype.Component;

@Component
public class QueueMsgProducer
{
  @Autowired
  private JmsTemplate jmsTemplate;

  private String queueName;

  public void setQueueName(String queueName) {
   this.queueName = queueName;
  }

  public void send(Object message) {
   jmsTemplate.convertAndSend(queueName, message);
  }
}
```

The following is the message listener class that listens for new messages and receives them.

```
//File Name: QueueListener.java
package com.springdemo;

import javax.jms.MapMessage;
import javax.jms.Message;
import javax.jms.MessageListener;
import javax.jms.TextMessage;

import org.springframework.stereotype.Component;

@Component
public class QueueListener implements MessageListener {

 public void onMessage(Message message) {
  System.out.println("Listening for message...");

  try {
   if (message instanceof TextMessage) {
```

```
        TextMessage textMessage = (TextMessage) message;
        System.out.println("Received Text Message: " +
                         textMessage.getText());
        }
        else if (message instanceof MapMessage) {
            MapMessage mapMessage = (MapMessage) message;
            System.out.println("Received Map Message: empid=" +
                         mapMessage.getString("empid") +
                         " empname=" +
                         mapMessage.getString("empname") +
                         " salary=" + mapMessage.getString("salary"));
        }
       }
       catch(Exception e){
        e.printStackTrace();
       }
      }
     }
```

Execute the main application 'JMSSendMessage.java' and the listener outputs as below.

```
Listening for message...
Received Text Message: This is a text message
Listening for message...
Received Map Message: empid=EMP1001 empname=Ibrahim salary=50000
Operation performed successfully.
```

7.6 EXAMPLE: PUBLISH/SUBSCRIBE MESSAGING

The bean instance creation of JmsTemplate always creates the object with referring to Queue by default. To tell JmsTemplate that it is Topic rather than Queue, you need to set the property 'pubSubDomain' to 'true'.

The following configuration tells JmsTemplate to use Queue (by default).

```
<bean id="jmsTemplate" class="org.springframework.jms.core.JmsTemplate">
   <constructor-arg ref="connectionFactory"/>
</bean>
```

The following configuration tells JmsTemplate to use Topic.

```
<bean id="jmsTemplate" class="org.springframework.jms.core.JmsTemplate">
   <constructor-arg ref="connectionFactory"/>
   <property name="pubSubDomain" value="true"/>
</bean>
```

Suppose you want to configure for both Queue and Topic in the same project. Then use different bean ids for JmsTemplate.

```
<beanid="jmsQueueTemplate" class="org.springframework.jms.core.JmsTemplate">
   <constructor-arg ref="connectionFactory"/>
</bean>

<bean id="jmsTopicTemplate" class="org.springframework.jms.core.
JmsTemplate">
   <constructor-arg ref="connectionFactory"/>
   <property name="pubSubDomain" value="true"/>
</bean>
```

The following application sends a text message to the Topic through TopicMsgProducer class.

```
//File Name: JMSSendMessage.java
package com.springdemo;

import org.springframework.context.support.AbstractApplicationContext;
import org.springframework.context.support.ClassPathXmlApplicationContext;
import com.springdemo.jms.TopicMsgProducer;

public class JMSSendMessage {
 public static void main(String[] args) {
  AbstractApplicationContext context =
              new ClassPathXmlApplicationContext("beans.xml");
  TopicMsgProducer topicMsgProducer =
             (TopicMsgProducer) context.getBean("topicMsgProducer");

  topicMsgProducer.send("This is a text message");

  System.out.println("Operation performed successfully.");
 }
}
```

The TopicMsgProducer class is given below, which contains the core logic to send messages to a Topic.

```
//File Name: TopicMsgProducer.java
package com.springdemo.jms;

import org.springframework.beans.factory.annotation.Autowired;
```

```
import org.springframework.jms.core.JmsTemplate;

public class TopicMsgProducer
{
  @Autowired
  private JmsTemplate jmsTopicTemplate;

  private String topicName;

  public void setTopicName(String topicName) {
   this.topicName = topicName;
  }

  public void send(Object message) {
    jmsTopicTemplate.convertAndSend(topicName, message);
  }
}
```

The following are two listeners who are subscribed to the same Topic and listening for new messages.

```
//File Name: TopicListener1.java
package com.springdemo;

import javax.jms.Message;
import javax.jms.MessageListener;
import javax.jms.TextMessage;

import org.springframework.stereotype.Component;

@Component
public class TopicListener1 implements MessageListener {

  public void onMessage(Message message) {
    System.out.println("TopicListener1: Listening for message...");

    try {
      if (message instanceof TextMessage) {
        TextMessage textMessage = (TextMessage) message;
        System.out.println("TopicListener1: Received Text Message: " +
                        textMessage.getText());
      }
```

```
    else {
      System.out.println("TopicListener1: Received message
                      is not a Text Message");
    }
  }
  catch(Exception e){
    e.printStackTrace();
  }
 }
}
```

The second listener class is given below.

```
//File Name: TopicListener2.java
package com.springdemo;

import javax.jms.Message;
import javax.jms.MessageListener;
import javax.jms.TextMessage;

import org.springframework.stereotype.Component;

@Component
public class TopicListener2 implements MessageListener {

  public void onMessage(Message message) {
    System.out.println("TopicListener2: Listening for message...");

    try {
      if (message instanceof TextMessage) {
        TextMessage textMessage = (TextMessage) message;
        System.out.println("TopicListener2: Received Text Message: " +
                      textMessage.getText());
      }
      else {
        System.out.println("TopicListener2: Received message
                      is not a Text Message");
      }
    }
    catch(Exception e){
      e.printStackTrace();
    }
  }
}
```

You can write many listeners to a same Topic as a Topic can be subscribed by many message consumers. The Spring bean configuration file under the "src" directory of the project is given below.

```
<?xml version="1.0" encoding="UTF-8"?>
<beans xmlns="http://www.springframework.org/schema/beans"
       xmlns:amq="http://activemq.apache.org/schema/core"
       xmlns:jms="http://www.springframework.org/schema/jms"
       xmlns:context="http://www.springframework.org/schema/context"
       xmlns:xsi="http://www.w3.org/2001/XMLSchema-instance"
       xsi:schemaLocation="http://www.springframework.org/schema/beans
       http://www.springframework.org/schema/beans/spring-beans-2.5.xsd
       http://activemq.apache.org/schema/core
       http://activemq.apache.org/schema/core/activemq-core-5.2.0.xsd
       http://www.springframework.org/schema/context
       http://www.springframework.org/schema/context/spring-context-
          2.5.xsd
       http://www.springframework.org/schema/jms
       http://www.springframework.org/schema/jms/spring-jms-2.5.xsd">

 <context:annotation-config />
 <context:component-scan base-package="com.springdemo"/>

 <!-- creates an ActiveMQ Connection Factory using the amq namespace -->
 <amq:connectionFactory id="connectionFactory"
                    brokerURL="tcp://localhost:61616"/>

 <!-- JmsTemplate Definition for Topic -->
 <bean id="jmsTopicTemplate"
      class="org.springframework.jms.core.JmsTemplate">
   <constructor-arg ref="connectionFactory"/>
   <property name="pubSubDomain" value="true"/>
 </bean>

<bean id="topicMsgProducer" class="com.springdemo.jms.TopicMsgProducer">
   <property name="topicName" value="DemoTopic"/>
 </bean>

 <bean id="topicListener1" class="com.springdemo.TopicListener1"/>
 <bean id="topicListener2" class="com.springdemo.TopicListener2"/>
```

```
<jms:listener-container connection-factory="connectionFactory"
                        cache="none" destination-type="topic">
  <jms:listener id="jmsTopicListener1" destination="DemoTopic"
                                ref="topicListener1"/>
  <jms:listener id="jmsTopicListener2" destination="DemoTopic"
                                ref="topicListener2"/>
</jms:listener-container>

</beans>
```

The result of the sample run of the 'JMSSendMessage.java' in Eclipse IDE is as shown below.

```
TopicListener1: Listening for message...
TopicListener1: Received Text Message: This is a text message
TopicListener2: Listening for message...
TopicListener2: Received Text Message: This is a text message
Operation performed successfully.
```

CHAPTER 8

JAVA MANAGEMENT EXTENSIONS (JMX)

Java Management eXtension (JMX) is a way to monitor and manage Java applications at runtime. The bean classes, whose objects can be accessed outside of the application at runtime, are called "Managed Beans" (MBeans). For example, we can access the value of attributes and methods of any MBean outside the running application.

8.1 JMX ANNOTATIONS

The following are some of the annotations that are used to declare/access MBeans.

`@ManagedResource`	Applied at class level, marks all instances of a class as JMX managed resources.
`@ManagedOperation`	Applied at method level, marks a method as JMX operation.
`@ManagedOperationParameter,`	Applied at method argument level, defines method
`@ManagedOperationParameters`	operation parameter(s).
`@ManagedAttribute`	Applied at getter and/or setter methods, makes a getter or setter method to access the corresponding attribute. If this annotation is applied on only getter method of an attribute, then the attribute become 'read-only', and if this annotation is applied on only setter method of an attribute, then the attribute become 'write-only' attribute.

8.2 JMX EXAMPLE

We will write a MBean in Spring and try to access it outside the runtime.

Store the following MBean class 'AppConfiguration.java' under `'com.springdemo.mbeans'` class.

```
//File Name: AppConfiguration.java
package com.springdemo.mbeans;
```

```
import org.springframework.jmx.export.annotation.ManagedAttribute;
import org.springframework.jmx.export.annotation.ManagedOperation;
import org.springframework.jmx.export.annotation.ManagedOperationParameter;
import org.springframework.jmx.export.annotation.ManagedOperationParameters;
import org.springframework.jmx.export.annotation.ManagedResource;

@ManagedResource
public class AppConfiguration {
 private int paginationSize;
 private boolean enableDebugLog;
 private boolean enableInfoLog;
 private String appTitle;

 @ManagedAttribute
 public int getPaginationSize() {
  return paginationSize;
 }

 @ManagedAttribute(defaultValue="10")
 public void setPaginationSize(int paginationSize) {
  this.paginationSize = paginationSize;
 }

 @ManagedAttribute
 public boolean isEnableDebugLog() {
  return enableDebugLog;
 }

 //Purposefully did not annotated, to make enableDebugLog as read-only
 public void setEnableDebugLog(boolean enableDebugLog) {
  this.enableDebugLog = enableDebugLog;
 }

 @ManagedAttribute
 public boolean isEnableInfoLog() {
  return enableInfoLog;
 }

 @ManagedAttribute(defaultValue="true")
 public void setEnableInfoLog(boolean enableInfoLog) {
  this.enableInfoLog = enableInfoLog;
 }
```

```
    @ManagedAttribute(defaultValue="Simple Application - Modified")
    public String getAppTitle() {
     return appTitle;
    }

    @ManagedAttribute(defaultValue="Simple Application")
    public void setAppTitle(String appTitle) {
     this.appTitle = appTitle;
    }

    @ManagedOperation(description="Enables/Disables Debug and Info log")
    @ManagedOperationParameters({
     @ManagedOperationParameter(name = "enableDebugLog",
                          description = "Debug Log Setting"),
     @ManagedOperationParameter(name = "enableInfoLog",
                          description = "Info Log Setting")})
    public void controlLogs(boolean enableDebugLog, boolean enableInfoLog) {
     setEnableDebugLog(enableDebugLog);
     setEnableInfoLog(enableInfoLog);
    }

    @ManagedOperation(
      description="Increase the pagination size by the given value")
    @ManagedOperationParameter(name = "value",
      description = "Value to be added to pagination size")
    public int addToPaginationSize(int value) {
     paginationSize += value;
     return paginationSize;
    }

    public String toString() {
     return "paginationSize = " + paginationSize +
          " enableDebugLog  = " + enableDebugLog +
          " enableInfoLog   = " + enableInfoLog +
          " appTitle        = " + appTitle;
    }
   }
```

Store the following Spring bean configuration 'beans.xml' file under "src" folder of the project.

```
<?xml version="1.0" encoding="UTF-8"?>
<beans xmlns="http://www.springframework.org/schema/beans"
```

```
xmlns:xsi="http://www.w3.org/2001/XMLSchema-instance"
xmlns:context="http://www.springframework.org/schema/context"
xsi:schemaLocation="http://www.springframework.org/schema/beans
http://www.springframework.org/schema/beans/spring-beans-3.0.xsd
http://www.springframework.org/schema/context
http://www.springframework.org/schema/context/spring-context3.0.xsd">

<!-- <context:mbean-server /> -->
<context:component-scan base-package="com.springdemo.mbeans"/>
<context:mbean-export />

<bean id="appConfiguration" class="com.springdemo.mbeans.
AppConfiguration">
  <property name="paginationSize" value="10"/>
  <property name="enableDebugLog" value="false"/>
  <property name="enableInfoLog" value="true"/>
  <property name="appTitle" value="Simple Application"/>
</bean>

<bean id="rmiRegistry"
     class="org.springframework.remoting.rmi.RmiRegistryFactoryBean"/>

<bean id="ConnectorServer"
   class="org.springframework.jmx.support.ConnectorServerFactoryBean"
   depends-on="rmiRegistry">

 <property name="serviceUrl" value="service:jmx:rmi://localhost/jndi/
                          rmi://localhost:1099/appConfiguration"/>
</bean>

</beans>
```

Store the following main application 'JMXDemo.java' under 'com.springdemo' package and execute it.

```
//File Name: JMXDemo.java
package com.springdemo;

import org.springframework.context.support.AbstractApplicationContext;
import org.springframework.context.support.ClassPathXmlApplicationContext;

import com.springdemo.mbeans.AppConfiguration;

public class JMXDemo {
```

```
  public static void main(String[] args) throws Exception {
   AbstractApplicationContext context =
          new ClassPathXmlApplicationContext("beans.xml");

   AppConfiguration appConfiguration =
          (AppConfiguration) context.getBean("appConfiguration");

    System.out.println("Configuration: \n" + appConfiguration);
    System.out.println("Press a key");
    System.in.read();
    System.out.println("Configuration: \n" + appConfiguration);
    //System.exit(0);
  }
}
```

The following is the output of the application:

```
Configuration:
paginationSize = 10 enableDebugLog = false enableInfoLog = true appTitle =
Simple Application
Press a key
```

The application waits for a key press. We made this wait intentionally, as we will access the MBean instance outside the runtime using 'jconsole' tool. You can access / modify the attributes and call the operation methods of the MBean.

Run jconsole: The `'jconsole'` is a tool that is provided with JDK. It is available under 'bin' directory of JDK installation (For example, `C:\Program Files\Java\jdk1.6.0_31\bin>`). Go to the 'bin' directory and issue the command.

`C:\Program Files\Java\jdk1.6.0_31\bin> jconsole`

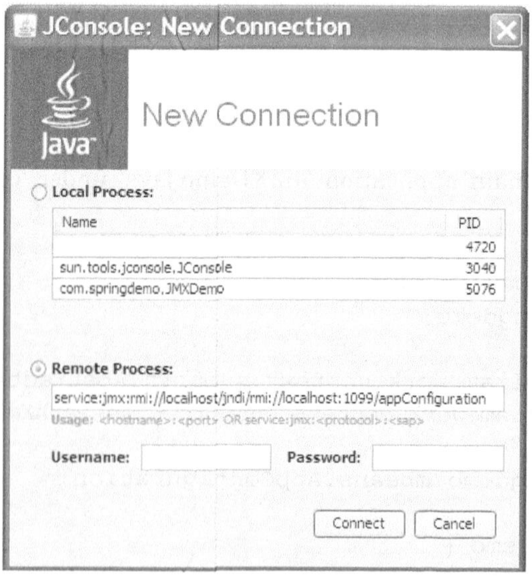

Enter the `'serviceUrl'` as specified in the Spring configuration XML file and click on “Connect”. Then, go to MBeans Tab.

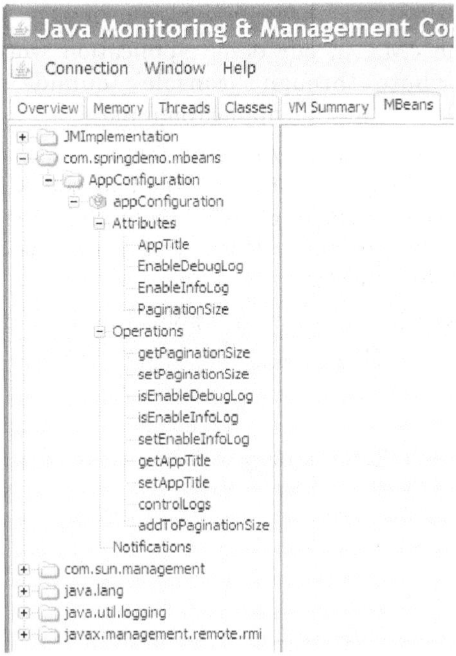

Expand our *mbeans* package. Click on ‘Operations’ under ‘appConfiguration’.

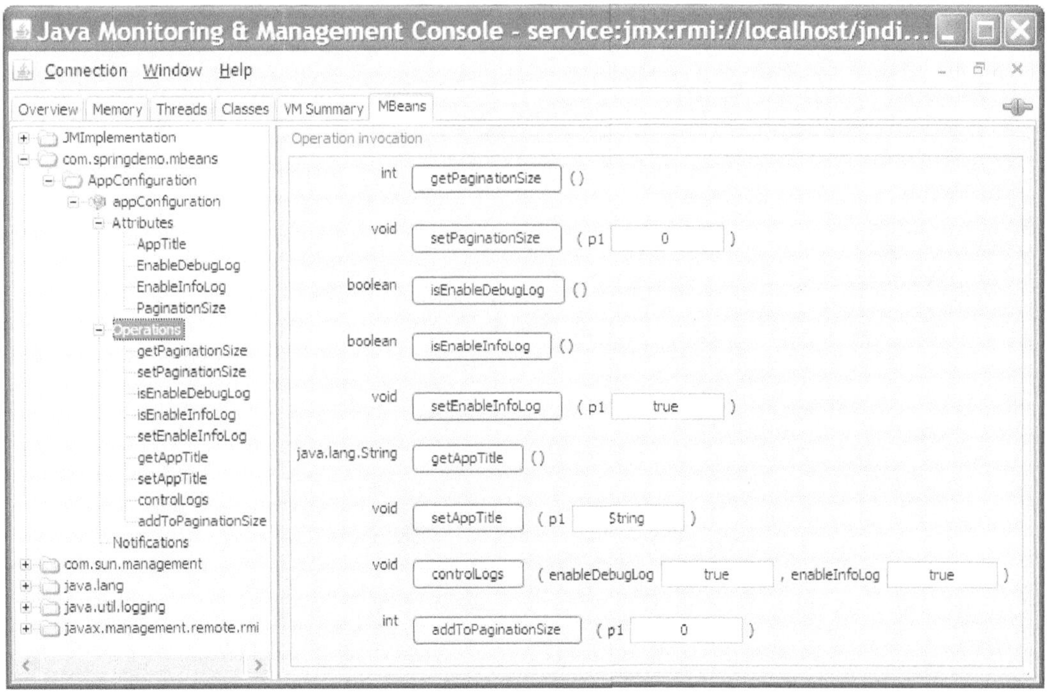

You can click on the corresponding buttons for invoking getter/setter methods and other methods (operations). Observe that there is no button for setting `enableDebugLog`, because we did not annotated its setter method as `@ManagedAttribute`.

The core concept of the JMX in our demo application works that if you change the value of any MBean attribute through 'jconsole' (outside of Java runtime to the application), it will be reflected in the application too.

For example, Type 20 in *setPaginationSize* textbox and click on *setPaginationSize* button. It will invoke the *setPaginationSize()* method in the MBean at the runtime. You can check the updated value via clicking on *getPaginationSize* button. Change *AppTitle* as "JMX Demo" (Click on *setAppTitle* button). Put *5* on *addToPaginationSize* text box and click on the corresponding button.

Now press the Enter key in the running application (our main Java application that is already running). Observe the output that the new values are updated for the attributes.

```
Configuration:
paginationSize = 10 enableDebugLog = false enableInfoLog = true appTitle =
Simple Application
Press a key

Configuration:
paginationSize = 25 enableDebugLog = false enableInfoLog = true appTitle =
JMX Demo
```

CHAPTER 9

ACCESSING E-MAILS

Spring provides API to send/receive e-mails. All the e-mails are stored in email server; we can send/receive mails to/from this email server. The **SMTP** (Simple Mail Transfer Protocol) is a mail protocol that is used to deliver emails from email client (such as Outlook, even any mail sending application) to the email server and used to deliver emails from one email server to another. Normally, SMTP uses port 25. The POP3 and IMAP are also mail protocols that are used to receive emails from an email server. The POP3 (Post Office Protocol) allows an email client to download emails from an email server and deletes them from the server. Normally, **POP3** uses port 110. The **IMAP** (Internet Message Access Protocol) is also similar to POP3 that allows an email client to download emails from an email server, but the emails will not be deleted in the email server even they got downloaded by an email client. It allows the users to keep their emails on the server, normally it uses port 143.

9.1 SPRING API FOR MAIL SUPPORT

The Spring Framework provides many classes/interfaces under the package 'org.springframework.mail' to access e-mails; it is the root level package for the Spring's email support.

The interface **'MailSender'** is used to send emails, the value object **'SimpleMailMessage'** class carries e-mail information such as 'from' and 'to' etc. and the interface **'JavaMailSender'** adds specialized features to 'MailSender' such as mail attachment (MIME message).

Install and configure mail server before executing our demo applications. There are many free/shareware versions of mail servers that can be downloaded from Internet; the following are two of them. Follow the corresponding manuals for installation and configuration.

- hMailServer (http://www.hmailserver.com/)
- IceWarp Mail Server (http://www.deerfield.com/download/icewarp/)

Gmail allows outside mail clients to access e-mail messages. To make our demo applications simple, we will use this gmail's support; use of gmail mail server instead of our own mail server. Of course, you need an Internet connection to communicate with gmail mail server.

9.2 EXAMPLE: SENDING AN E-MAIL

Download mail.jar for the corresponding JDK version and JavaMail library javamail-1.4.5.jar and include them in the project's classpath.

The following is our core class to send mails.

```
File Name: SendMail.java
package com.springdemo.mail;

import org.springframework.mail.MailSender;
import org.springframework.mail.SimpleMailMessage;

public class SendMail {

 MailSender mailSender;
 SimpleMailMessage mailProperties;

 public void setMailSender(MailSender mailSender) {
  this.mailSender = mailSender;
 }

 public void send(SimpleMailMessage mailProperties) throws Exception {
  mailSender.send(mailProperties);
 }
}
```

The following is the Spring bean configuration file and store this file as 'beans.xml' in "src" directory of the project.

```
<?xml version="1.0" encoding="UTF-8"?>
<beans xmlns="http://www.springframework.org/schema/beans"
 xmlns:xsi="http://www.w3.org/2001/XMLSchema-instance"
 xmlns:context="http://www.springframework.org/schema/context"
 xmlns:tx="http://www.springframework.org/schema/tx"
 xsi:schemaLocation="http://www.springframework.org/schema/beans
 http://www.springframework.org/schema/beans/spring-beans-3.0.xsd
 http://www.springframework.org/schema/context
 http://www.springframework.org/schema/context/spring-context-3.0.xsd
 http://www.springframework.org/schema/tx
 http://www.springframework.org/schema/tx/spring-tx-2.5.xsd">

 <bean id="mailSender"
       class="org.springframework.mail.javamail.JavaMailSenderImpl">
```

```
  <property name="host" value="smtp.gmail.com"/>
  <property name="port" value="465"/>
  <property name="protocol" value="smtps"/>
  <property name="username" value="gmailid@gmail.com"/>
  <!-- Replace stars by the mail account password -->
  <property name="password" value="********"/>
  <property name="javaMailProperties">
   <props>
    <prop key="mail.smtps.auth">true</prop>
    <prop key="mail.smtps.starttls.enable">true</prop>
    <prop key="mail.smtps.debug">true</prop>
   </props>
  </property>
 </bean>

 <bean id="sendMail" class="com.springdemo.mail.SendMail">
  <property name="mailSender" ref="mailSender"/>
 </bean>

</beans>
```

The following is the main application.

```
//File Name: SendMailDemo.java
package com.springdemo;

import org.springframework.context.support.AbstractApplicationContext;
import org.springframework.context.support.ClassPathXmlApplicationContext;
import org.springframework.mail.SimpleMailMessage;

import com.springdemo.mail.SendMail;

public class SendMailDemo {

 public static void main(String[] args) throws Exception {
  AbstractApplicationContext context =
            new ClassPathXmlApplicationContext("beans.xml");
  SendMail sendMail = (SendMail) context.getBean("sendMail");
  SimpleMailMessage mailProperties = new SimpleMailMessage();
  mailProperties.setFrom("bmdibrahim@gmail.com");
  mailProperties.setTo("bmohamedibrahim@yahoo.co.in");
```

```
        mailProperties.setSubject("Test Mail Subject");
        mailProperties.setText("Test Mail Message Text");
        sendMail.send(mailProperties);
        System.out.println("Operation performed successfully.");
    }
}
```

In this application, we are sending a mail from gmail to yahoo id. Execute the main application and check the inbox of yahoo account (I used my gmail and yahoo credentials, replace these information based on your credentials).

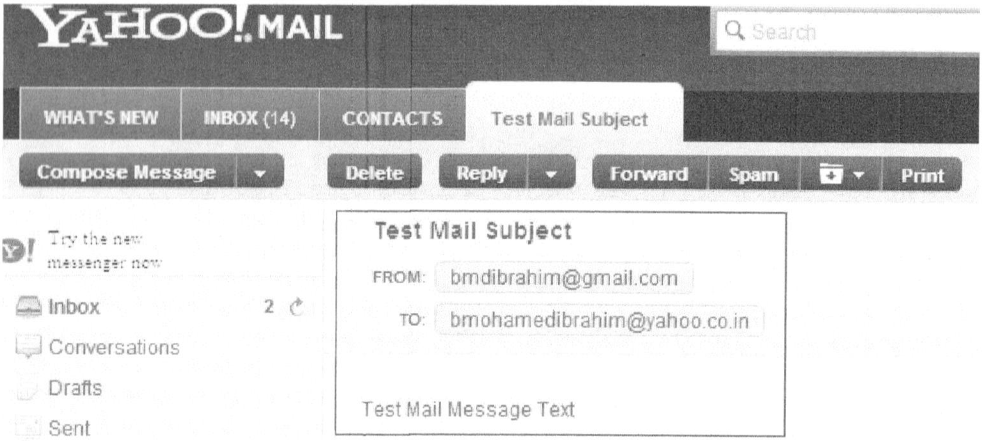

9.3 EXAMPLE: SENDING AN E-MAIL WITH ATTACHMENT

The `MimeMessageHelper` class is used to send MIME (Multipurpose Internet Mail Extensions) data in emails.

The following is the business class that sends a mail with attached document file. The '`addAttachment`' method of the '`MimeMessageHelper`' class is used to add an attachment. Repeat this method for adding multiple attachments.

```
File Name: SendMail.java
package com.springdemo.mail;

import java.io.File;

import javax.mail.internet.MimeMessage;

import org.springframework.core.io.FileSystemResource;
import org.springframework.mail.javamail.JavaMailSenderImpl;
import org.springframework.mail.javamail.MimeMessageHelper;

public class SendMail {
```

```
  JavaMailSenderImpl mailSender;

  public void setMailSender(JavaMailSenderImpl mailSender) {
    this.mailSender = mailSender;
  }

  public void sendWithAttachment() throws Exception {
    MimeMessage mimeMessage = mailSender.createMimeMessage();
    //Send 'true' as second parameter to indicate a multipart message
    MimeMessageHelper helper = new MimeMessageHelper(mimeMessage, true);

    helper.setTo("bmohamedibrahim@yahoo.co.in");
    helper.setCc(new String[]
              {"bmdibrahim@gmail.com", "bmdibrahim@rediffmail.com"});
    helper.setSubject("Test Mail with Attachment");
    helper.setText("This is a test message. Kindly receive
                 the attached MS-Word document");

    FileSystemResource file =
        new FileSystemResource(new File("C:/AppointmentLetter.doc"));
    helper.addAttachment("AppointmentLetter.doc", file);

    mailSender.send(mimeMessage);
  }
}
```

The following is the bean configuration file (beans.xml).

```
<?xml version="1.0" encoding="UTF-8"?>
<beans xmlns="http://www.springframework.org/schema/beans"
  xmlns:xsi="http://www.w3.org/2001/XMLSchema-instance"
  xmlns:context="http://www.springframework.org/schema/context"
  xmlns:tx="http://www.springframework.org/schema/tx"
  xsi:schemaLocation="http://www.springframework.org/schema/beans
  http://www.springframework.org/schema/beans/spring-beans-3.0.xsd
  http://www.springframework.org/schema/context
 http://www.springframework.org/schema/context/spring-context-3.0.xsd
  http://www.springframework.org/schema/tx
  http://www.springframework.org/schema/tx/spring-tx-2.5.xsd">

  <bean id="mailSender"
      class="org.springframework.mail.javamail.JavaMailSenderImpl">
```

```
    <property name="host" value="smtp.gmail.com"/>
    <property name="port" value="465"/>
    <property name="protocol" value="smtps"/>

    <!-- Specify your gmail id -->
    <property name="username" value="gmailid@gmail.com"/>
    <!— Replace stars by password —>
    <property name="password" value="**********"/>

    <property name="javaMailProperties">
     <props>
      <prop key="mail.smtps.auth">true</prop>
       <prop key="mail.smtps.starttls.enable">true</prop>
      <prop key="mail.smtps.debug">true</prop>
     </props>
    </property>
  </bean>

  <bean id="sendMail" class="com.springdemo.mail.SendMail">
    <property name="mailSender" ref="mailSender"/>
  </bean>

</beans>
```

Execute the following main application.

```
//File Name: SendMailAttachmentDemo.java
package com.springdemo;

import org.springframework.context.support.AbstractApplicationContext;
import org.springframework.context.support.ClassPathXmlApplicationContext;

import com.springdemo.mail.SendMail;

public class SendMailAttachmentDemo {

 public static void main(String[] args) throws Exception {
  AbstractApplicationContext context =
              new ClassPathXmlApplicationContext("beans.xml");
  SendMail sendMail = (SendMail) context.getBean("sendMail");
  sendMail.sendWithAttachment();
```

```
    System.out.println("Operation performed successfully.");
  }
}
```

Check mail in e-mail client.

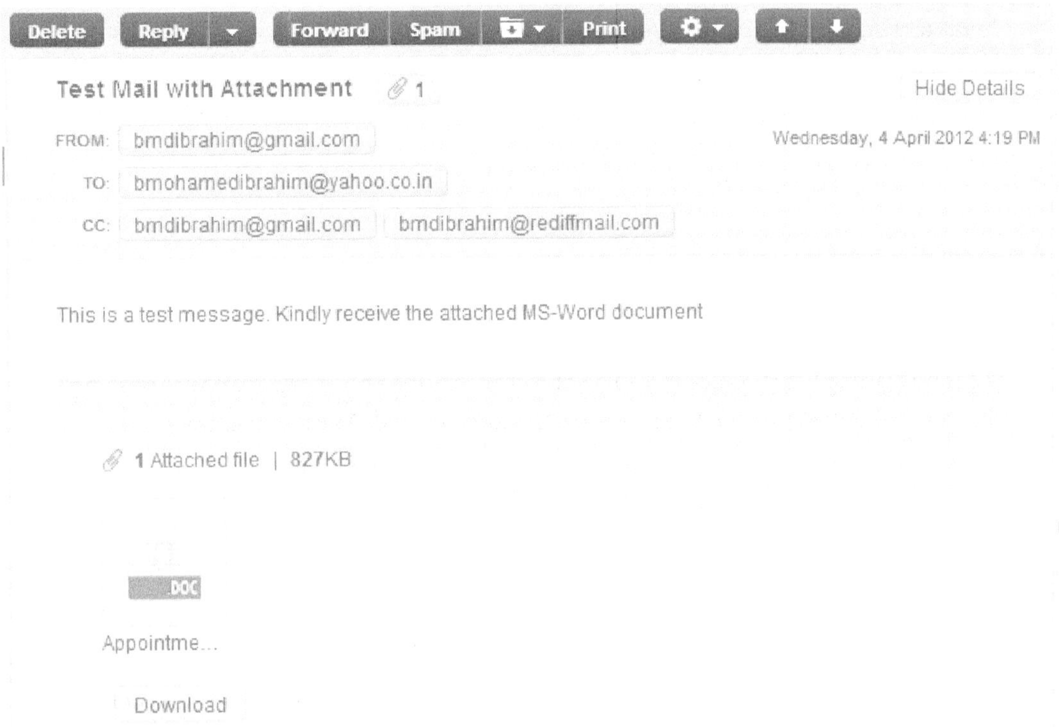

9.4 EXAMPLE: SENDING AN E-MAIL WITH INLINE RESOURCES

Inline resources are embedded in the body of the email message, not as separate attachment. The mail-sending core class is given below and keep all other file as they are in the previous example.

```
File Name: SendMail.java
package com.springdemo.mail;

import java.io.File;

import javax.mail.internet.MimeMessage;

import org.springframework.core.io.FileSystemResource;
```

```
import org.springframework.mail.javamail.JavaMailSenderImpl;
import org.springframework.mail.javamail.MimeMessageHelper;

public class SendMail {

 JavaMailSenderImpl mailSender;

 public void setMailSender(JavaMailSenderImpl mailSender) {
  this.mailSender = mailSender;
 }

 public void sendWithAttachment() throws Exception {
  MimeMessage mimeMessage = mailSender.createMimeMessage();

  //Send 'true' as second parameter to indicate a multipart message
  MimeMessageHelper helper = new MimeMessageHelper(mimeMessage, true);

  helper.setTo("bmohamedibrahim@yahoo.co.in");
  helper.setSubject("Test Mail with Inline Attachment");

  //Second parameter declares the text is HTML
  helper.setText("<html><body>Happy Birth Day<br> <img src='cid:id1' />
             <br>Best Regards,<br>Ibrahim</body></html>", true);

  FileSystemResource file =
          new FileSystemResource(new File("C:/BirthDayWishes.jpg"));
  helper.addInline("id1", file);
  //addInline() method calls can be repeated

  mailSender.send(mimeMessage);
 }
}
```

Check mail with e-mail client.

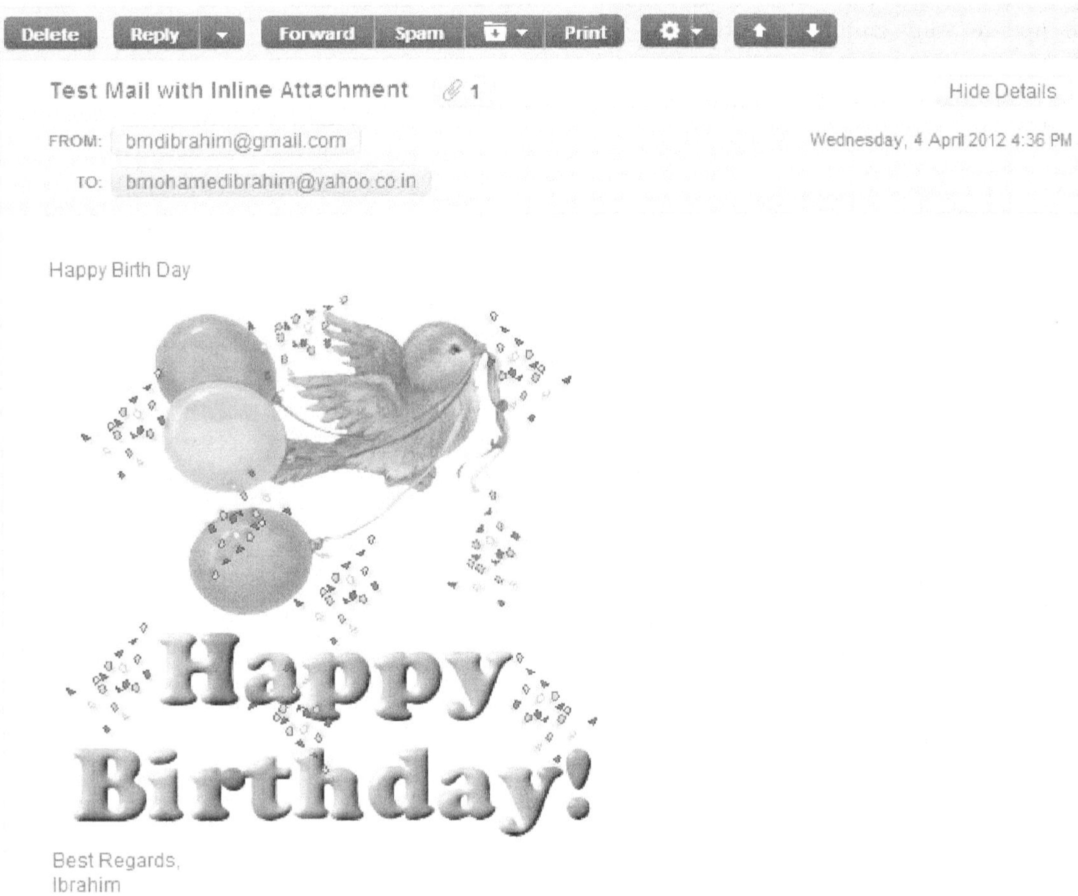

9.5 EXAMPLE: E-MAIL CLIENT APPLICATION—ACCESSING E-MAILS

Only mail servers will receive the emails that are sent by the users. The received mails in the mail box can be accessed via any email clients such as Outlook. Now we will try to write an e-mail client application which will retrieve e-mails from the mail server. I am using gmail account in this demo application, change the configuration according to your mail server settings if you want to access mails from your mail server.

Download and include Spring integration core and integration mail (*spring-integration-core-2.0.0.RELEASE.jar* and *spring-integration-mail-2.0.3.RELEASE.jar*) libraries in the classpath of the project.

You should use SSL to connect with gmail account for reading mails. The following property settings will do for us.

```
props.setProperty("mail.imap.socketFactory.class",
                "javax.net.ssl.SSLSocketFactory");
props.setProperty("mail.imap.socketFactory.fallback", "false");
```

Here is the core class to download e-mails from gmail mail server. Do not forget to update your gmail credentials in this code.

```
//File Name: ReceiveMail.java
package com.springdemo.mail;

import java.util.Date;
import java.util.Properties;

import javax.mail.Address;
import javax.mail.Authenticator;
import javax.mail.Flags;
import javax.mail.Message;
import javax.mail.MessagingException;
import javax.mail.PasswordAuthentication;

import org.springframework.integration.mail.ImapMailReceiver;

public class ReceiveMail {
 public void receive() throws MessagingException {

  ImapMailReceiver mailReceiver = null;
  Properties props = null;
  try {
   props = new Properties();
   props.setProperty("mail.imap.host", "imap.gmail.com");
   props.setProperty("mail.imap.port", "993");
   props.setProperty("mail.imap.auth.login.disable", "true");
   props.setProperty("mail.imap.auth", "true");
   props.setProperty("mail.imap.ssl.enable", "true");
   props.setProperty("mail.store.protocol", "imaps");
   // props.setProperty("mail.debug", "true");
   props.setProperty("mail.imap.socketFactory.class",
                "javax.net.ssl.SSLSocketFactory");
   props.setProperty("mail.imap.socketFactory.fallback", "false");
   props.setProperty("mail.imap.connectionpoolsize", "3");

   mailReceiver = new ImapMailReceiver
        ("imaps://gmailid:password@imap.gmail.com:993/inbox");

  // Example: ("imaps://bmdibrahim:password@imap.gmail.com:993/inbox");

   mailReceiver.setJavaMailProperties(props);
```

```
mailReceiver.setJavaMailAuthenticator(new Authenticator() {
 protected PasswordAuthentication getPasswordAuthentication() {
return new PasswordAuthentication("gmailid@gmail.com", "password");
 }
});
 mailReceiver.setShouldDeleteMessages(false);
 mailReceiver.setShouldMarkMessagesAsRead(false);

System.out.println("Retrieving messages. Please wait...");

mailReceiver.setMaxFetchSize(5); //Set as needed
Message msg[] = mailReceiver.receive();

for (int i = 0; i < msg.length; i++) {
 Message message = msg[i];
 int messageNumber = message.getMessageNumber();
 Address from[] = message.getFrom();
 Date dateReceived = message.getReceivedDate();
 String subject = message.getSubject();
 Object content = message.getContent();
 String contentType = message.getContentType();
 Flags flags = message.getFlags();

 System.out.println("Mail Message Number:" + messageNumber);
 System.out.println("From:" + from[0]);
 System.out.println("Received Date: " + dateReceived);
 System.out.println("Subject: " + subject);
 System.out.println("Content Type:" + contentType);
 if (contentType.startsWith("multipart"))
  System.out.println("Mail contains multi-part data.
              May contain Attachments");
 else
  System.out.println("Content:\n" + content);

 //All these flags are not applicable for 'INBOX',
 //however given for reference
 Flags.Flag[] systemFlags = flags.getSystemFlags();
 for(int j=0; j < systemFlags.length; j++) {
  if (systemFlags[j] == Flags.Flag.ANSWERED)
   System.out.println("This message has been answered");
  else if (systemFlags[j] == Flags.Flag.DELETED)
   System.out.println("This message is marked deleted");
```

```
        else if (systemFlags[j] == Flags.Flag.DRAFT)
         System.out.println("This message is a draft");
        else if (systemFlags[j] == Flags.Flag.RECENT)
         System.out.println("This message is recent");
        else if (systemFlags[j] == Flags.Flag.SEEN)
         System.out.println("This message is seen");
      }
      System.out.println("=====================================");
     }
    }
    catch (Exception e) {
     e.printStackTrace();
    }
   }
  }
```

Store the following 'beans.xml' bean configuration file under 'src' directory of the project.

```
<?xml version="1.0" encoding="UTF-8"?>
<beans xmlns="http://www.springframework.org/schema/beans"
  xmlns:xsi="http://www.w3.org/2001/XMLSchema-instance"
  xmlns:context="http://www.springframework.org/schema/context"
  xsi:schemaLocation="http://www.springframework.org/schema/beans
  http://www.springframework.org/schema/beans/spring-beans-3.0.xsd
  http://www.springframework.org/schema/context
 http://www.springframework.org/schema/context/spring-context 3.0.xsd">

<bean id="receiveMail" class="com.springdemo.mail.EmailReceiverService" />

</beans>
```

Execute the following main application, which invokes the `receive()` method of ReceiveMail class. Then, the downloaded emails will be printed on the screen. Adjust the parameter value to the `setMaxFetchSize()` method to restrict number of emails to read (downloaded by this email client). Note that this application will download all kind of messages (such as read, non-read, ...) in the order they are received by the email server.

```
//File Name: ReceiveMailDemo.java
package com.springdemo;

import org.springframework.context.support.AbstractApplicationContext;
import org.springframework.context.support.ClassPathXmlApplicationContext;
```

```
import com.springdemo.mail.EmailReceiverService;

public class ReceiveMailDemo {

 public static void main(String[] args) throws Exception {
  AbstractApplicationContext context =
          new ClassPathXmlApplicationContext("beans.xml");

  EmailReceiverService emailReceiverService =
          (EmailReceiverService) context.getBean("receiveMail");
  emailReceiverService.receive();
  System.out.println("Operation performed successfully.");
 }
}
```

9.6 EXAMPLE: E-MAIL CLIENT APPLICATION—LISTENING FOR NEW E-MAILS

The `receive()` method of the following class will be called by the Spring container whenever a new email is received by the configured mail server.

```
//File Name: ReceiveEmail.java
package com.springdemo.mail;

import javax.mail.Address;
import javax.mail.BodyPart;
import javax.mail.internet.MimeMessage;
import javax.mail.internet.MimeMultipart;

public class ReceiveEmail {

 public void receive(MimeMessage message) {
  try {
   String messageID = message.getMessageID();
   Address from[] = message.getFrom();
   String subject = message.getSubject();
   Object content = message.getContent();
   String contentType = message.getContentType();

   System.out.println("Mail Message ID: " + messageID);
   System.out.println("From: " + from[0]);
   System.out.println("Subject: " + subject);
   System.out.println("Content Type: " + contentType);
   if (contentType.startsWith("multipart")) {
```

```
      System.out.println("Mail contains multi-part data.");
      MimeMultipart multipart = (MimeMultipart)content;
      BodyPart bodypart = multipart.getBodyPart(0);
      System.out.println(bodypart.getContent());
    }
    else {
      System.out.println("Content:\n" + (String)content);
    }

    System.out.println("=====================================");
   }
   catch(Exception e){
     System.out.println(e.getMessage());
   }
  }
 }
```

Store the following Spring configuration file 'beans.xml' under the "src" directory of the project. It contains the mail listener settings to download the received email from the mail server and it pass the downloaded email as argument to `receive()` method of `ReceiveEmail` class.

The property `'should-mark-messages-as-read'` is set to `'true'` to mark as read on the mail server for those downloaded messages. Set the property `'should-delete-messages'` to `'true'` to delete those downloaded emails on the mail server.

```
<?xml version="1.0" encoding="UTF-8"?>

<beans xmlns="http://www.springframework.org/schema/beans"
  xmlns:xsi="http://www.w3.org/2001/XMLSchema-instance"
  xmlns:mail="http://www.springframework.org/schema/integration/mail"
  xmlns:int="http://www.springframework.org/schema/integration"
  xmlns:util="http://www.springframework.org/schema/util"
  xsi:schemaLocation="http://www.springframework.org/schema/beans
  http://www.springframework.org/schema/beans/spring-beans-3.0.xsd
  http://www.springframework.org/schema/integration/mail
  http://www.springframework.org/schema/integration/mail/
                              spring-integration-mail-2.0.xsd
  http://www.springframework.org/schema/util
  http://www.springframework.org/schema/util/spring-util-2.0.xsd">

 <util:properties id="javaMailProperties">
  <prop key="mail.imap.socketFactory.class">
```

```
   javax.net.ssl.SSLSocketFactory
  </prop>
  <prop key="mail.imap.socketFactory.fallback">false</prop>
  <prop key="mail.store.protocol">imaps</prop>
  <!– <prop key="mail.debug">true</prop> –>
 </util:properties>

 <mail:inbound-channel-adapter id="imapAdapter"
    store-uri="imaps://gmailid:password@imap.gmail.com:993/inbox"
    channel="recieveEmailChannel"
    should-delete-messages="false"
    should-mark-messages-as-read="true"
    auto-startup="true"
    java-mail-properties="javaMailProperties">
  <int:poller fixed-delay="5000"/>
 </mail:inbound-channel-adapter>

 <int:channel id="recieveEmailChannel">
  <int:interceptors>
   <int:wire-tap channel="logger"/>
  </int:interceptors>
 </int:channel>

 <int:logging-channel-adapter id="logger" level="DEBUG"/>

 <int:service-activator input-channel="recieveEmailChannel"
                  ref="receiveEmail" method="receive"/>

 <bean id="receiveEmail" class="com.springdemo.mail.ReceiveEmail"/>

</beans>
```

Execute the following main application to start up.

```
//File Name: ReceiveMailDemo.java
package com.springdemo;

import org.springframework.context.support.AbstractApplicationContext;
import org.springframework.context.support.ClassPathXmlApplicationContext;

public class ReceiveMailDemo {
```

```
  public static void main(String args[]) throws Exception {
   AbstractApplicationContext context =
         new ClassPathXmlApplicationContext("beans.xml");
   System.out.println("Listening for new e-mails...");
  }
}
```

A sample output is given below.

```
Listening for new e-mails...
```

Now send a mail to bmdibrahim@gmail.com through any e-mail client. (The e-mail id -bmdibrahim@gmail.com is registered in the Spring configuration file to listen for new e-mails)

```
Mail Message ID: <1333611510.96369.YahooMailNeo@web193103.
mail.sg3.yahoo.com>
From: Mohamed Ibrahim <bmohamedibrahim@yahoo.co.in>
Subject: Test Mail
Content Type: multipart/alternative; boundary="-814770868-1259807177
-1333611510=:96369"
Mail contains multi-part data.
This is a test mail.
______________
Thanks & Regards,
Mohamed Ibrahim
```

Check with Gmail email client.

Whenever a new mail is received by the configured e-mail account, then our application will download that e-mail immediately.

CHAPTER 10

UNIT TESTING WITH JUNIT AND SPRING

Unit Testing is Software testing process in which the smallest specific functionality of an application, called a unit, is tested to determine whether it behaves exactly as expected. It applies to various smallest testable parts of the application. It can be done manually, or automatically using test automation tools such as JUnit and TestNG.

10.1 JUnit

Unit testing using any automation tool is more preferable over manual testing, as manual testing is a time-consuming process. JUnit is an open-source testing framework, and the latest version of JUnit supports the use of annotations, which simplifies development of test cases.

Download the latest version of JUnit and place the junit library jar file in the classpath of our project. For our demonstration applications, the JUnit version 4.10 is used which can be downloaded from Maven Repository or from JUnit's home page (http://junit.org).

10.2 SUPPORTED ANNOTATIONS IN JUnit

Some of the annotations that are provided by JUnit 4.x:

`@Test`	Declares a method as test method.
`@BeforeClass`	Executes the method only once, before all of the test methods in a test case class are executed.
`@AfterClass`	Executes the method only once, after all of the test methods in a test case class are executed.
`@Before`	Executes the method every time before executing a test method.
`@After`	Executes the method every time after a test method is executed.
`@Test(expected= exception_class)`	Fails the test case method, if the method does not throw the specified exception.
`@Ignore`	Ignores the test case method for execution. It is very helpful when you changed the source code and not updated the test case method yet.

10.3 SOME TEST METHODS IN JUnit

Method	Description
`assertsEquals (expected, actual)`	Tests that two values are the same.
`assertsEquals(expected, actual, tolerance)`	Test that float or double values match. The tolerance is the number of decimals which must be the same.
`assertTrue(boolean condition)`	Checks that the boolean condition is true.
`assertSame(expected, actual)`	Checks that both object reference variables refer to the same object.
`assertNotSame(expected, actual)`	Checks that both object reference variables refer to not the same object.
`assertNull(object)`	Checks that the object is null.
`assertNotNull(object)`	Checks that the object is not null.
`fail(String)`	Forces the test to fail. The parameter string specifies the description.

10.4 SPRING'S SUPPORT TO JUnit

Spring Framework supports JUnit, and here are some of the annotations that can be used in Spring based test applications.

Annotation	Description
`@RunWith(class)`	Setting `'springJUnit4ClassRunner.class'` as parameter to this annotation tells JUnit to use Spring's Test Context Framework test runner instead of the default JUnit's built-in test runner. Example: `@RunWith(SpringJUnit4ClassRunner.class)`
`@ContextConfiguration (locations)`	Specifies the locations where to find the application context for test classes. It can accept an array of locations. Example: `@ContextConfiguration (locations = "classpath:beans.xml")`
`@BeforeTransaction`	Executes before a transactional test method (`@Transactional`) is started.
`@AfterTransaction`	Executes after a transactional test method (`@Transactional`) has ended.
`@Rollback(boolean)`	Defines whether the transaction for the annotated test method should be rolled back after the test method has completed or not.

`@Timed(millis=value)`	Makes the test case method fail if the test method is not finished execution in the specified milliseconds.
`@Repeat(value)`	Makes the test case method to execute the specified number of times.

10.5 EXAMPLE TEST CLASS USING JUnit ANNOTATIONS

Create a package named 'com.springdemo.arithmetic' in the SpringDemo project, and store the following class.

```
//File Name: ArithmeticOperations.java
package com.springdemo.arithmetic;

public class ArithmeticOperations {

 public int addition(int a, int b) {
  int c = a + b;
  System.out.println("\nIn addition method. a[" + a + "] b["
                + b + "] c[" + c + "]\n");
  return c;
 }

 public int subtract(int a, int b) {
  int c = a - b;
  System.out.println("\nIn subtract method. a[" + a + "] b["
                + b + "] c[" + c + "]\n");
  return c;
 }

 public double multiply(double a, double b) {
  double c = a * b;
  System.out.println("\nIn multiply method. a[" + a + "] b["
                + b + "] c[" + c + "]\n");
  return c;
 }

 public double divide(double a, double b) throws Exception {
  if (b == 0)
   throw new Exception("Dividing a number by zero");
  double c;
  c = a / b;
  System.out.println("\nIn divide method. a[" + a + "] b["
                + b + "] c[" + c + "]\n");
  return c;
 }
}
```

Store the following Spring configuration file 'beans.xml' in the "src" directory of the project.

```
<?xml version="1.0" encoding="UTF-8"?>
<beans xmlns="http://www.springframework.org/schema/beans"
    xmlns:xsi="http://www.w3.org/2001/XMLSchema-instance"
    xmlns:context="http://www.springframework.org/schema/context"
    xsi:schemaLocation="http://www.springframework.org/schema/beans
    http://www.springframework.org/schema/beans/spring-beans-3.0.xsd
    http://www.springframework.org/schema/context
  http://www.springframework.org/schema/context/spring-context 3.0.xsd">

 <context:component-scan base-package="com.springdemo"/>

 <bean id="arithOperations"
      class="com.springdemo.arithmetic.ArithmeticOperations"/>

</beans>
```

Create a package named 'com.springdemo.test' and place all the test classes. Place the following test class in this package.

```
//File Name: ArithmeticOperationsTest.java
package com.springdemo.test;

import static junit.framework.Assert.*;

import org.junit.After;
import org.junit.AfterClass;
import org.junit.Before;
import org.junit.BeforeClass;
import org.junit.Ignore;
import org.junit.Test;
import org.junit.runner.RunWith;
import org.springframework.beans.factory.annotation.Autowired;
import org.springframework.test.annotation.Repeat;
import org.springframework.test.annotation.Timed;
import org.springframework.test.context.ContextConfiguration;
import org.springframework.test.context.junit4.SpringJUnit4ClassRunner;

import com.springdemo.arithmetic.ArithmeticOperations;

@RunWith(SpringJUnit4ClassRunner.class)
```

```
@ContextConfiguration(locations = "classpath:beans.xml")
public class ArithmeticOperationsTest {

    @Autowired
    ArithmeticOperations arithOperations;

   int a = 10, b = 5;

   @BeforeClass
   public static void beforeAllTestCases() {
     System.out.println("Called the method - beforeAllTestCases");
   }

   @Before
   public void beforeATestCase() {
     System.out.println("Called the method - beforeATestCase");
   }

   @Test
   public void additionTest() {
     System.out.println("Called the method - additionTest");
     int c = arithOperations.addition(a, b);
     assertEquals(15, c);
   }

   @Test
   public void subtractTest() {
     System.out.println("Called the method - subtractTest");
     int c = arithOperations.subtract(a, b);
     assertEquals(5, c);
   }

   @Test
   public void multiplyTest() {
     System.out.println("Called the method - multiplyTest");
     double c = arithOperations.multiply(a, b);
     assertEquals(50.0, c);
   }

   @Test
   public void divideTest() {
     System.out.println("Called the method - divideTest");
```

```
    Double c = null;
      try {
        c = arithOperations.divide(a, b);
      }
      catch (Exception e) {
        e.printStackTrace();
      }
    assertEquals(2.0, c);
  }

  @Test (expected = Exception.class)
  public void divideExceptionTest() throws Exception {
    System.out.println("Called the method - divideExceptionTest");
    double c = arithOperations.divide(a, 0);
    assertEquals(2.0, c);
  }

  @Test
  @Timed(millis = 100)
  public void waitFailTest() {
    System.out.println("Called the method - waitFailTest");
    for (long i = 1L; i < 99999L; i++) ;
  }

  @Test
  public void failTest() {
    System.out.println("Called the method - failTest");
    fail("This is intentionally to make fail this test case.");
  }

  @Ignore
  @Test
  public void failTest2() {
    System.out.println("Called the method - failTest2
                                  - Ignored for testing");
    fail("This is intentionally to make fail this test case.");
  }

  @Test
  public void objectNullTest() {
    System.out.println("Called the method - objectNullTest");
    assertNull(arithOperations);
```

```
    }

    @Test
    public void objectNotNullTest() {
      System.out.println("Called the method - objectNotNullTest");
      assertNotNull(arithOperations);
    }

    @Test
    public void sameObjectTest() {
      System.out.println("Called the method - sameObjectTest");
      ArithmeticOperations arithOperations2 = arithOperations;
      System.out.println(arithOperations2.addition(50, 1));
      assertSame(arithOperations, arithOperations2);
    }

    @Test
    public void notSameObjectTest() {
      System.out.println("Called the method - notSameObjectTest");
      ArithmeticOperations arithOperations2 = new ArithmeticOperations();
      System.out.println(arithOperations2.addition(50, 1));
      assertSame(arithOperations, arithOperations2);
    }

    @Test
    public void conditionTrueTest() {
      System.out.println("Called the method - conditionTrueTest");
      assertTrue(a==b);
    }

    @Test
    @Repeat(10)
    public void repeatTest() {
      System.out.println("Called the method - repeatTest");
    }

    @After
    public void afterATestCase() {
      System.out.println("Called the method - afterATestCase");
    }

    @AfterClass
    public static void afterAllTestCases() {
      System.out.println("Called the method - afterAllTestCases");
    }
  }
```

Execute the test script in Eclipse: Select this test class 'ArithmeticOperationsTest.java' → Right click, Run As → JUnit Test.

The results of test cases are given below.

The screen output is given below.

```
Called the method - beforeAllTestCases
Called the method - beforeATestCase
Called the method - additionTest

In addition method. a[10] b[5] c[15]

Called the method - afterATestCase
```

```
Called the method - beforeATestCase
Called the method - subtractTest

In subtract method. a[10] b[5] c[5]

Called the method - afterATestCase
Called the method - beforeATestCase
Called the method - multiplyTest

In multiply method. a[10.0] b[5.0] c[50.0]

Called the method - afterATestCase
Called the method - beforeATestCase
Called the method - divideTest

In divide method. a[10.0] b[5.0] c[2.0]

Called the method - afterATestCase
Called the method - beforeATestCase
Called the method - divideExceptionTest
Called the method - afterATestCase
Called the method - beforeATestCase
Called the method - waitFailTest
Called the method - afterATestCase
Called the method - beforeATestCase
Called the method - failTest
Called the method - afterATestCase
Called the method - beforeATestCase
Called the method - objectNullTest
Called the method - afterATestCase
Called the method - beforeATestCase
Called the method - objectNotNullTest
Called the method - afterATestCase
Called the method - beforeATestCase
Called the method - sameObjectTest

In addition method. a[50] b[1] c[51]

51
Called the method - afterATestCase
Called the method - beforeATestCase
Called the method - notSameObjectTest
```

```
In addition method. a[50] b[1] c[51]

51
Called the method - afterATestCase
Called the method - beforeATestCase
Called the method - conditionTrueTest
Called the method - afterATestCase
Called the method - beforeATestCase
Called the method - repeatTest
Called the method - afterATestCase
Called the method - beforeATestCase
Called the method - repeatTest
Called the method - afterATestCase
Called the method - beforeATestCase
Called the method - repeatTest
Called the method - afterATestCase
Called the method - beforeATestCase
Called the method - repeatTest
Called the method - afterATestCase
Called the method - beforeATestCase
Called the method - repeatTest
Called the method - afterATestCase
Called the method - beforeATestCase
Called the method - repeatTest
Called the method - afterATestCase
Called the method - beforeATestCase
Called the method - repeatTest
Called the method - afterATestCase
Called the method - beforeATestCase
Called the method - repeatTest
Called the method - afterATestCase
Called the method - beforeATestCase
Called the method - repeatTest
Called the method - afterATestCase
Called the method - beforeATestCase
Called the method - repeatTest
Called the method - afterATestCase
Called the method - afterAllTestCases
```

CHAPTER 11

WEB APPLICATION DEVELOPMENT WITH SPRING WEBMVC

Spring Framework provides its own **Model-View-Controller (MVC)** web framework, which acquires Spring's features such as Inversion of Control (Dependency Injection), and it highly decouples the component dependencies and simplifies the configuration and development of flexible loosely coupled web applications.

11.1 SPRING WEB MVC DATA BINDING TAGS

Spring Web MVC provides data binding-aware tags for handling web form elements, and these tags can be used in JSPs by adding the following taglib declaration at the top of a JSP file.

```
<%@taglib prefix="form" uri="http://www.springframework.org/tags/form" %>
```

11.1.1 `<form:form>` Tag

It renders the HTML form element and it is the root tag of all form elements.

General format:

```
<form:form commandName="command_object"
         method="FORM_method"
         action="action_url" >
  ...
</form:form>
```

The object specified in the commandName attribute loads the object (Java bean object) into pageContext so that its members can be accessed in the nested elements of this form tag. If it is not used, then the command name is default to 'command'. We can also use modelAttribute in alternate to this commandName attribute.

The method attribute specifies the HTML form submission method such as GET and POST.

The form will be submitted to the URL specified in the action attribute.

11.1.2 <form:label> Element

It renders the HTML label element.

General format:

```
<form:label for="HTML_Ref_ID"
         path="binding_property">

Label Text

</form:label>
```

The HTML <label> element is used to supply a visible text label to a form control. The 'for' attribute specifies the form's input control that this label is for and the value specified in this attribute should be same as the "id" value of the input control. The 'path' attribute refers the path to errors object for data binding.

11.1.3 <form:input> Element

It renders the HTML input (type = "text") element.

General format:

```
<form:input path="binding_property"
         disabled=true
         maxlength="max_length"
         readonly=true/>
```

The path attribute specifies the path to the property of form command object for data binding. The "disabled" attribute with the value "true" will disable the element.

11.1.4 <form:password> Element

It renders the HTML input (type = "password") element.

General format:

```
<form:password path="binding_property"
            disabled=true|false
            maxlength="max_length"
            readonly=true
            showPassword=true/>
```

The path attribute specifies the path to the property of form command object for data binding. The attribute showPassword defines the password value to be shown or not, default to false.

11.1.5 <form:hidden> Element

It renders the HTML input (type = "hidden") element.

General format:

```
<form:hidden path="binding_property"/>
```

The path attribute specifies the path to the property of form command object for data binding.

11.1.6 <form:checkbox> Element

It renders the HTML input (type = "checkbox") element.

General format:

```
<form:checkbox path="binding_property"
            value="value"
            label="label_to_display"
            disabled=true/>
```

The path attribute specifies the path to the property of form command object for data binding.

11.1.7 <form:checkboxes> Element

It renders multiple HTML input (type = "checkbox") elements.

General format:

```
<form:checkbox path="binding_property"
            items="data_collection_for_checkboxes"
            itemLabel="label_for_each_checkbox"
            itemValue="value_for_each_checkbox"
            disabled=true/>
```

The path attribute specifies the path to the property of form command object for data binding. A Collection, Map or Array of objects is specified in 'items' attribute as input to create check boxes. A property of the class of the input objects is specified in 'itemLabel' as label of each checkbox; and the same/another property may be applied for 'itemValue' attribute as value of each check boxes.

11.1.8 <form:radiobutton> Element

It renders the HTML input (type = "radio") element.

General format:

```
<form:radiobutton path="binding_property"
            value="value"
            label="label_to_display"
            disabled=true/>
```

The path attribute specifies the path to the property of form command object for data binding.

11.1.9 <form:radiobuttons> Element

It renders multiple HTML input (type = "radio") elements.

General format:

```
<form:radiobuttons path="binding_property"
            items="data_collection_for_radiobuttons"
```

```
                    itemLabel="label_for_each_radiobutton"
                    itemValue="value_for_each_radiobutton"
                    disabled=true/>
```

The path attribute specifies the path to the property of form command object for data binding. A Collection, Map or Array of objects is specified in 'items' attribute as input to create radio buttons. A property of the class of the input objects is specified in 'itemLabel' as label of each radio button; and the same/another property may be applied for 'itemValue' attribute as value of each radio buttons.

11.1.10 `<form:select>` Element

It renders HTML select (List box, Drop down List box) element.

General format:

```
<form:select path="binding_property"
             items="data_collection_for_radiobuttons"
             itemLabel="label_for_each_radiobutton"
             itemValue="value_for_each_radiobutton"
             multiple="true"
             size="Number_of_options_visible"
             disabled=true/>
```

The path attribute specifies the path to the property of form command object for data binding. A Collection, Map or Array of objects is specified in 'items' attribute as input to create option items (<option>). A property of the class of the input objects is specified in 'itemLabel' as label of each options (text between <option> and </option>); and the same/another property may be applied for 'itemValue' attribute as value of each options (value attribute of <option>). The attribute 'multiple' determines whether the user can select multiple options or not.

11.1.11 `<form:option>` Element

It renders HTML option (inside the select element) element.

General format:

```
<form:option label="label_to_display"
         value="value_to_pass"
         disabled=true/>
```

This element should be used inside <form:select> and </form:select> element to provide option(s) which produces HTML option element(s). These <form:option> elements can be used as an alternate to "items" attribute of <form:select> element.

11.1.12 `<form:options>` Element

It renders HTML option (inside the select element) elements.

General format:

```
<form:options items="data_collection_for_radiobuttons"
          itemLabel="label_for_each_radiobutton"
```

```
        itemValue="value_for_each_radiobutton"
        disabled=true/>
```

This element should be used inside <form:select> and </form:select> element to provide options which produces HTML option elements. These <form:options> element can be used as an alternate to "items" attribute of <form:select> element. A Collection, Map or Array of objects is specified in 'items' attribute as input to create option items (<option>). A property of the class of the input objects is specified in 'itemLabel' as label of each options (text between <option> and </option>); and the same/another property may be applied for 'itemValue' attribute as value of each options (value attribute of <option>).

11.1.13 <form:textarea> Element

It renders HTML textarea element.

General format:

```
<form:textarea path="binding_property"
          rows="number_of_rows_visible"
          cols="number _of_columns_visible_per_row"
         disabled=true
         readonly=true/>
```

The path attribute specifies the path to the property of form command object for data binding. It creates a HTML textarea element with the specified rows and columns.

11.1.14 <form:errors> Tag

It renders HTML textarea element.

General format:

```
<form:errors path="binding_property |*"
         cssClass="css_class"
         cssStyle="css_style"
         element="element_to_render_the_output"/>
```

The path attribute specifies the path to the property of form command object to retrieve the associated error message, the value "*" renders all the error messages associated with the fields. The cssClass and cssStyle attributes are used to define style of the display of messages and the attribute element specified the HTML element that is used to render the enclosing errors instead of rendering to the default "span" element.

11.2 SPRING WEB MVC

The Spring Web Model-View-Controller (MVC) framework works on Front Controller design pattern. The main aim of the MVC pattern is to separate the business logic and application data from the presentation layer. The MVC (Model-View-Controller) works as described below.

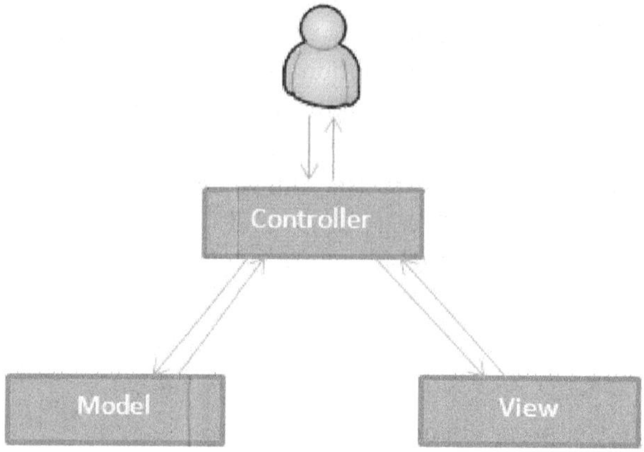

Model: Represents data of an application.

View: Represents presentation of the application (display).

Controller: Receives requests from the user, process the request, communicate with appropriate Model and View, and response back to the user.

11.2.1 DispatcherServlet

This Spring provided servlet acts as an Front Controller that dispatches the requests to handlers (controllers).

This DispatcherServlet servlet inherits HttpServlet, and this servlet should be declared in the web.xml file under WEB-INF directory of the web application as any other servlet mapping is declared in a web application. This mapping is required to map the incoming requests that the DispatcherServlet should handle.

```
<servlet>
 <servlet-name>SpringWebDemo</servlet-name>
 <servlet-class>
   org.springframework.web.servlet.DispatcherServlet
 </servlet-class>
 <load-on-startup>1</load-on-startup>
</servlet>

<servlet-mapping>
 <servlet-name>SpringWebDemo</servlet-name>
 <url-pattern>*.demo</url-pattern>
</servlet-mapping>
```

With the above mapping, the DispatcherServlet will handle all requests that end with ".demo"; for example, create.demo and delete.demo. You can change this extension according to your project.

Upon initialization of this DispatcherServlet, the Spring Framework will look for a file named "<servlet-name>-servlet.xml" file in the WEB-INF directory of the project. In our example configuration, the file name is SpringWebDemo-servlet.xml (servlet-name of DispacherServlet declaration in web.xml). All the Spring specific beans and configurations are defined in this file.

We can use different file name instead of the default "<servlet-name>-servlet.xml" Spring web context file, and even can specify the directory the context file instead of the default location WEB-INF. This can be configured using the Servlet initialization parameter "contextConfigLocation" as shown in the below example.

```
<servlet>
  <servlet-name>SpringWebDemo</servlet-name>
  <servlet-class>
    org.springframework.web.servlet.DispatcherServlet
  </servlet-class>
  <init-param>
    <param-name>contextConfigLocation</param-name>
    <param-value>/WEB-INF/beans.xml</param-value>
  </init-param>
  <load-on-startup>1</load-on-startup>
</servlet>

<servlet-mapping>
  <servlet-name>SpringWebDemo</servlet-name>
  <url-pattern>*.demo</url-pattern>
</servlet-mapping>
```

We can also specify multiple configuration files separated by commas, as pram-value of the initialization parameter "contextConfigLocation".

It is also preferable to specify the "contextConfigLocation" setting outside of servlet declaration, as shown below.

```
<context-param>
  <param-name>contextConfigLocation</param-name>
  <param-value>/WEB-INF/beans.xml</param-value>
</context-param>

<servlet>
  <servlet-name>SpringWebDemo</servlet-name>
  <servlet-class>
    org.springframework.web.servlet.DispatcherServlet
  </servlet-class>
```

```
    <load-on-startup>1</load-on-startup>
  </servlet>

  <servlet-mapping>
    <servlet-name>SpringWebDemo</servlet-name>
    <url-pattern>*.demo</url-pattern>
  </servlet-mapping>
```

11.3 @Controller

This @Controller annotation declares a class as a controller. Then, the dispatcher will scan these controller classes for mapping the required methods.

To make auto-detection of these controller classes to the Spring context, use the following context schema in the beans definition (in our case, put it in the `SpringWebDemo-servlet.xml` file).

```
<?xml version="1.0" encoding="UTF-8"?>
<beans xmlns="http://www.springframework.org/schema/beans"
  xmlns:xsi="http://www.w3.org/2001/XMLSchema-instance"
  xmlns:p="http://www.springframework.org/schema/p"
  xmlns:context="http://www.springframework.org/schema/context"
  xsi:schemaLocation="http://www.springframework.org/schema/beans
  http://www.springframework.org/schema/beans/spring-beans-3.0.xsd
  http://www.springframework.org/schema/context
  http://www.springframework.org/schema/context/spring-context-
  3.0.xsd">

<context:component-scan base-package="com.springdemo.web"/>

...
...
</bean>
```

Note: The attribute `base-package` specifies the base package name in which the Spring will scan for components such as `@Controller`.

11.4 @RequestMapping

This annotation can be applied at class level and/or method level to map the request URLs onto an class / a particular method. The @RequestMapping at class level maps a specific request path that are common to all the methods in the controller class, and then @RequestMapping at method level is relative to the class level path. If @RequestMapping is not used at class level, then all the @RequestMapping at the methods are simply absolute, not relative.

General format

```
@RequestMapping("mapping_url")
@RequestMapping(value="mapping_url",
            method=RequestMethod.GET | RequestMethod.POST)
```

Some of the acceptable constants available in RequestMethod enumeration are given below.

- DELETE
- GET
- HEAD
- OPTIONS
- POST
- PUT
- TRACE

The following are some of the supported argument types of a @RequestMapping annotated methods (handler methods).

- Servlet Request/Response objects

```
javax.servlet.ServletRequest
javax.servlet.http.HttpServletRequest
javax.servlet.ServletResponse
javax.servlet.http.HttpServletResponse
```

- Servlet Session object

```
javax.servlet.http.HttpSession
```

- WebRequest—Used to access request parameters and access request/session attributes.

```
org.springframework.web.context.request.WebRequest
```

- InputStream/Reader—Used to access request's content.

```
java.io.InputStream
java.io.Reader
```

- OutputStream/Writer—Used to send response content.

```
java.io.OutputStream
java.io.Writer
```

- @RequestParam annotated argument—Used to access a specific request parameter. The value will be converted into the declared argument type of the argument automatically.

```
@RequestParam("<request_parameter_name>") data-type argument-name
```

Example,

```
@RequestParam("username") String uname
@RequestParam("age") int age
```

- @RequestBody annotated argument – Used to access the HTTP Request body. Example,

```
@RequestBody  String  body
```

- Map/Model/ModelMap – Used to carry data among models and views.

```
java.util.Map
org.springframework.ui.Model
org.springframework.ui.ModelMap
```

- Command/Form Objects – Request parameters are automatically bind to these objects. They are instances of Java bean classes with setter/getter methods.
- Errors/BindingResult – Carries validation results for a preceding command/form object argument. Note that the order of arguments in the method (signature) is very important.

```
org.springframework.validation.Errors
org.springframework.validation.BindingResult
```

Example,

```
    String save(@ModelAttribute("user") User user, BindingResult
result)
```

The argument "result" carries validation errors of "user" object (if any error binded).

- `@PathVariable` annotated argument – Used to access URI template variables (applied in RESTful Web Services).
- `@MatrixVariable` annotated argument – Used to access the name-value pairs located in URI path segments.
- `@RequestHeader` annotated argument – Used to access specific Servlet request HTTP headers. The parameter values are converted to the argument type automatically.

The following are some of the supported return types of a `@RequestMapping` annotated method (handler method).

- A String value that is interpreted as the logical view name. The model can be implicitly determined using `"command"` (object name) object, or using `@ModelAttribute` argument, or even can be defined programmatically as Model argument to the method.
- A ModelAndView object
- A Model object
- A Map object
- A View object. The model implicitly determined through command objects or can be defined programmatically as Model argument to the method.

- void (if the method handles the response itself by writing the response directly using the argument of type ServletResponse)

11.5 @ModelAttribute

This annotation is used to prepare the model data, which can be applied at method level and method parameter level, does the following two functions accordingly.

- Injecting data objects to the model; that can be sent to View such as JSPs for the initial population of forms.
- Used to read data from an existing model and assigning it to handler method parameters.

General format,

```
@ModelAttribute(["name_of_model_attribute_to_bind_to"])
    @ModelAttribute([value="name_of_model_attribute_to_bind_to"])
```

The attribute 'value' is optional, which refers the name of the object. If not used, then the return type name in case of methods and parameter type name in case of method parameters will be taken as default value.

This `@ModelAttribute` annotation used in a `@Controller` annotated class behaves as below, for a HTTP request.

- The method(s) which is marked as `@ModelAttribute` will be executed in a `@Controller` class before executing any respective handler method (Method annotated with `@RequestMapping`).
- The data returned by this `@ModelAttribute` annotated method will be stored in a temporary Map object with the object name specified in the `@ModelAttribute` annotation, which will be added to Model after the execution of the handler method if the handler method does not have a `@ModelAttribute` parameter with the same object name ('value').
- The required request handler method (Method annotated with `@RequestMapping`) will be called. If the request handler method has a parameter annotated with `@ModelAttribute`, then,
- It would search in the temporary Map object with the specified object name (value of 'value' attribute of `@ModelAttribute`). If it finds, then the object value from the temporary Map object will be used for this parameter.
- If it does not find, and if there is a `@SessionAttribures` annotation is used in the same `@Controller class`, then it will search for the specified object name (value of 'value' attribute of `@ModelAttribute`) that matches in `@SessionAttribures` name. If there is a match then the object is retrieved from the session and uses for this handler method parameter.
- If the object is not resolved through the said temporary Map or `@SessionAttribures`, then it creates an instance of the parameter-type and passes it as the handler method parameter. (Note: As it creates the object for the handler method parameter, the parameter type should be a class, otherwise error will be raided as other parameter types such as an object cannot be

created if the parameter type is not a concrete class type such as such as interfaces and abstract classes.

- Once the handler is executed, the parameters marked with `@ModelAttribute(s)` are added to the Model.

11.6 @SessionAttributes

This annotation is used on `@Controller` class level to declare Model attributes to be stored in session. All the Model attributes whose names are defined in this `@SessionAttributes` annotation will be automatically persisted and restored between the subsequent requests.

General format,

```
@SessionAttributes("name_of_session_attribute_in_the_model")
@SessionAttributes({"name1", "name2", "name3", ...  })
```

The parameter to the `@SessionAttributes` refers the name(s) of the session attributes in the Model, which will be stored in the session or some conversational storage. The persistence of these Model attributes is defined by `SessionAttributeStore` interface implementation; Spring Framework will use `HttpSession` as the persistence storage by default as its `DefaultSessionAttributeStore` class (implements `SessionAttributeStore`) relies on `HttpSession` as the storage for Servlet environment.

This `@SessionAttributes` annotation used in a `@Controller` annotated class behaves as below.

- `@SessionAttributes` is initialized when a corresponding attribute(s) is put into Model by either using a method annotated with `@ModelAttribute` or explicitly.
- Whenever a handler method with the model attribute parameter is invoked, then its corresponding session attribute specified in `@SessionAttributes` will be updated by the data from HTTP parameters (form).
- If SessionStatus interface is specified as parameter to an handler method, and a method call `setComplete()` to the SessionStatus object inside the handler method will remove the active session attribute defined in the `@SessionAttributes`. The active session `attribute(s)` is the actual session attribute used by the corresponding handler method that is passed as argument to the handler method using `@ModelAttribute`.

Limitation: The `@SessionAttributes` attributes will not be available across the `@Controller` classes even though they are using `HttpSession` for persistence. These attributes are not behave as session attributes that we create using `setAttribute()` method of `HttpSession` object.

11.7 @RequestParam

This annotation is applied on a handler method parameter, which binds the corresponding request data. It retrieves the corresponding request parameter value from the HTTP request, converts data to the handler method parameter type and assigns it.

General format,

```
@RequestParam(value="name_of_request_paramter_to_bind_to",
              required="true|false",
              defaultValue="default_value")
```

The “required” attribute set to "true" by default, which leads to an exception in case of the specified parameter is missing in the request. If it is set to "false", then a 'null' value will be assigned to the corresponding handler method parameter in case the request parameter is not available in the request; we can specify a default value to the parameter using the "defaultValue" attribute, which will take effect in case the corresponding request parameter is not present in the request or it is empty. The "defaultValue" attribute implicitly sets the "required" to false.

11.8 @RequestBody

This annotation is applied on a handler method parameter, which binds the value of the HTTP request body.

General format,

```
@RequestBody(required="true|false")
```

The "required" attribute set to "true" by default, which leads to an exception in case there is no body content. If it is set to "false", then a 'null' value will be assigned to the corresponding handler method parameter in case there is no body content.

This @RequestBody annotation is used to work with request data sent in structured format such as XML and JSON.

11.9 @ResponseBody

This annotation is applied at method level and indicates the method returns HTTP response body. That is, the return value is to be written straight to the HTTP response body.

General format,

```
@ResponseBody
```

The @RequestBody and @ResponseBody annotations are used to work with request/ response of data in structured format such as XML and JSON.

11.10 @InitBinder

This annotation is used commonly for specifying custom data type conversion for form data. This @InitBinder annotation can be applied to any method with void return type and any number of arguments of any type (as like a @RequestMapping annotated method) except command/form objects as argument(s) and their corresponding validation result objects.

General format,

```
@InitBinder
```

Usually the `@InitBinder` annotated methods are having method prototypes with arguments of type `WebDataBinder` along with `WebRequest` for initializing the `WebDataBinder` which is used for populating command/form object arguments of the handler methods in the same `@Controller` annotated class.

11.11 @CookieValue

This annotation can be applied to a parameter of `@RequestMapping` annotated handler method, which binds the value of the specified HTTP cookie object to the parameter.

General format,

```
@CookieValue(value="name_of_cookie_to_bind_to"
          required="true|false",
          defaultValue="default_value")
```

The "`required`" attribute set to "`true`" by default, which leads to an exception in case of the header is missing in the request. If it is set to "`false`", then a 'null' value will be assigned to the corresponding handler method parameter in case the header is missing in the request; we can specify a default value to the parameter using the "`defaultValue`" attribute, which will take effect as the result of fallback. The "`defaultValue`" attribute implicitly sets the "`required`" to false.

11.12 @RequestHeader

This annotation can be applied to a parameter of `@RequestMapping` annotated handler method, which binds the value of the specified web request header such as Keep-Alive, Accept-Encoding, and Host.

General format,

```
@RequestHeader(value="name_of_request_header_to_bind_to"
          required="true|false",
          defaultValue="default_value")
```

The "`required`" attribute set to "`true`" by default, which leads to an exception in case of the header is missing in the request. If it is set to "`false`", then a 'null' value will be assigned to the corresponding handler method parameter in case the header is missing in the request; we can specify a default value to the parameter using the "`defaultValue`" attribute, which will take effect as the result of fallback. The "`defaultValue`" attribute implicitly sets the "`required`" to false.

11.13 HANDLING VIEWS

Views in Spring are addressed by a logical view name and are resolved by a view resolver and all the handler methods in a controller class must resolve to a logical view name, either explicitly (for example, by returning a String, View, or ModelAndView) or implicitly.

The view resolver "`InternalResourceViewResolver`" is used to handle Servlet/JSP based views.

The "redirect:" prefixed to the return String of a handler method in a controller instructs the container that a redirect is needed. The rest of the string (after "redirect:") will be taken as redirect URL.

The "forward:" prefixed to the return String of a handler method in a controller forwards the request to the specified URL (URL specified after "forward:").

11.14 EXAMPLE APPLICATIONS

This part demonstrates the main components of Spring MVC in terms of small applications. These applications are written to illustrate the concepts of Spring MVC and not full-fledged applications.

11.14.1 Simple Input/Output

This application gets your name from a web-page and displays the same with welcome message.

Install Maven: Download the latest version of Maven, a Project Management Tool, from its official web site (http://maven.apache.org/download.cgi) in Zip format. I downloaded Maven version 3.0.5; unzip the file and include its bin directory in to the PATH variable so that you can access "mvn" in any command prompt/shell window.

Create a Web Project: Go to your workspace directory in the command prompt/ shell window and invoke "mvn" command as shown below.

```
C:\Development\Install\eclipse-juno\workspace>mvn archetype:generate
        -DgroupId=SpringDemo -DartifactId=SpringDemoWeb
        -DarchetypeArtifactId=maven-archetype-webapp
        -DinteractiveMode=false
[INFO] Scanning for projects...
[INFO]
[INFO] ------------------------------------------------------------
[INFO] Building Maven Stub Project (No POM) 1
[INFO] ------------------------------------------------------------
[INFO]
[INFO] >>> maven-archetype-plugin:2.2:generate (default-cli)
@ standalone-pom >>>
[INFO]
[INFO] <<< maven-archetype-plugin:2.2:generate (default-cli)
@ standalone-pom <<<
[INFO]
[INFO] --- maven-archetype-plugin:2.2:generate (default-cli)
@ standalone-pom
[INFO] Generating project in Batch mode
[INFO] ------------------------------------------------------------
[INFO] Using following parameters for creating project from Old (1.x)
Archetype: maven-archetype-webapp:1.0
```

```
[INFO] ------------------------------------------------------------
[INFO] Parameter: groupId, Value: SpringDemo
[INFO] Parameter: packageName, Value: SpringDemo
[INFO] Parameter: package, Value: SpringDemo
[INFO] Parameter: artifactId, Value: SpringDemoWeb
[INFO] Parameter: basedir, Value: C:\Development\Install\eclipse-juno
                                                          \workspace
[INFO] Parameter: version, Value: 1.0-SNAPSHOT
[INFO] project created from Old (1.x) Archetype in dir:
C:\Development\Install\eclipse-juno\workspace\SpringDemoWeb
[INFO] ------------------------------------------------------------
[INFO] BUILD SUCCESS
[INFO] ------------------------------------------------------------
[INFO] Total time: 16.526s
[INFO] Finished at: Tue May 07 10:40:52 SGT 2013
[INFO] Final Memory: 7M/18M
[INFO] ------------------------------------------------------------
```

Then, a directory named "SpringDemoWeb" will be created with "src" directory and pom.xml.

```
C:\Development\Install\eclipse-juno\workspace\SpringDemoWeb>dir
Directory of C:\Development\Install\eclipse-juno\workspace\SpringDemoWeb

05/07/2013  10:40 AM    <DIR>          .
05/07/2013  10:40 AM    <DIR>          ..
05/07/2013  10:40 AM               745 pom.xml
05/07/2013  10:40 AM    <DIR>          src
```

Add the project to Eclipse IDE: I am using Eclipse IDE (Eclipse Juno/4.2) for application development; we need to add the created Maven project into Eclipse, this can be done using Eclipse Maven plug-in or through the following command at command prompt.

Go to the project directory and issue the "mvn eclipse:eclipse" command to convert the project as Eclipse Java project, add `"-Dwtpversion=2.0"` to specify Web Tools Platform (WTP) version that converts the project as Eclipse Web project.

```
C:\Development\Install\eclipse-juno\workspace\SpringDemoWeb> mvn
                                 eclipse:eclipse -Dwtpversion=2.0
[INFO] Scanning for projects...
[INFO]
[INFO] ------------------------------------------------------------
[INFO] Building SpringDemoWeb Maven Webapp 1.0-SNAPSHOT
```

```
[INFO] ------------------------------------------------------------
[INFO]
[INFO] >>> maven-eclipse-plugin:2.9:eclipse (default-cli) @ SpringDemoWeb
>>>
[INFO]
[INFO] <<< maven-eclipse-plugin:2.9:eclipse (default-cli) @ SpringDemoWeb
<<<
[INFO]
[INFO] ---maven-eclipse-plugin:2.9:eclipse (default-cli) @ SpringDemoWeb
---
[INFO] Adding support for WTP version 2.0.
[INFO] Using Eclipse Workspace: C:\Development\Install\eclipse
juno\workspace
[WARNING] Workspace defines a VM that does not contain a valid jre/lib
rt.jar: C:\Program Files\Java\jre6
[INFO] no substring wtp server match.
[INFO] Using as WTP server : Apache Tomcat v6.0
[INFO] Adding default classpath container:
org.eclipse.jdt.launching.JRE_CONTAINER
[INFO] Not writing settings - defaults suffice
[INFO] Wrote Eclipse project for "SpringDemoWeb" to
C:\Development\Install\eclipse-juno\workspace\SpringDemoWeb.
[INFO]
[INFO]------------------------------------------------------------
[INFO] BUILD SUCCESS
[INFO]------------------------------------------------------------
[INFO] Total time: 8.414s
[INFO] Finished at: Tue May 07 10:55:38 SGT 2013
[INFO] Final Memory: 5M/15M
[INFO] ------------------------------------------------------------
```

Invoke Eclipse IDE, File → Import → Existing Projects into Workspace → Select the “SpringDemoWeb” directory for “Select root directory” → Finish.

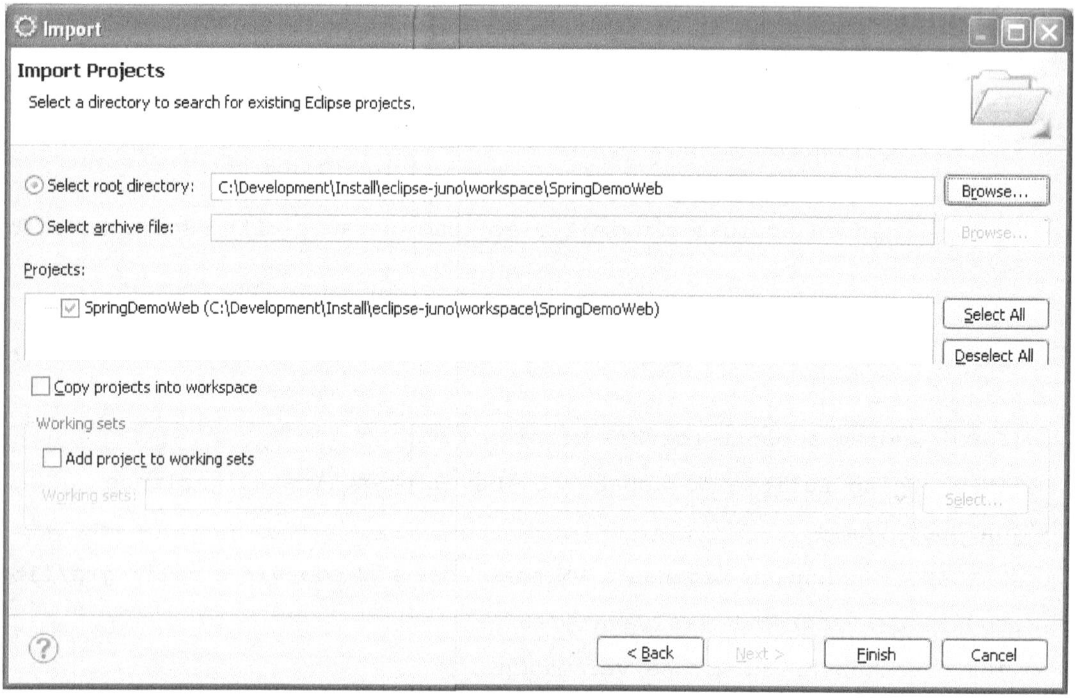

Edit pom.xml: POM stands for "Project Object Model". This pom.xml file in a Maven project specifies all the configurations in order to build the project.

Open the pom.xml and update it content as given below.

```
<project xmlns="http://maven.apache.org/POM/4.0.0"
        xmlns:xsi="http://www.w3.org/2001/XMLSchema-instance"
        xsi:schemaLocation="http://maven.apache.org/POM/4.0.0
        http://maven.apache.org/maven-v4_0_0.xsd">

  <modelVersion>4.0.0</modelVersion>
  <groupId>SpringDemo</groupId>
  <artifactId>SpringDemoWeb</artifactId>
  <packaging>war</packaging>
  <version>1.0-SNAPSHOT</version>
  <name>SpringDemoWeb Maven Webapp</name>

  <properties>
   <spring.version>3.2.2.RELEASE</spring.version>
   <junit.version>4.11</junit.version>
   <jdk.version>1.6</jdk.version>
  </properties>
```

```
<dependencies>
 <!-- Spring 3 dependencies starts -->
 <dependency>
  <groupId>org.springframework</groupId>
  <artifactId>spring-core</artifactId>
  <version>${spring.version}</version>
 </dependency>

 <dependency>
  <groupId>org.springframework</groupId>
  <artifactId>spring-web</artifactId>
  <version>${spring.version}</version>
 </dependency>

 <dependency>
  <groupId>org.springframework</groupId>
  <artifactId>spring-webmvc</artifactId>
  <version>${spring.version}</version>
 </dependency>
 <!-- Spring 3 dependencies ends -->

 <dependency>
  <groupId>junit</groupId>
  <artifactId>junit</artifactId>
  <version>${junit.version}</version>
  <scope>test</scope>
 </dependency>
</dependencies>

<build>
 <finalName>SpringDemoWeb</finalName>
 <plugins>
  <plugin>
   <groupId>org.apache.maven.plugins</groupId>
   <artifactId>maven-compiler-plugin</artifactId>
   <version>3.0</version>
   <configuration>
      <source>${jdk.version}</source>
      <target>${jdk.version}</target>
   </configuration>
  </plugin>
```

```
    <plugin>
     <groupId>org.mortbay.jetty</groupId>
     <artifactId>maven-jetty-plugin</artifactId>
     <version>6.1.26</version>
     <configuration>
      <connectors>
    <connector
        implementation="org.mortbay.jetty.nio.SelectChannelConnector">
     <port>8080</port>
    </connector>
     </connectors>
    </configuration>
   </plugin>
  </plugins>
 </build>
</project>
```

Spring Configuration File: Create the following "SpringDemoWeb-servlet.xml" file under `src/main/webapp/WEB-INF` directory of the project.

```
<beans xmlns="http://www.springframework.org/schema/beans"
    xmlns:context="http://www.springframework.org/schema/context"
    xmlns:p="http://www.springframework.org/schema/p"
    xmlns:xsi="http://www.w3.org/2001/XMLSchema-instance"
    xsi:schemaLocation="
    http://www.springframework.org/schema/beans
    http://www.springframework.org/schema/beans/spring-beans-3.0.xsd
    http://www.springframework.org/schema/context
    http://www.springframework.org/schema/context/spring-context-
    3.0.xsd">

  <context:component-scan base-package="com.springdemo.controller" />
  <bean
  class="org.springframework.web.servlet.view.InternalResourceViewResolver"
   p:prefix="/WEB-INF/jsp/" p:suffix=".jsp" />

</beans>
```

Update web.xml: Update the "web.xml" file under `src/main/webapp/WEB-INF` as shown below.

```
<web-app xmlns="http://java.sun.com/xml/ns/javaee"
         xmlns:xsi="http://www.w3.org/2001/XMLSchema-instance"
         xsi:schemaLocation="http://java.sun.com/xml/ns/javaee
         http://java.sun.com/xml/ns/javaee/web-app_2_5.xsd"
         version="2.5">

  <display-name>Spring Demo Web Application</display-name>

  <servlet>
   <servlet-name>SpringDemoWeb</servlet-name>
   <servlet-class>
     org.springframework.web.servlet.DispatcherServlet
   </servlet-class>
   <load-on-startup>1</load-on-startup>
  </servlet>

  <servlet-mapping>
   <servlet-name>SpringDemoWeb</servlet-name>
   <url-pattern>/</url-pattern>
  </servlet-mapping>

  <context-param>
   <param-name>contextConfigLocation</param-name>
   <param-value>/WEB-INF/SpringDemoWeb-servlet.xml</param-value>
  </context-param>

  <listener>
   <listener-class>
    org.springframework.web.context.ContextLoaderListener
   </listener-class>
  </listener>
</web-app>
```

Create Java Files: Create a directory named "java" under "src/main" and then crate a package named "com.springdemo.controller" under "src/main/java". Add the following controller class.

```
//File Name: DisplayNameController.java
package com.springdemo.controller;

import org.springframework.stereotype.Controller;
```

```
import org.springframework.ui.ModelMap;
import org.springframework.web.bind.annotation.RequestMapping;
import org.springframework.web.bind.annotation.RequestParam;

@Controller
public class DisplayNameController {

 @RequestMapping(value = "/")
 public String input() {
  return "inputname";
 }

 @RequestMapping(value = "/displayname")
 public String display(@RequestParam("userName") String userName,
                    ModelMap model) {

   model.addAttribute("resultMessage", "Welcome " + userName);
   return "displayname";
 }
}
```

Add JSP Files: Create a folder named "jsp" under src/main/webapp/WEB-INF. And add the following JSP files.

```
<!-- File Name: inputname.jsp →
<html>
 <head>
  <title>Spring Demo -Web MVC</title>
 </head>

 <body>
  <form name="form" action="/SpringDemoWeb/displayname">
   Enter your name:
   <input type="text" name="userName" maxlength="40" size="30">
   <br>
   <input type="submit" value="Submit It">
  </form>
 </body>
</html>
```

```
<!-- File Name: displayname.jsp ->
<html>
 <head>
  <title>Spring Demo -Web MVC</title>
 </head>

 <body>
  ${resultMessage}
 </body>
</html>
```

Compile and Package the Project: Use Maven to compile and package the project. Then the project will be compiled and the .war file will be generated in the "target" directory of the project.

Note: Internet connection will be required at least first time to import the libraries and plug-ins used in the pom.xml file.

```
C:\Development\Install\eclipse-juno\workspace\SpringDemoWeb> mvn
                                   eclipse:eclipse -Dwtpversion=2.0
[INFO] Scanning for projects...
[INFO] ------------------------------------------------------------
[INFO] Building SpringDemoWeb Maven Webapp 1.0-SNAPSHOT
[INFO] ------------------------------------------------------------
[INFO] >>> maven-eclipse-plugin:2.9:eclipse (default-cli) @ SpringDemoWeb
>>>
[INFO] <<< maven-eclipse-plugin:2.9:eclipse (default-cli) @ SpringDemoWeb
<<<
[INFO] --- maven-eclipse-plugin:2.9:eclipse (default-cli) @ SpringDemoWeb
---
[INFO] Adding support for WTP version 2.0.
[INFO] Using Eclipse Workspace: C:\Development\Install\eclipse
juno\workspace
[WARNING] Workspace defines a VM that does not contain a valid jre/lib/
rt.jar: C:\Program Files\Java\jre6
[INFO] no substring wtp server match.
[INFO] Using as WTP server : Apache Tomcat v6.0
[INFO] Wrote Eclipse project for "SpringDemoWeb" to
C:\Development\Install\eclipse-juno\workspace\SpringDemoWeb.
[INFO]
[INFO] ------------------------------------------------------------
[INFO] BUILD SUCCESS
[INFO] ------------------------------------------------------------
[INFO] Total time: 5.675s
[INFO] Finished at: Tue May 07 16:36:47 SGT 2013
```

```
[INFO] Final Memory: 6M/15M
[INFO] ------------------------------------------------------------------------
C:\Development\Install\eclipse-juno\workspace\SpringDemoWeb> mvn clean
                                              compile package
[INFO] Scanning for projects...
[INFO]
[INFO] ------------------------------------------------------------------------
[INFO] Building SpringDemoWeb Maven Webapp 1.0-SNAPSHOT
[INFO] ------------------------------------------------------------------------
...
...
[INFO] Building war: C:\Development\Install\eclipse-juno
            \workspace\SpringDemoWeb\target\SpringDemoWeb.war
[INFO] ------------------------------------------------------------------------
[INFO] BUILD SUCCESS
[INFO] ------------------------------------------------------------------------
```

Then, our project structure in Eclipse Package Explorer is as shown below.

Deploying Application on Application Server: Observe that a war file named "SpringDemoWeb.war" is created in the "target" folder of the application. You can deploy this war file in any Servlet-enabled application server/Servlet container.

I am using Jetty Servlet container to test our application, to do so I am using Maven Jetty Plug-in and already configured in the pom.xml file of our project.

Invoke the `"mvn jetty:run"` command to invoke the Jetty server.

```
C:\Development\Install\eclipse-juno\workspace\SpringDemoWeb> mvn
jetty:run
[INFO] Scanning for projects...
[INFO]
[INFO] ------------------------------------------------------------
[INFO] Building SpringDemoWeb Maven Webapp 1.0-SNAPSHOT
[INFO] ------------------------------------------------------------
....
....
INFO: FrameworkServlet 'SpringDemoWeb': initialization completed in
436 ms
INFO::Started SelectChannelConnector@0.0.0.0:8080
[INFO] Started Jetty Server
```

Invoke a browser with the URL: http://localhost:8080/SpringDemoWeb/

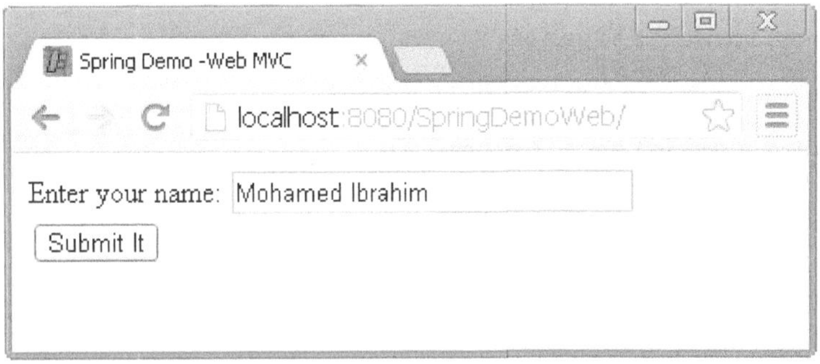

Click on “Submit It”.

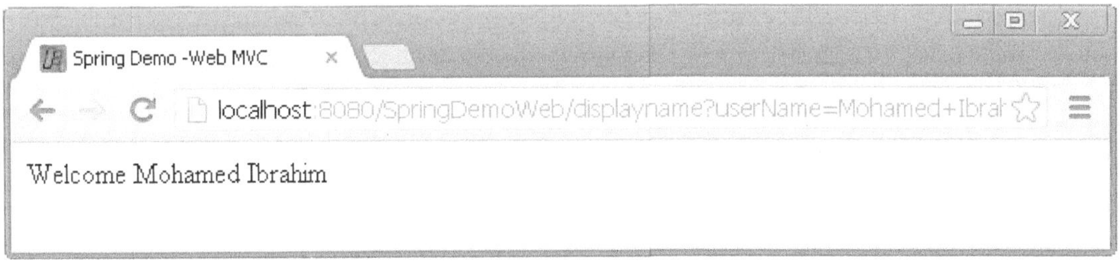

11.14.2 CRUD Operations with Employee Data

This application illustrates how to do Create/Read/Update/Delete (CRUD) operations with database through Spring MVC. Please refer the above application for the configuration; this part contains only the core information.

Create user in MySQL database: In our demo application, MySQL is used as database for persisting data. You can use any other database; then change the configuration accordingly. Create a user and database in MySQL database. I created a database named ‘demodb’ for the user ‘ibrahim’ with password ‘pword’ (Refer earlier chapters for creating user/database in MySQL).

In DOS window:

```
C:\> mysql -u ibrahim -ppword demodb
Welcome to the MySQL monitor.  Commands end with ; or \g.
Your MySQL connection id is 3
Server version: 5.5.17 MySQL Community Server (GPL)
...
...
mysql>
```

Data Access Objects:

Create a package named 'com.springdemo.entity' and add the following file.

```
//FileName: Employee.java
package com.springdemo.entity;

import java.io.Serializable;
import java.util.Date;

import javax.persistence.Column;
import javax.persistence.Entity;
import javax.persistence.GeneratedValue;
import javax.persistence.Id;
import javax.persistence.Table;
import javax.persistence.Temporal;
import javax.persistence.TemporalType;

import org.hibernate.annotations.GenericGenerator;

@Entity
@Table(name = "EMPLOYEE")
public class Employee implements Serializable {

 private static final long serialVersionUID = 4515666565548935l2L;

 @Id
 @GeneratedValue(generator = "idGen")
 @GenericGenerator(name = "idGen", strategy = "uuid.hex")
 @Column(name = "ID", length = 32)
 private String id;

 @Column(name = "EMP_NUMBER", length = 10, nullable = false)
 private String empNumber;

 @Column(name = "EMP_NAME", length = 50, nullable = false)
```

```
private String empName;

@Column(name = "DESIGNATION", length = 100)
private String designation;

@Temporal(value = TemporalType.DATE)
@Column(name = "DOJ")
private Date dateOfJoining;

@Column(name = "BASIC_PAY", precision = 7, scale = 2, nullable = false)
private double basicPay;

@Column(name = "ALLOWANCES", precision = 7, scale = 2)
private double allowances;

@Column(name = "DEDUCTIONS", precision = 7, scale = 2)
private double deductions;

@Column(name = "NET_PAY", precision = 7, scale = 2)
private double netPay;

public String getId() {
 return id;
}

public void setId(String id) {
 this.id = id;
}

public String getEmpNumber() {
 return empNumber;
}

public void setEmpNumber(String empNumber) {
 this.empNumber = empNumber;
}

public String getEmpName() {
 return empName;
}

public void setEmpName(String empName) {
```

```
    this.empName = empName;
  }

  public String getDesignation() {
    return designation;
  }

  public void setDesignation(String designation) {
    this.designation = designation;
  }

  public Date getDateOfJoining() {
    return dateOfJoining;
  }

  public void setDateOfJoining(Date dateOfJoining) {
    this.dateOfJoining = dateOfJoining;
  }

  public double getBasicPay() {
    return basicPay;
  }

  public void setBasicPay(double basicPay) {
    this.basicPay = basicPay;
  }

  public double getAllowances() {
    return allowances;
  }

  public void setAllowances(double allowances) {
    this.allowances = allowances;
  }

  public double getDeductions() {
    return deductions;
  }

  public void setDeductions(double deductions) {
    this.deductions = deductions;
  }
```

```
 public double getNetPay() {
  return netPay;
 }

 public void setNetPay(double netPay) {
  this.netPay = netPay;
 }

}
```

Create a package named 'com.springdemo.dao' user "src" directory and add the following file.

```
//FileName: EmployeeDAO.java
package com.springdemo.dao;

import java.util.List;
import com.springdemo.entity.Employee;

public interface EmployeeDAO {

 public Employee get(String id);
 public void save(Employee employee);
 public void update(Employee employee);
 public void delete(String id);
 public List<Employee> list();
}
```

Create a package named "com.springdemo.daoimpl" under "src" directory and add the following file.

```
//FileName: EmployeeDAOImpl.java
package com.springdemo.daoimpl;

import java.util.List;

import org.hibernate.SessionFactory;
import org.springframework.beans.factory.annotation.Autowired;
import org.springframework.orm.ObjectRetrievalFailureException;
import org.springframework.stereotype.Repository;
import org.springframework.transaction.annotation.Transactional;
```

```
import com.springdemo.dao.EmployeeDAO;
import com.springdemo.entity.Employee;

@Repository
@Transactional
public class EmployeeDAOImpl implements EmployeeDAO {

 @Autowired
 private SessionFactory sessionFactory;

 @SuppressWarnings("unchecked")
 @Transactional(readOnly = true)
 public Employee get(String id) {
  List<Employee> list = sessionFactory.getCurrentSession()
                       .createQuery("from Employee where id = :id")
                       .setString("id", id).list();

  if (!list.isEmpty())
   return list.get(0);

  return null;
 }

 @SuppressWarnings("unchecked")
 @Transactional(readOnly = false)
 public void save(Employee employee) {
  List<Employee> list = sessionFactory.getCurrentSession()
             .createQuery("from Employee where empNumber = :empNumber")
             .setString("empNumber", employee.getEmpNumber()).list();
  if (list != null && !list.isEmpty())
   throw new org.hibernate.exception.ConstraintViolationException(
                       "Duplicate Employee Number", null, null);

  sessionFactory.getCurrentSession().save(employee);
 }


 @Transactional(readOnly = false)
 public void update(Employee employee) {
  sessionFactory.getCurrentSession().merge(employee);
 }
```

```
    @Transactional(readOnly = false)
    public void delete(String id) {
     Employee employee = get(id);
     if (employee == null)
     throw new ObjectRetrievalFailureException(Employee.class, employee);

     sessionFactory.getCurrentSession().delete(employee);
    }

    @SuppressWarnings("unchecked")
    @Transactional(readOnly = true)
    public List<Employee> list() {
     return sessionFactory.getCurrentSession()
              .createQuery("from Employee").list();
    }
}
```

Controller: Create a package named 'com.springdemo.controller' under "src" directory and add the following file.

```
//FileName: EmployeeController.java
package com.springdemo.controller;

import java.text.SimpleDateFormat;
import java.util.Date;
import java.util.List;

import org.springframework.beans.factory.annotation.Autowired;
import org.springframework.beans.propertyeditors.CustomDateEditor;
import org.springframework.stereotype.Controller;
import org.springframework.ui.ModelMap;
import org.springframework.validation.BindingResult;
import org.springframework.validation.ObjectError;
import org.springframework.web.bind.WebDataBinder;
import org.springframework.web.bind.annotation.InitBinder;
import org.springframework.web.bind.annotation.ModelAttribute;
import org.springframework.web.bind.annotation.RequestMapping;
import org.springframework.web.bind.annotation.RequestParam;

import com.springdemo.dao.EmployeeDAO;
import com.springdemo.entity.Employee;
import com.springdemo.validator.EmployeeValidator;
```

```
@Controller
public class EmployeeController {

 @Autowired
 private EmployeeDAO employeeDAO;

 @RequestMapping("Employee/create.demo")
 public ModelMap create(ModelMap modelMap) {
  modelMap.addAttribute("employee", new Employee());
  return modelMap;
 }

 @RequestMapping("Employee/save.demo")
 public String save(@ModelAttribute("employee") Employee employee,
                 BindingResult result) {
  new EmployeeValidator().validate(employee, result);
  if (result.hasErrors()) {
   return "Employee/create";
  }
  try {
  employee.setNetPay(employee.getBasicPay() + employee.getAllowances()
                  - employee.getDeductions());
   employeeDAO.save(employee);
  }
  catch (Exception e) {
   if (e.getCause() instanceof
       org.hibernate.exception.ConstraintViolationException ||
    e instanceof org.hibernate.exception.ConstraintViolationException)
{
    result.addError(new ObjectError("employee", null, null,
   "Database constraint violated. Duplicate Entry Attempted. Same record
     already exists in the system."));
   }
   else {
    result.addError(new ObjectError("employee", null, null,
      "Error occured while saving Employee record. Error Message [" +
       e.getMessage() + "]"));
   }
   e.printStackTrace();
  }
```

```
  if (result.hasErrors()) {
   return "Employee/create";
  }
  String info = "Employee record is saved successfully";
  return "redirect:list.demo?MSG=" + info;
 }

 @RequestMapping(value = "Employee/edit.demo")
 public ModelMap edit(@RequestParam("employeeId") String employeeId,
               ModelMap modelMap) {
  String ERROR = "";
  Employee employee = null;
  try {
   employee = employeeDAO.get(employeeId);
   modelMap.addAttribute("employee", employee);
  }
  catch (Exception e) {
   e.printStackTrace();
   ERROR = "Error occurred [" + e.getMessage() + "]";
  }
  if (ERROR.length() > 0)
   modelMap.addAttribute("MSG", ERROR);
  return modelMap;
 }

 @RequestMapping(value = "Employee/update.demo")
 public String update(@ModelAttribute("employee") Employee employee,
               BindingResult result) {
  new EmployeeValidator().validate(employee, result);
  if (result.hasErrors()) {
   return "Employee/edit";
  }

  try {
  employee.setNetPay(employee.getBasicPay() + employee.getAllowances()
               - employee.getDeductions());
   employeeDAO.update(employee);
  }
  catch (Exception e) {
   if (e.getCause() instanceof
      org.hibernate.exception.ConstraintViolationException ||
```

```
      e instanceof org.hibernate.exception.ConstraintViolationException)
   {
      result.addError(new ObjectError("employee", null, null,
               "Database constraint violated. Another record with same
                details already exists."));
    }
    else {
      result.addError(new ObjectError("employee", null, null,
                "Error occured while updating Employee record. Error
                Message [" + e.getMessage() + "]"));
    }
    e.printStackTrace();
   }

   if (result.hasErrors()) {
    return "Employee/edit";
   }

   String info = "Employee record is updated";
   return "redirect:list.demo?MSG=" + info;
  }

  @RequestMapping("Employee/delete.demo")
  public String delete(@RequestParam("employeeId") String employeeId) {
   String ERROR = "";
   String INFO = "Employee record is deleted";
   try {
    employeeDAO.delete(employeeId);
   }
   catch (Exception e) {
    ERROR = "Error occurred: [" + e.getMessage() + "]";
    e.printStackTrace();
   }
   if (ERROR.length() == 0) {
    return "redirect:list.demo?MSG=" + INFO;
   }
   else {
    return "redirect:list.demo?MSG=" + ERROR;
   }
  }

  @RequestMapping("Employee/list.demo")
```

```
public ModelMap list(@RequestParam(value = "MSG", defaultValue = "")
                    String MSG, ModelMap modelMap) {
 List<Employee> employeeList = null;
 try {
  employeeList = employeeDAO.list();

  if ((employeeList == null) || (employeeList.size() == 0))
   MSG = "No Employee record found";
 }
 catch (Exception e) {
  MSG = "Error occurred. ERROR [" + e.getMessage() + "]";
  e.printStackTrace();
 }
 modelMap.addAttribute("MSG", MSG);
 modelMap.addAttribute("employeeList", employeeList);
 return modelMap;
}

@InitBinder
protected void initBinder(WebDataBinder binder) {
 SimpleDateFormat dateFormat = new SimpleDateFormat("dd-MM-yyyy");
 dateFormat.setLenient(false);
 binder.registerCustomEditor(Date.class,
                         new CustomDateEditor(dateFormat, true));
}
}
```

Form Data Validator: Create a package named 'com.springdemo.validator' under "src" directory and add the following file.

```
package com.springdemo.validator;

import org.springframework.validation.Errors;
import org.springframework.validation.ValidationUtils;
import org.springframework.validation.Validator;

import com.springdemo.entity.Employee;

public class EmployeeValidator implements Validator {

 public void validate(Object object, Errors errors) {
  ValidationUtils.rejectIfEmptyOrWhitespace(errors, "empNumber",
```

```
                "empNumber.required", "Employee Number is required");

    ValidationUtils.rejectIfEmptyOrWhitespace(errors, "empName",
                "empName.required", "Employee Name is required");

    ValidationUtils.rejectIfEmptyOrWhitespace(errors, "basicPay",
                "basicPay.required", "Basic Pay is required");
  }

  @SuppressWarnings("rawtypes")
  public boolean supports(Class clazz) {
    return Employee.class.isAssignableFrom(clazz);
  }
}
```

pom.xml: Update the content of the pom.xml which is located under root of the project as below.

```
<project xmlns="http://maven.apache.org/POM/4.0.0"
       xmlns:xsi="http://www.w3.org/2001/XMLSchema-instance"
       xsi:schemaLocation="http://maven.apache.org/POM/4.0.0
       http://maven.apache.org/maven-v4_0_0.xsd">
  <modelVersion>4.0.0</modelVersion>
  <groupId>SpringDemo</groupId>
  <artifactId>SpringDemoWeb</artifactId>
  <packaging>war</packaging>
  <version>1.0-SNAPSHOT</version>
  <name>SpringDemoWeb Maven Webapp</name>

  <properties>
   <spring.version>3.2.2.RELEASE</spring.version>
   <junit.version>4.11</junit.version>
   <jdk.version>1.6</jdk.version>
  </properties>

  <dependencies>
   <!-- Spring 3 dependencies starts ->
   <dependency>
     <groupId>org.springframework</groupId>
     <artifactId>spring-core</artifactId>
     <version>${spring.version}</version>
   </dependency>
```

```
<dependency>
  <groupId>org.springframework</groupId>
  <artifactId>spring-web</artifactId>
  <version>${spring.version}</version>
</dependency>

<dependency>
  <groupId>org.springframework</groupId>
  <artifactId>spring-webmvc</artifactId>
  <version>${spring.version}</version>
</dependency>

<dependency>
  <groupId>org.springframework</groupId>
  <artifactId>spring-orm</artifactId>
  <version>${spring.version}</version>
</dependency>
<!-- Spring 3 dependencies ends -->

<dependency>
  <groupId>org.hibernate</groupId>
  <artifactId>hibernate-core</artifactId>
  <version>4.1.0.Final</version>
</dependency>

<dependency>
  <groupId>mysql</groupId>
  <artifactId>mysql-connector-java</artifactId>
  <version>5.1.17</version>
</dependency>

<dependency>
  <groupId>commons-dbcp</groupId>
  <artifactId>commons-dbcp</artifactId>
  <version>20030825.184428</version>
</dependency>

<dependency>
  <groupId>commons-pool</groupId>
  <artifactId>commons-pool</artifactId>
  <version>20030825.183949</version>
</dependency>
```

```
    <dependency>
     <groupId>taglibs</groupId>
     <artifactId>standard</artifactId>
     <version>1.1.2</version>
    </dependency>

    <dependency>
     <groupId>junit</groupId>
     <artifactId>junit</artifactId>
     <version>${junit.version}</version>
     <scope>test</scope>
    </dependency>
   </dependencies>

   <build>
    <finalName>SpringDemoWeb</finalName>
    <plugins>
     <plugin>
      <groupId>org.apache.maven.plugins</groupId>
      <artifactId>maven-compiler-plugin</artifactId>
      <version>3.0</version>
      <configuration>
       <source>${jdk.version}</source>
       <target>${jdk.version}</target>
      </configuration>
     </plugin>

     <plugin>
      <groupId>org.mortbay.jetty</groupId>
      <artifactId>maven-jetty-plugin</artifactId>
      <version>6.1.26</version>
      <configuration>
       <scanIntervalSeconds>10</scanIntervalSeconds>
       <connectors>
        <connector
          implementation="org.mortbay.jetty.nio.SelectChannelConnector">
         <port>8080</port>
        </connector>
       </connectors>
      </configuration>
```

```
    </plugin>
   </plugins>
  </build>
</project>
```

web.xml: Update the following as the content of web.xml which is located at SpringDemoWeb/src/main/webapp/WEB-INF direcoty.

```
<web-app xmlns="http://java.sun.com/xml/ns/javaee"
        xmlns:xsi="http://www.w3.org/2001/XMLSchema-instance"
        xsi:schemaLocation="http://java.sun.com/xml/ns/javaee
        http://java.sun.com/xml/ns/javaee/web-app_2_5.xsd"
        version="2.5">

  <display-name>Spring Demo Web Application</display-name>

  <servlet>
   <servlet-name>SpringDemoWeb</servlet-name>
   <servlet-class>
     org.springframework.web.servlet.DispatcherServlet
   </servlet-class>
   <load-on-startup>1</load-on-startup>
  </servlet>

  <servlet-mapping>
   <servlet-name>SpringDemoWeb</servlet-name>
   <url-pattern>*.demo</url-pattern>
  </servlet-mapping>

  <context-param>
   <param-name>contextConfigLocation</param-name>
   <param-value>/WEB-INF/SpringDemoWeb-servlet.xml</param-value>
  </context-param>

  <listener>
   <listener-class>
     org.springframework.web.context.ContextLoaderListener
   </listener-class>
  </listener>
</web-app>
```

Spring Configuration File: Store the following Spring configuration file 'SpringDemoWeb-servlet.xml' under SpringDemoWeb/src/main/webapp/WEB-INF directory.

```
<?xml  version="1.0" encoding="UTF-8"?>
<beans xmlns="http://www.springframework.org/schema/beans"
    xmlns:xsi="http://www.w3.org/2001/XMLSchema-instance"
    xmlns:tx="http://www.springframework.org/schema/tx"
    xmlns:p="http://www.springframework.org/schema/p"
    xmlns:context="http://www.springframework.org/schema/context"
    xsi:schemaLocation="http://www.springframework.org/schema/beans
    http://www.springframework.org/schema/beans/spring-beans-3.1.xsd
    http://www.springframework.org/schema/context
    http://www.springframework.org/schema/context/spring-context-
    3.0.xsd
    http://www.springframework.org/schema/tx
    http://www.springframework.org/schema/tx/spring-tx-3.1.xsd">

  <context:annotation-config/>
  <context:component-scan base-package="com.springdemo"/>

  <bean
  class="org.springframework.web.servlet.view.InternalResourceViewResolver"
   p:prefix="/WEB-INF/jsp/" p:suffix=".jsp"/>

  <bean id="propertyConfigurer"
        class="org.springframework.beans.factory.config
                          .PropertyPlaceholderConfigurer"
    p:location="/WEB-INF/jdbc.properties"/>

  <bean id="dataSource" class="org.apache.commons.dbcp.BasicDataSource"
   destroy-method="close" p:driverClassName="${jdbc.driverClassName}"
   p:url="${jdbc.databaseurl}" p:username="${jdbc.username}"
   p:password="${jdbc.password}"/>

  <bean id="sessionFactory"
   class="org.springframework.orm.hibernate4.LocalSessionFactoryBean">
   <property name="dataSource" ref="dataSource"/>
   <property name="annotatedClasses">
    <list>
     <value>com.springdemo.entity.Employee</value>
    </list>
   </property>
   <property name="hibernateProperties">
    <props>
```

```
    <prop key="hibernate.dialect">${jdbc.dialect}</prop>
    <prop key="hibernate.show_sql">true</prop>
   <!—At first time execution use 'create',
       Once the database tables are created,
       change 'create' to 'update' -->
    <prop key="hibernate.hbm2ddl.auto">create</prop>
    <prop key="hibernate.c3p0.minPoolSize">5</prop>
    <prop key="hibernate.c3p0.maxPoolSize">20</prop>
    <prop key="hibernate.c3p0.timeout">600</prop>
    <prop key="hibernate.c3p0.max_statement">50</prop>
    <prop key="hibernate.c3p0.testConnectionOnCheckout">false</prop>
   </props>
  </property>
 </bean>

 <tx:annotation-driven transaction-manager="transactionManager"/>

 <bean id="transactionManager"
 class="org.springframework.orm.hibernate4.HibernateTransactionManager">
  <property name="sessionFactory" ref="sessionFactory"/>
 </bean>

</beans>
```

Store the following 'jdbc.properties' which is referred in Spring configuration file, under the same directory where the SpringDemoWeb-servlet.xml file is stored.

```
jdbc.driverClassName= com.mysql.jdbc.Driver
jdbc.dialect=org.hibernate.dialect.MySQLDialect
jdbc.databaseurl=jdbc:mysql://localhost:3306/demodb
jdbc.username=ibrahim
jdbc.password=pword
```

<u>JSPs</u>: Store the following JSP files under the specified directories.

Store the 'include.jsp' under the `/webapp/WEB-INF/jsp` directory.

```
<%@ taglib prefix="c" uri="http://java.sun.com/jsp/jstl/core"%>
<%@ taglib prefix="fmt" uri="http://java.sun.com/jsp/jstl/fmt"%>
<%@ taglib prefix="spring" uri="http://www.springframework.org/tags"%>
<%@ taglib prefix="form" uri="http://www.springframework.org/tags/
form"%>
<%@ taglib prefix="fn" uri="http://java.sun.com/jsp/jstl/functions"%>
```

Store the following 'list.jsp' under /webapp/WEB-INF/jsp/Employee directory.

```
<%@ include file="/WEB-INF/jsp/include.jsp"%>

<head>
<title>List of Employee Records</title>

<script type="text/javascript">
 function callAddNew() {
  form.action = '/SpringDemoWeb/Employee/create.demo';
  form.submit();
 }
</script>

</head>

<body>
 <form:form name="form" action="" method="post">
  <br>
   <table border="0" cellspacing="0" cellpadding="0" width="100%">
    <tr>
     <td width="20"> </td>
     <td>
      <table border="0" cellspacing="0" cellpadding="0" width="100%">
       <tr>
        <td height=50><h2>Employee List</h2></td>
       </tr>
       <tr>
        <td height=50><c:if test="${fn:length(MSG) > 0}">
          <div>${MSG}</div>
         </c:if></td>
       </tr>
       <tr>
        <td>
         <table border="1" cellspacing="0" cellpadding="0" width="100%">
          <tbody>
           <tr align="left">
            <th>Emp Number</th>
            <th>Emp Name</th>
            <th>Designation</th>
            <th>DOJ</th>
            <th>BasicPay</th>
```

```
<th>Allowances</th>
<th>Deductions</th>
<th>NetPay</th>
</tr>

<c:forEach var="employee" items="${employeeList}"
        varStatus="i">
  <tr onclick="document.location.href=
'/SpringDemoWeb/Employee/edit.demo?employeeId=${employee.id}';">
    <td>${employee.empNumber}</td>
    <td>${employee.empName}</td>
    <td>${employee.designation}</td>
    <td><fmt:formatDate pattern="dd-MM-yyyy"
                value="${employee.dateOfJoining}" /></td>
    <td>${employee.basicPay}</td>
    <td>${employee.allowances}</td>
    <td>${employee.deductions}</td>
    <td>${employee.netPay}</td>
  </tr>
</c:forEach>
</tbody>
</table>
</td>
</tr>

<tr>
<td height=50 align="center">
  <input value="Add New" type="button" name="butNew"
   onclick="callAddNew();">
</td>
</tr>
</table>
</td>
<td width="20"> </td>
</tr>
</table>
</form:form>
</body>
</html>
```

Store the following 'create.jsp' under /webapp/WEB-INF/jsp/Employee directory.

```
<%@ include file="/WEB-INF/jsp/include.jsp"%>

<html>
<head>
<title>Create Employee Record</title>

<script type="text/javascript">
 function callSave() {
  form.action = '/SpringDemoWeb/Employee/save.demo';
  form.submit();
 }
</script>

</head>

<body>
 <form:form name="form" action="" method="post"
modelAttribute="employee">
  <br>
  <table border="0" cellspacing="0" cellpadding="0" width="100%">
   <tr>
    <td width="20"> </td>
    <td>
     <table border="0" cellspacing="0" cellpadding="0" width="100%">
      <tr>
       <td height=50><h2>Create Employee Record</h2></td>
      </tr>
      <tr>
       <td>
        <spring:hasBindErrors name="employee">
         <div class="errors">
          <ul>
           <c:forEach var="err" items="${errors.allErrors}">
            <li><c:out value="${err.defaultMessage}" /></li>
           </c:forEach>
          </ul>
         </div>
        </spring:hasBindErrors>
       </td>
      </tr>
      <tr>
```

```
 <td height=20></td>
</tr>
<tr>
 <td>
  <table border="0" cellspacing="0" cellpadding="5">
   <tr>
    <td>Emp Number :</td>
    <td><form:input path="empNumber" maxlength="10" /></td>
   </tr>

   <tr>
    <td>Emp Name :</td>
    <td><form:input path="empName" maxlength="50" /></td>
   </tr>

   <tr>
    <td>Designation :</td>
    <td><form:input path="designation" maxlength="100" /></td>
   </tr>

   <tr>
    <td>DOJ :</td>
    <td><form:input path="dateOfJoining" maxlength="10" />
       (dd-MM-yyyy)</td>
   </tr>

   <tr>
    <td>Basic Pay :</td>
    <td><form:input path="basicPay" maxlength="10" /></td>
   </tr>

   <tr>
    <td>Allowances :</td>
    <td><form:input path="allowances" maxlength="10" /></td>
   </tr>

   <tr>
    <td>Deductions :</td>
    <td><form:input path="deductions" maxlength="10" /></td>
   </tr>
  </table>
 </td>
```

```
      </tr>
      <tr>
       <td>
         <input value="Save" type="button" name="btnNew"
          onclick="callSave();">
       </td>
      </tr>
     </table>
    </td>
    <td width="20"> </td>
   </tr>
  </table>
 </form:form>
</body>
</html>
```

Store the following 'edit.jsp' under `/webapp/WEB-INF/jsp/Employee` directory.

```
<%@ include file="/WEB-INF/jsp/include.jsp"%>

<html>
<head>
<title>Edit Employee Record</title>

<script type="text/javascript">
 function callUpdate() {
  form.action = '/SpringDemoWeb/Employee/update.demo';
  form.submit();
 }
</script>

</head>

<body>
  <form:form name="form" action="" method="post" modelAttribute="employee">
  <form:hidden path="id"/>
  <br>
  <table border="0" cellspacing="0" cellpadding="0" width="100%">
   <tr>
    <td width="20"> </td>
    <td>
```

```
<table border="0" cellspacing="0" cellpadding="0" width="100%">
 <tr>
  <td height=50><h2>Edit Employee Record</h2></td>
 </tr>
 <tr>
  <td>
   <spring:hasBindErrors name="employee">
    <div class="errors">
     <ul>
      <c:forEach var="err" items="${errors.allErrors}">
       <li><c:out value="${err.defaultMessage}" /></li>
      </c:forEach>
     </ul>
    </div>
   </spring:hasBindErrors>
  </td>
 </tr>
 <tr>
  <td height=20></td>
 </tr>
 <tr>
  <td>
   <table border="0" cellspacing="0" cellpadding="5">
    <tr>
     <td>Emp Number :</td>
     <td>
      <form:input path="empNumber" maxlength="10" readonly="true" />
     </td>
    </tr>

    <tr>
     <td>Emp Name :</td>
     <td><form:input path="empName" maxlength="50" /></td>
    </tr>

    <tr>
     <td>Designation :</td>
     <td><form:input path="designation" maxlength="100" /></td>
    </tr>

    <tr>
     <td>DOJ :</td>
```

```
         <td><form:input path="dateOfJoining" maxlength="10" />
          (dd-MM-yyyy)</td>
        </tr>

        <tr>
         <td>Basic Pay :</td>
         <td><form:input path="basicPay" maxlength="10" /></td>
        </tr>

        <tr>
         <td>Allowances :</td>
         <td><form:input path="allowances" maxlength="10" /></td>
        </tr>

        <tr>
         <td>Deductions :</td>
         <td><form:input path="deductions" maxlength="10" /></td>
        </tr>
       </table>
      </td>
     </tr>
     <tr>
      <td>
        <input class="hand" onclick="callUpdate();" value="Update"
             type="button">   
        <input class="hand" value="Delete" type="button"
         onclick="javascript:
         if (confirm('Are you sure you want to delete this record?',
                  'Delete Employee')) {
           document.form.action='/SpringDemoWeb/Employee/delete.demo
           ?employeeId=${employee.id}'; document.form.submit(); }">
       </td>
     </tr>
    </table>
   </td>
   <td width="20"> </td>
  </tr>
 </table>
</form:form>
</body>
</html>
```

Compile and Package the Project: Compile and package this web project using Maven. As result, SpringDemoWeb.war file will be generated at the 'target' directory of the project. You can deploy this war file in any application server/Servlet container.

Before compile and package, import the required libraries (Internet connection is needed).

```
C:\Development\Install\eclipse-juno\workspace\SpringDemoWeb> mvn
                                                   eclipse:eclipse
[INFO] Scanning for projects...
[INFO]
[INFO] ------------------------------------------------------------
[INFO] Building SpringDemoWeb Maven Webapp 1.0-SNAPSHOT
[INFO] ------------------------------------------------------------
...
...
[INFO] Wrote Eclipse project for "SpringDemoWeb" to
C:\Development\Install\eclipse-juno\workspace\SpringDemoWeb.
[INFO]
[INFO] ------------------------------------------------------------
[INFO] BUILD SUCCESS
[INFO] ------------------------------------------------------------
[INFO] Total time: 5.953s
[INFO] Finished at: Sat May 11 19:33:10 SGT 2013
[INFO] Final Memory: 6M/15M
[INFO] ------------------------------------------------------------
```

Compile and package the project.

```
C:\Development\Install\eclipse-juno\workspace\SpringDemoWeb> mvn clean
                                                   compile package
[INFO] Scanning for projects...
[INFO]
[INFO] ------------------------------------------------------------
[INFO] Building SpringDemoWeb Maven Webapp 1.0-SNAPSHOT
[INFO] ------------------------------------------------------------
...
...
[INFO] Building war: C:\Development\Install\eclipse-
juno\workspace\SpringDemoWeb\target\SpringDemoWeb.war
[INFO] ------------------------------------------------------------
[INFO] BUILD SUCCESS
[INFO] ------------------------------------------------------------
```

Run the application: In our demonstration, Jetty Servlet container is used for the deployment of this web application and it is already configured in the pom.xml file.

```
C:\Development\Install\eclipse-juno\workspace\SpringDemoWeb>mvn
jetty:run
[INFO] Scanning for projects...
[INFO]
[INFO] ------------------------------------------------------------------------
[INFO] Building SpringDemoWeb Maven Webapp 1.0-SNAPSHOT
[INFO] ------------------------------------------------------------------------
INFO: HHH000400: Using dialect: org.hibernate.dialect.MySQLDialect
INFO: Loading XML bean definitions from ServletContext resource [/WEB-
INF/SpringDemoWeb-servlet.xml]
INFO: Loading properties file from ServletContext resource [/WEB-INF/
jdbc.properties]
Hibernate: drop table if exists EMPLOYEE
Hibernate: create table EMPLOYEE (ID varchar(32) not null, ALLOWANCES
double precision, BASIC_PAY double precision not null, DOJ date, DEDUCTIONS
double precision, DESIGNATION varchar(100), EMP_NAME varchar(50) not
null, EMP_NUMBER var
INFO: Mapped URL path [/displayname] onto handler 'displayNameController'
INFO: Mapped URL path [/displayname.*] onto handler
'displayNameController'
INFO: Mapped URL path [/displayname/] onto handler 'displayNameController'
INFO: Root mapping to handler 'displayNameController'
INFO: Mapped URL path [/Employee/edit.demo] onto handler
'employeeController'
INFO: Mapped URL path [/Employee/list.demo] onto handler
'employeeController'
INFO: Mapped URL path [/Employee/save.demo] onto handler
'employeeController'
INFO: Mapped URL path [/Employee/delete.demo] onto handler
'employeeController'
INFO: Mapped URL path [/Employee/create.demo] onto handler
'employeeController'
INFO: Mapped URL path [/Employee/update.demo] onto handler
'employeeController'
[INFO] Started Jetty Server
```

Check with MySQL database 'demodb' that a table named 'EMPLOYEE' is created with the specified columns. It is performed through ORM.

```
mysql> show tables;
+-------------------+
| Tables_in_demodb  |
+-------------------+
| employee          |
+-------------------+
1 row in set (0.00 sec)
```

```
mysql> desc employee;
+-------------+--------------+------+-----+---------+-------+
| Field       | Type         | Null | Key | Default | Extra |
+-------------+--------------+------+-----+---------+-------+
| ID          | varchar(32)  | NO   | PRI | NULL    |       |
| ALLOWANCES  | double       | YES  |     | NULL    |       |
| BASIC_PAY   | double       | NO   |     | NULL    |       |
| DOJ         | date         | YES  |     | NULL    |       |
| DEDUCTIONS  | double       | YES  |     | NULL    |       |
| DESIGNATION | varchar(100) | YES  |     | NULL    |       |
| EMP_NAME    | varchar(50)  | NO   |     | NULL    |       |
| EMP_NUMBER  | varchar(10)  | NO   |     | NULL    |       |
| NET_PAY     | double       | YES  |     | NULL    |       |
+-------------+--------------+------+-----+---------+-------+
9 rows in set (0.00 sec)
```

Access the Web Application: Access our deployed web application through the URL: http://localhost:8080/SpringDemoWeb/Employee/list.demo

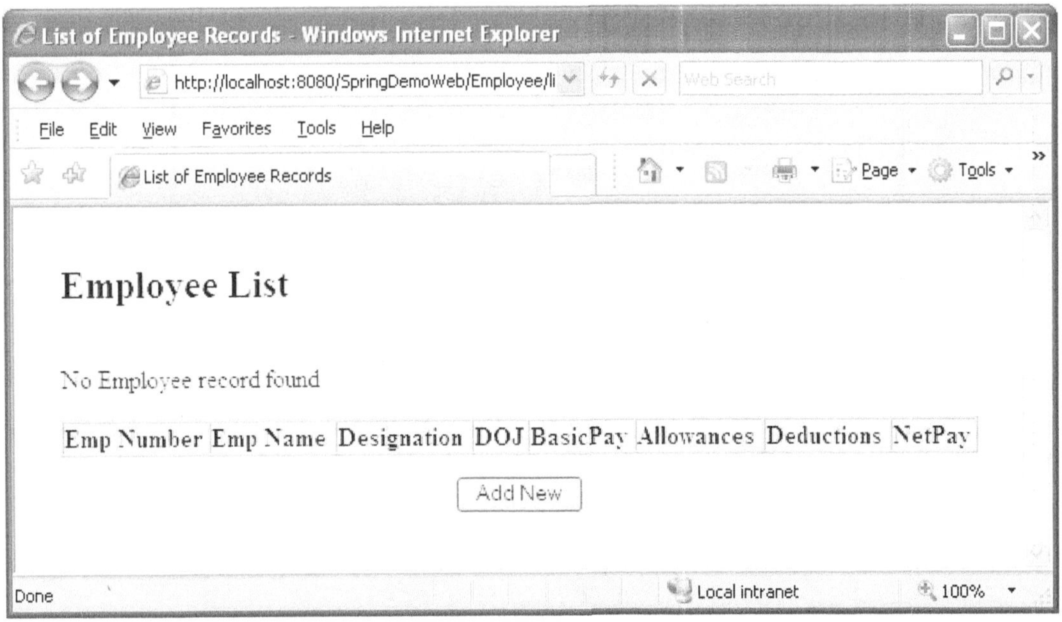

Add a Employee Record by clicking on 'Add New' button.

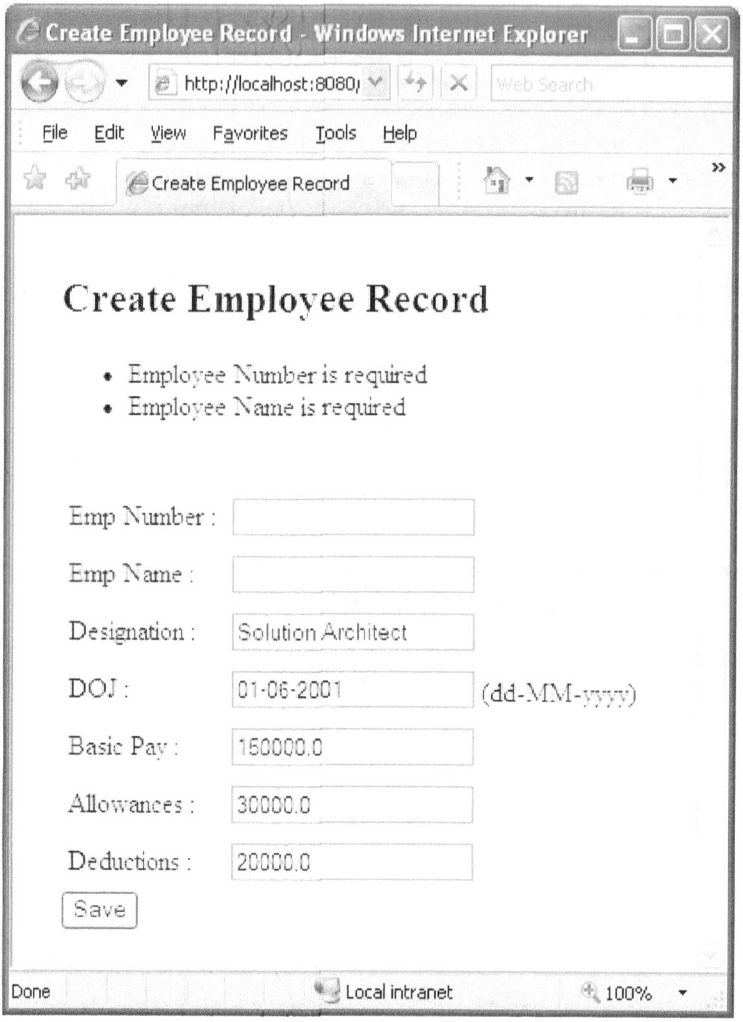

If no entry is made for Emp Number / Emp Name, then error message will be displayed.

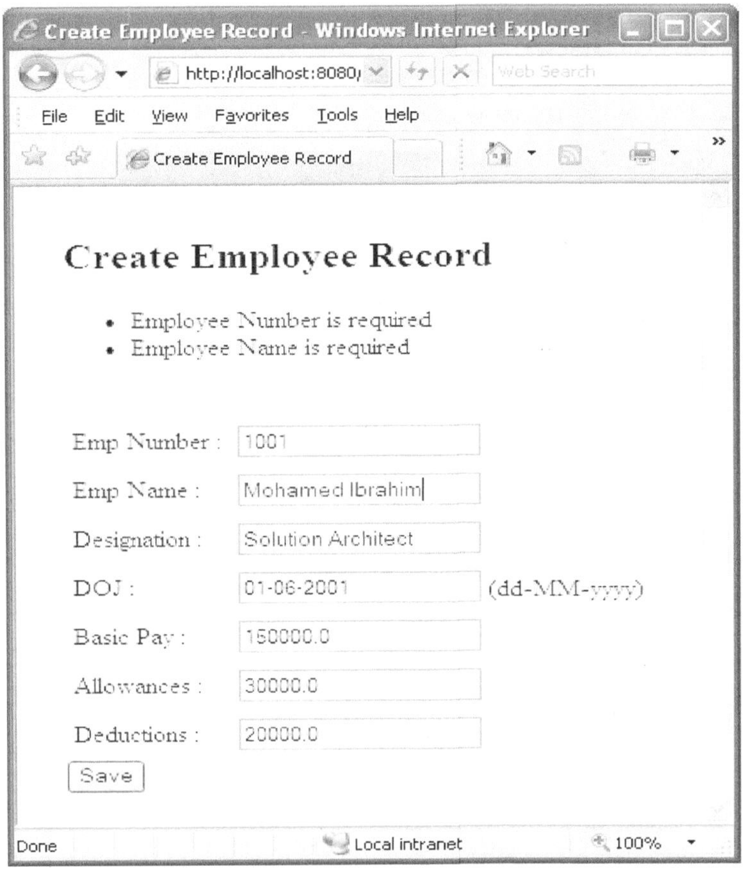

Click on 'Save'.

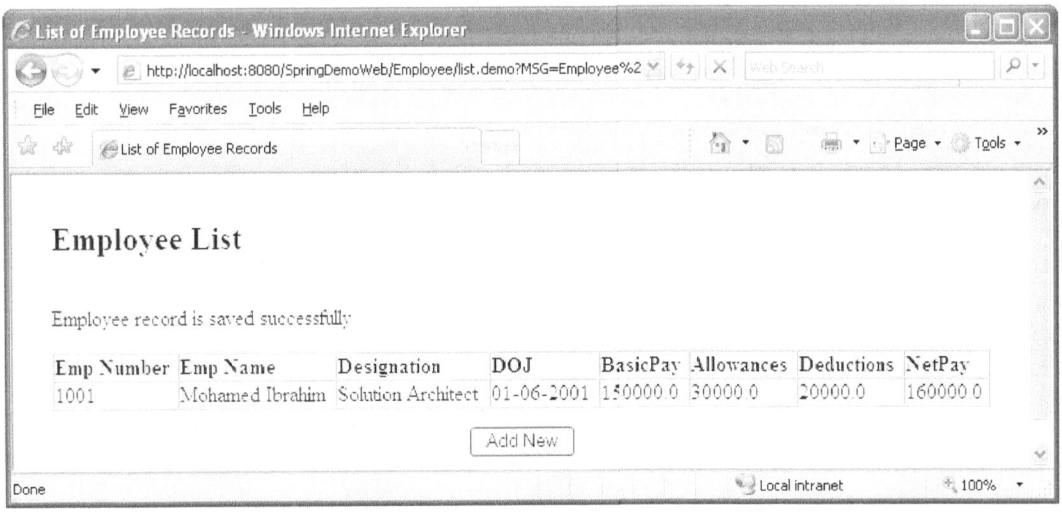

You can add many Employee records, and you can edit a record by clicking on any row in the list. In this screen, either you can update the record or delete the record.

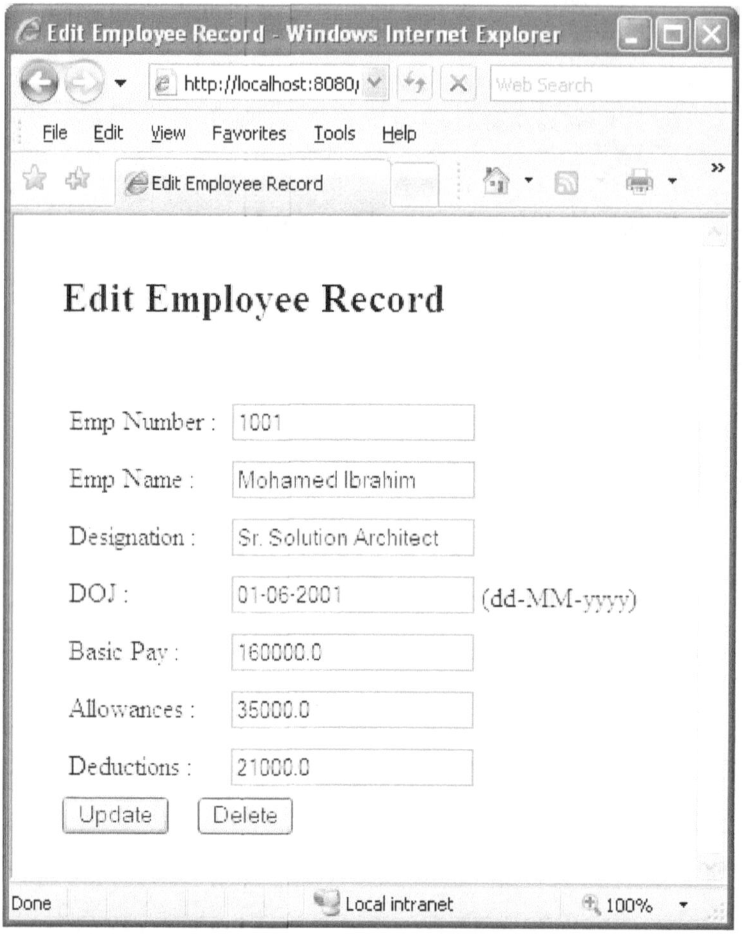
Edit Employee Record - Windows Internet Explorer
http://localhost:8080/
Web Search
File Edit View Favorites Tools Help
Edit Employee Record
Edit Employee Record
Emp Number : 1001
Emp Name : Mohamed Ibrahim
Designation : Sr. Solution Architect
DOJ : 01-06-2001 (dd-MM-yyyy)
Basic Pay : 160000.0
Allowances : 35000.0
Deductions : 21000.0
Update
Delete
Done
Local intranet
100%

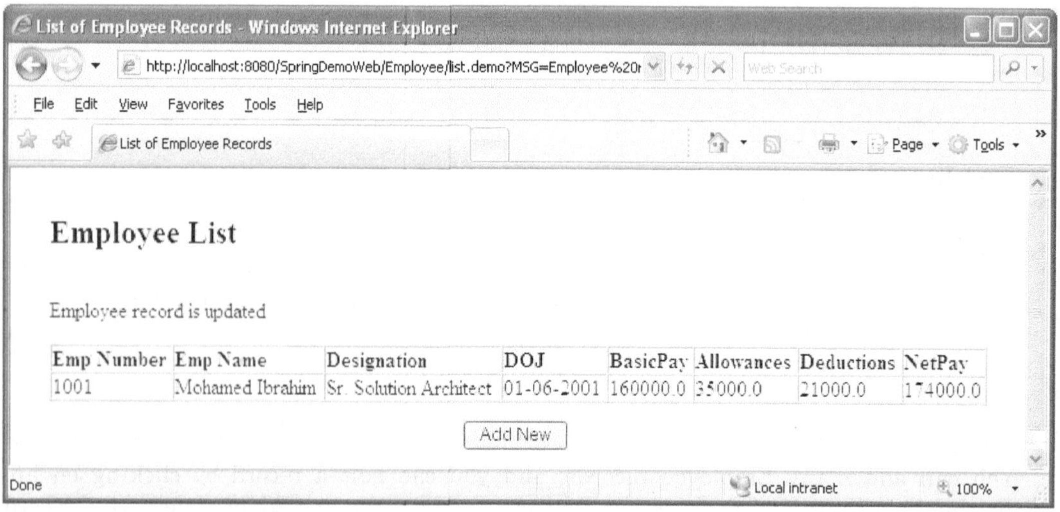
List of Employee Records - Windows Internet Explorer
http://localhost:8080/SpringDemoWeb/Employee/list.demo?MSG=Employee%20r
Web Search
File Edit View Favorites Tools Help
List of Employee Records
Page Tools
Employee List
Employee record is updated
Emp Number Emp Name Designation DOJ BasicPay Allowances Deductions NetPay
1001 Mohamed Ibrahim Sr. Solution Architect 01-06-2001 160000.0 35000.0 21000.0 174000.0
Add New
Done
Local intranet
100%

11.14.3 File Upload Application

This application uploads the choosen file to the server where this web application is running. The uploaded files will be stored in the local directory of the server. Follow the same configuration and execution procedure of the above web applciations.

web.xml

```
<web-app xmlns="http://java.sun.com/xml/ns/javaee"
       xmlns:xsi="http://www.w3.org/2001/XMLSchema-instance"
     xsi:schemaLocation="http://java.sun.com/xml/ns/javaee
     http://java.sun.com/xml/ns/javaee/web-app_2_5.xsd"
    version="2.5">

 <display-name>Spring Demo Web Application</display-name>

 <servlet>
  <servlet-name>SpringDemoWeb</servlet-name>
  <servlet-class>
    org.springframework.web.servlet.DispatcherServlet
  </servlet-class>
  <load-on-startup>1</load-on-startup>
 </servlet>

 <servlet-mapping>
  <servlet-name>SpringDemoWeb</servlet-name>
  <url-pattern>/</url-pattern>
 </servlet-mapping>

 <context-param>
  <param-name>contextConfigLocation</param-name>
  <param-value>/WEB-INF/SpringDemoWeb-servlet.xml</param-value>
 </context-param>

 <listener>
  <listener-class>
    org.springframework.web.context.ContextLoaderListener
  </listener-class>
 </listener>
</web-app>
```

pom.xml

```
<project xmlns="http://maven.apache.org/POM/4.0.0"
         xmlns:xsi="http://www.w3.org/2001/XMLSchema-instance"
         xsi:schemaLocation="http://maven.apache.org/POM/4.0.0
         http://maven.apache.org/maven-v4_0_0.xsd">
```

```
<modelVersion>4.0.0</modelVersion>
<groupId>SpringDemo</groupId>
<artifactId>SpringDemoWeb</artifactId>
<packaging>war</packaging>
<version>1.0-SNAPSHOT</version>
<name>SpringDemoWeb Maven Webapp</name>

<properties>
 <spring.version>3.2.2.RELEASE</spring.version>
 <junit.version>4.11</junit.version>
 <jdk.version>1.6</jdk.version>
</properties>

<dependencies>
 <dependency>
  <groupId>org.springframework</groupId>
  <artifactId>spring-core</artifactId>
  <version>${spring.version}</version>
 </dependency>

 <dependency>
  <groupId>org.springframework</groupId>
  <artifactId>spring-web</artifactId>
  <version>${spring.version}</version>
 </dependency>

 <dependency>
  <groupId>org.springframework</groupId>
  <artifactId>spring-webmvc</artifactId>
  <version>${spring.version}</version>
 </dependency>

 <dependency>
  <groupId>taglibs</groupId>
  <artifactId>standard</artifactId>
  <version>1.1.2</version>
 </dependency>

 <dependency>
  <groupId>commons-fileupload</groupId>
  <artifactId>commons-fileupload</artifactId>
  <version>1.3</version>
 </dependency>
```

```
    <dependency>
     <groupId>org.apache.commons</groupId>
     <artifactId>commons-io</artifactId>
     <version>2.4</version>
    </dependency>
  </dependencies>

  <build>
    <finalName>SpringDemoWeb</finalName>
    <plugins>
     <plugin>
      <groupId>org.apache.maven.plugins</groupId>
      <artifactId>maven-compiler-plugin</artifactId>
      <version>3.0</version>
      <configuration>
       <source>${jdk.version}</source>
       <target>${jdk.version}</target>
      </configuration>
     </plugin>

     <plugin>
      <groupId>org.mortbay.jetty</groupId>
      <artifactId>maven-jetty-plugin</artifactId>
      <version>6.1.26</version>
      <configuration>
       <scanIntervalSeconds>10</scanIntervalSeconds>
       <connectors>
        <connector implementation=
               "org.mortbay.jetty.nio.SelectChannelConnector">
         <port>8080</port>
        </connector>
       </connectors>
      </configuration>
     </plugin>
    </plugins>
  </build>
</project>
```

SpringDemoWeb-servlet.xml

```
<?xml  version="1.0" encoding="UTF-8"?>
<beans xmlns="http://www.springframework.org/schema/beans"
       xmlns:xsi="http://www.w3.org/2001/XMLSchema-instance"
```

```
        xmlns:tx="http://www.springframework.org/schema/tx"
        xmlns:p="http://www.springframework.org/schema/p"
        xmlns:context="http://www.springframework.org/schema/context"
       xsi:schemaLocation="http://www.springframework.org/schema/beans
       http://www.springframework.org/schema/beans/spring-beans-3.1.xsd
        http://www.springframework.org/schema/context
       http://www.springframework.org/schema/context/spring-context-
       3.0.xsd
        http://www.springframework.org/schema/tx
        http://www.springframework.org/schema/tx/spring-tx-3.1.xsd">

  <context:annotation-config />
  <context:component-scan base-package="com.springdemo" />

  <bean
  class="org.springframework.web.servlet.view.InternalResourceViewResolver"
   p:prefix="/WEB-INF/jsp/" p:suffix=".jsp" />

 <bean id="multipartResolver"
 class="org.springframework.web.multipart.commons.CommonsMultipartResolver"
 />

 </beans>
```

Java Files:

Create necessary packages to place the following Java files.

```
//FileName: FileUpload.java
package com.springdemo.valueobject;

import java.util.List;

import org.springframework.web.multipart.MultipartFile;

public class FileUpload {

 private List<MultipartFile> files;

 public FileUpload() {
 }
```

```
 public List<MultipartFile> getFiles() {
  return files;
 }

 public void setFiles(List<MultipartFile> files) {
  this.files = files;
 }

}
```

```
//FileName: FileUploadValidator.java
package com.springdemo.validator;

import java.util.Arrays;
import java.util.List;

import org.springframework.validation.Errors;
import org.springframework.validation.Validator;
import org.springframework.web.multipart.MultipartFile;

import com.springdemo.valueobject.FileUpload;

public class FileUploadValidator implements Validator {

 private String allowedFileTypes[] = { "txt", "doc", "pdf",
                                        "jpg", "jpeg", "png" };

 @Override
 public boolean supports(Class<?> clazz) {
  return FileUploadValidator.class.equals(clazz);
 }

 public void validate(Object obj, Errors errors) {
  FileUpload fileUpload = (FileUpload) obj;
  List<MultipartFile> files = fileUpload.getFiles();

  if (files != null && files.size() > 0) {
   for (MultipartFile multipartFile : files) {
    String fileName = multipartFile.getOriginalFilename();
```

```
    if (fileName.length() == 0) {
     //Write logic for mandatory files
     continue;
    }
    int fileTypeExtensionIndex = fileName.lastIndexOf('.');
    if ((fileTypeExtensionIndex != -1) &&
      (fileName.length() > (fileTypeExtensionIndex + 1))) {
     String fileNameExtension =
           fileName.substring(fileTypeExtensionIndex + 1);

    if (!Arrays.asList(allowedFileTypes)
            .contains(fileNameExtension.toLowerCase())) {
      errors.reject("error.upload", "The file type ["
               + fileNameExtension + "] is not supported for upload");
     }

     if (multipartFile.getSize() == 0) {
      errors.reject("error.upload", "The empty file ["
               + fileName + "] is not supported for upload");
     }

     if (multipartFile.getSize() > 1048576) {
      errors.reject("error.upload", "The file [" + fileName
            + "] exceeds 1 MB size. File size should be within 1 MB");
     }
    }
    else {
     errors.reject("error.upload", "The file name without extension ["
               + fileName + "] is not supported for upload");
    }
   }
  }
 }
}
```

```
//FileName: FileUploadController.java
package com.springdemo.controller;

import java.io.File;
import java.util.ArrayList;
import java.util.List;
```

```
import org.springframework.stereotype.Controller;
import org.springframework.ui.ModelMap;
import org.springframework.validation.BindingResult;
import org.springframework.web.bind.annotation.ModelAttribute;
import org.springframework.web.bind.annotation.RequestMapping;
import org.springframework.web.bind.annotation.RequestMethod;
import org.springframework.web.multipart.MultipartFile;

import com.springdemo.validator.FileUploadValidator;
import com.springdemo.valueobject.FileUpload;

@Controller
public class FileUploadController {
 @RequestMapping(value = "/input", method = RequestMethod.GET)
 public String displayForm() {
  return "FileUpload/input";
 }

 @RequestMapping(value = "/upload", method = RequestMethod.POST)
 public String save(@ModelAttribute("fileUpload") FileUpload fileUpload,
                BindingResult result, ModelMap modelMap) {

  new FileUploadValidator().validate(fileUpload, result);
  if (result.hasErrors()) {
   return "FileUpload/input";
  }

  String MSG = "";
  List<MultipartFile> files = fileUpload.getFiles();
  List<String> uploadedFileNames = new ArrayList<String>();

  for (MultipartFile multipartFile : files) {
   String fileName = multipartFile.getOriginalFilename();
   if (fileName.length() == 0)
    continue;
   try {
     multipartFile.transferTo(new File("C:/UPLOADED_FILES/"
                   + multipartFile.getOriginalFilename()));
    uploadedFileNames.add(fileName);
   }
```

```
    catch (Exception e) {
     MSG = "Error occurred while uploading file [" + fileName + "]";
     e.printStackTrace();
    }
   }

   modelMap.addAttribute("uploadedFiles", uploadedFileNames);
   modelMap.addAttribute("MSG", MSG);
   return "FileUpload/uploadsuccess";
  }
 }
```

JSP Files:

Store the following JSP files under /webapp/WEB-INF/jsp/FileUpload/ directory of this SpringDemoWeb project.

File Name: /webapp/WEB-INF/jsp/FileUpload/input.jsp

```
<%@ include file="/WEB-INF/jsp/include.jsp"%>

<html>
<head>
<title>File Upload Input Form</title>
</head>

<body>
<form:form method="post" action="/SpringDemoWeb/upload"
        modelAttribute="fileUpload" enctype="multipart/form-data">
  <br>
  <table border="0" cellspacing="0" cellpadding="0" width="100%">
   <tr>
    <td width="20"> </td>
    <td>
     <table border="0" cellspacing="0" cellpadding="0" width="100%">
      <tr>
       <td height=50><h2>Upload Files</h2></td>
      </tr>
      <tr>
       <td>
        <spring:hasBindErrors name="fileUpload">
         <div class="errors">
          <ul>
```

```
            <c:forEach var="err" items="${errors.allErrors}">
             <li><c:out value="${err.defaultMessage}" /></li>
            </c:forEach>
           </ul>
          </div>
         </spring:hasBindErrors>
        </td>
       </tr>
       <tr>
        <td height=20></td>
       </tr>
       <tr>
        <td>
         <table border="0" cellspacing="0" cellpadding="5">
         <tr>
          <td>File 1 :</td>
          <td><input type="file" name="files[0]" size="50" /></td>
         </tr>

         <tr>
          <td>File 2 :</td>
          <td><input type="file" name="files[1]" size="50" /></td>
         </tr>

         <tr>
          <td>File 3 :</td>
          <td><input type="file" name="files[2]" size="50" /></td>
         </tr>
        </table>
        </td>
       </tr>
       <tr>
        <td><input value="Upload" type="submit"></td>
       </tr>
      </table>
     </td>
     <td width="20"> </td>
    </tr>
   </table>
  </form:form>
 </body>
</html>
```

File Name: /webapp/WEB-INF/jsp/FileUpload/uploadsuccess.jsp

```
<%@ include file="/WEB-INF/jsp/include.jsp"%>

<html>
<head>
<title>File Upload Result</title>
</head>

<body>
 <br>
 <table border="0" cellspacing="0" cellpadding="0" width="100%">
  <tr>
   <td width="20"> </td>
   <td>
    <table border="0" cellspacing="0" cellpadding="0" width="100%">
     <tr>
      <td height=50><h2>Upload Files</h2></td>
     </tr>
     <tr>
      <td>${MSG}</td>
     </tr>
     <tr>
      <td height=20></td>
     </tr>
     <tr>
      <td>
       The uploaded files are:
       <ol>
        <c:forEach var="file" items="${uploadedFiles}">
         <li>${file}</li>
        </c:forEach>
       </ol>
      </td>
     </tr>
    </table>
   </td>
   <td width="20"> </td>
  </tr>
 </table>
</body>
</html>
```

Run the Application: Use the following Maven commands in the DOS command prompt of the SpringDemoWeb directory.

```
mvn eclipse:eclipse
mvn clean compile package install
```

Invoke the browser with the URL: `http://localhost:8080/SpringDemoWeb/input`

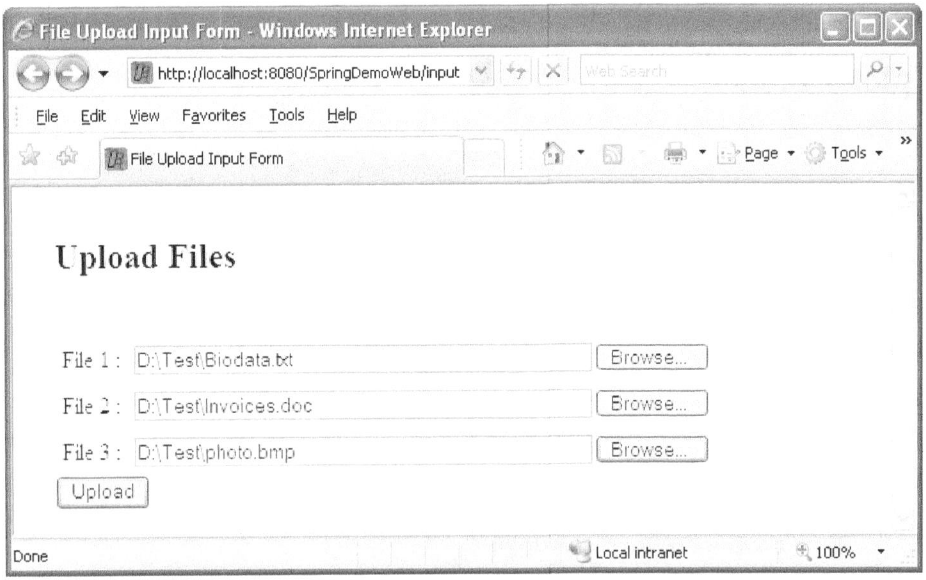

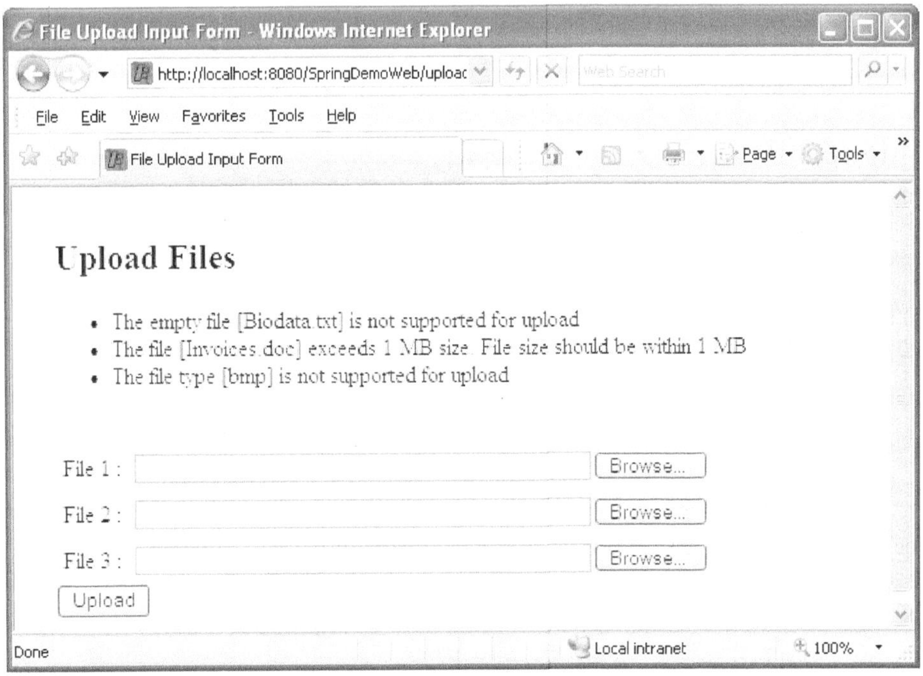

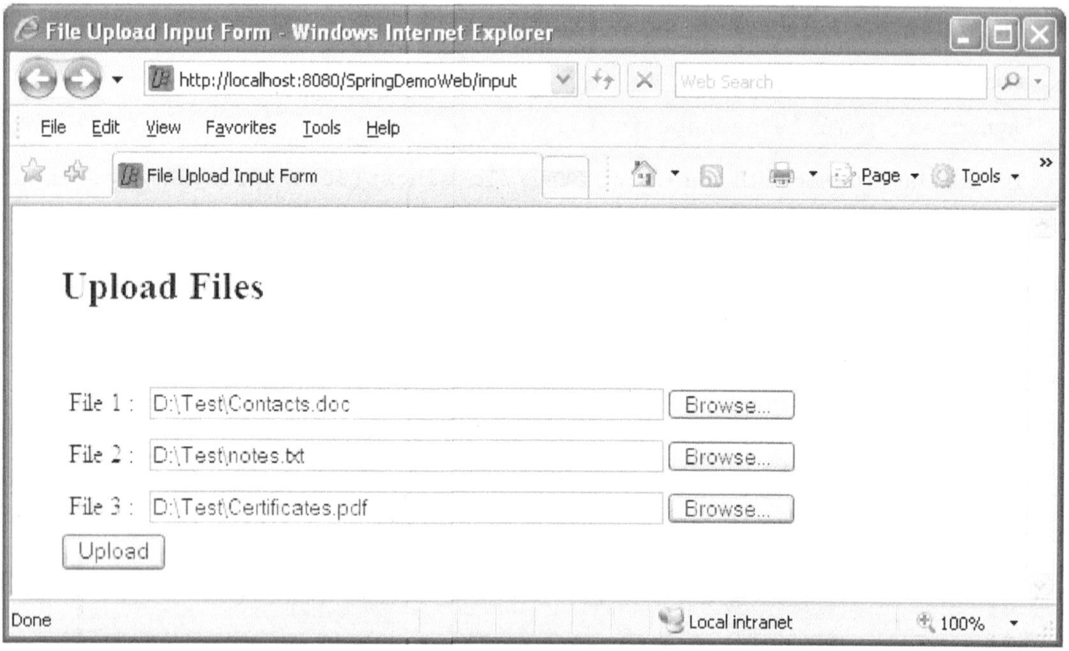

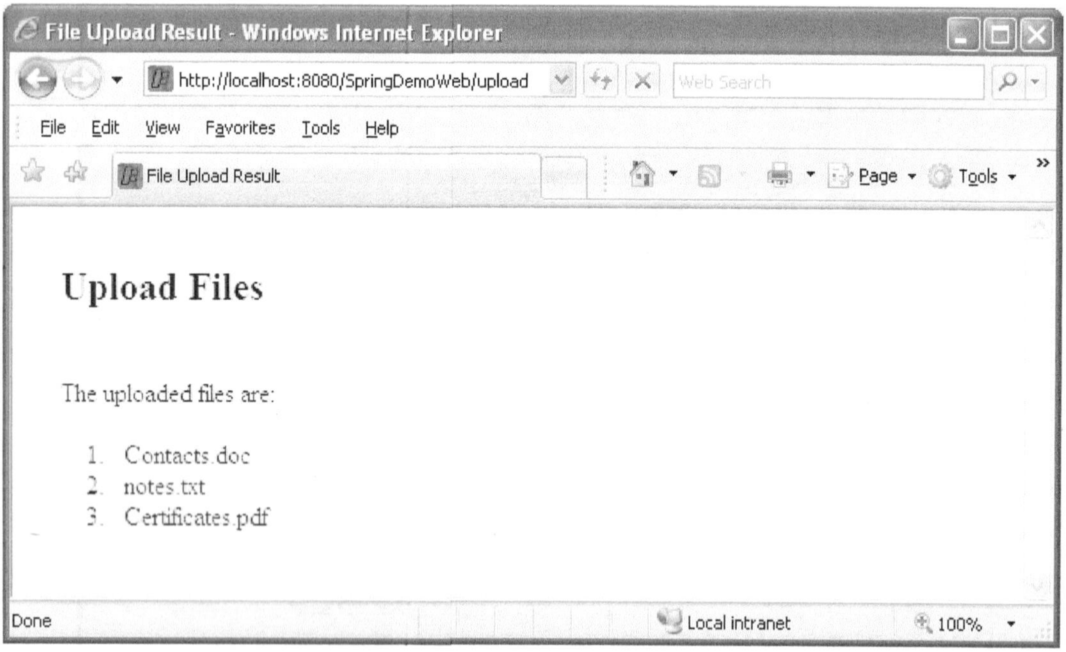

Check the files under `C:\UPLOADED_FILES` folder.

11.14.4 Web Application using Apache Tiles for Layout Templates

Apache Tiles is a templatimg framework, simplifies the development of user interface design of web applciations. A Tile is a reusable markup fragment which can be assembled to develop the user interfaces of an web applciation. In this demonstation application, Apache Tiles 3 is used. Follow the previous project for configuration and running the applciation; only important files are given below for reference.

This applciation is given to illustate how to use Apache Tiles with Spring Framework. The complete logic for login and CRUD operations of records are not implemented. Readers are advided to refer previous examples to do the required code implementations.

pom.xml

Store it on the root of the project (under SpringDemoWeb)

```
<project xmlns="http://maven.apache.org/POM/4.0.0"
        xmlns:xsi="http://www.w3.org/2001/XMLSchema-instance"
        xsi:schemaLocation="http://maven.apache.org/POM/4.0.0
        http://maven.apache.org/maven-v4_0_0.xsd">
  <modelVersion>4.0.0</modelVersion>
  <groupId>SpringDemo</groupId>
  <artifactId>SpringDemoWeb</artifactId>
  <packaging>war</packaging>
  <version>1.0-SNAPSHOT</version>
  <name>SpringDemoWeb Maven Webapp</name>

  <properties>
   <spring.version>3.2.2.RELEASE</spring.version>
   <junit.version>4.11</junit.version>
   <jdk.version>1.6</jdk.version>
   <tiles.version>3.0.1</tiles.version>
  </properties>

  <dependencies>
   <dependency>
    <groupId>org.springframework</groupId>
    <artifactId>spring-core</artifactId>
    <version>${spring.version}</version>
   </dependency>

   <dependency>
    <groupId>org.springframework</groupId>
    <artifactId>spring-web</artifactId>
    <version>${spring.version}</version>
   </dependency>
```

```
<dependency>
  <groupId>org.springframework</groupId>
  <artifactId>spring-webmvc</artifactId>
  <version>${spring.version}</version>
</dependency>

<dependency>
  <groupId>taglibs</groupId>
  <artifactId>standard</artifactId>
  <version>1.1.2</version>
</dependency>

<dependency>
  <groupId>javax.servlet.jsp.jstl</groupId>
  <artifactId>javax.servlet.jsp.jstl-api</artifactId>
  <version>1.2.1</version>
</dependency>

<dependency>
  <groupId>org.apache.tiles</groupId>
  <artifactId>tiles-request-api</artifactId>
  <version>1.0.1</version>
</dependency>

<dependency>
  <groupId>org.apache.tiles</groupId>
  <artifactId>tiles-request-jsp</artifactId>
  <version>1.0.1</version>
</dependency>

<dependency>
  <groupId>org.apache.tiles</groupId>
  <artifactId>tiles-servlet</artifactId>
  <version>3.0.1</version>
</dependency>

<dependency>
  <groupId>org.apache.tiles</groupId>
  <artifactId>tiles-template</artifactId>
  <version>3.0.1</version>
</dependency>
```

```
<dependency>
 <groupId>org.apache.tiles</groupId>
 <artifactId>tiles-api</artifactId>
 <version>${tiles.version}</version>
</dependency>

<dependency>
 <groupId>org.apache.tiles</groupId>
 <artifactId>tiles-core</artifactId>
 <version>${tiles.version}</version>
</dependency>

<dependency>
 <groupId>org.apache.tiles</groupId>
 <artifactId>tiles-jsp</artifactId>
 <version>${tiles.version}</version>
</dependency>

<dependency>
 <groupId>org.apache.tiles</groupId>
 <artifactId>tiles-servlet</artifactId>
 <version>${tiles.version}</version>
</dependency>

<dependency>
 <groupId>org.apache.tiles</groupId>
 <artifactId>tiles-template</artifactId>
 <version>${tiles.version}</version>
</dependency>

<dependency>
 <groupId>org.apache.tiles</groupId>
 <artifactId>tiles-extras</artifactId>
 <version>${tiles.version}</version>
</dependency>

<dependency>
 <groupId>org.apache.tiles</groupId>
 <artifactId>tiles-autotag-core-runtime</artifactId>
 <version>1.1.0</version>
</dependency>
```

```
    <dependency>
     <groupId>commons-logging</groupId>
     <artifactId>commons-logging</artifactId>
     <version>1.1.1</version>
    </dependency>

    <dependency>
     <groupId>commons-beanutils</groupId>
     <artifactId>commons-beanutils</artifactId>
     <version>1.8.0</version>
    </dependency>

    <dependency>
     <groupId>log4j</groupId>
     <artifactId>log4j</artifactId>
     <version>1.2.17</version>
    </dependency>

    <dependency>
     <groupId>commons-digester</groupId>
     <artifactId>commons-digester</artifactId>
     <version>2.0</version>
    </dependency>

    <dependency>
     <groupId>org.slf4j</groupId>
     <artifactId>slf4j-api</artifactId>
     <version>1.7.2</version>
    </dependency>

    <dependency>
     <groupId>org.slf4j</groupId>
     <artifactId>slf4j-simple</artifactId>
     <version>1.7.2</version>
    </dependency>

   </dependencies>

  <build>
   <finalName>SpringDemoWeb</finalName>
   <plugins>
```

```
  <plugin>
   <groupId>org.apache.maven.plugins</groupId>
   <artifactId>maven-compiler-plugin</artifactId>
   <version>3.0</version>
   <configuration>
    <source>${jdk.version}</source>
    <target>${jdk.version}</target>
   </configuration>
  </plugin>

  <plugin>
   <groupId>org.mortbay.jetty</groupId>
   <artifactId>maven-jetty-plugin</artifactId>
   <version>6.1.26</version>
   <configuration>
    <scanIntervalSeconds>10</scanIntervalSeconds>
    <connectors>
     <connector implementation=
              "org.mortbay.jetty.nio.SelectChannelConnector">
      <port>8080</port>
     </connector>
    </connectors>
   </configuration>
  </plugin>
 </plugins>
 </build>
</project>
```

---

web.xml

Store this web configuration file uder SpringWebDemo/src/main/webapp/WEB-INF

```
<web-app xmlns:xsi="http://www.w3.org/2001/XMLSchema-instance"
       xmlns="http://java.sun.com/xml/ns/javaee"
       xmlns:web="http://java.sun.com/xml/ns/javaee/web-app_2_5.xsd"
       xsi:schemaLocation="http://java.sun.com/xml/ns/javaee
       http://java.sun.com/xml/ns/javaee/web-app_3_0.xsd"
       id="WebApp_ID" version="3.0">

 <display-name>Spring Demo Web Application</display-name>
```

```
  <servlet>
   <servlet-name>SpringDemoWeb</servlet-name>
   <servlet-class>
     org.springframework.web.servlet.DispatcherServlet
   </servlet-class>
   <load-on-startup>1</load-on-startup>
  </servlet>

  <servlet-mapping>
   <servlet-name>SpringDemoWeb</servlet-name>
   <url-pattern>/</url-pattern>
  </servlet-mapping>

  <context-param>
   <param-name>contextConfigLocation</param-name>
   <param-value>/WEB-INF/SpringDemoWeb-servlet.xml</param-value>
  </context-param>

  <listener>
   <listener-class>
     org.springframework.web.context.ContextLoaderListener
   </listener-class>
  </listener>
</web-app>
```

Spring Configuration File:

Store the Spring Configuration file (SpringDemoWeb-servlet.xml) under `SpringWebDemo/src/main/webapp/WEB-INF`.

```
<?xml version="1.0" encoding="UTF-8"?>
<beans xmlns="http://www.springframework.org/schema/beans"
      xmlns:xsi="http://www.w3.org/2001/XMLSchema-instance"
      xmlns:p="http://www.springframework.org/schema/p"
      xmlns:context="http://www.springframework.org/schema/context"
      xmlns:mvc="http://www.springframework.org/schema/mvc"
     xsi:schemaLocation="http://www.springframework.org/schema/beans
    http : //www.springframework.org/schema/beans/spring-beans-3.0.xsd
    http : //www.springframework.org/schema/context
    http : //www.springframework.org/schema/context/spring-context-
    3.0.xsd
      http://www.springframework.org/schema/mvc
      http://www.springframework.org/schema/mvc/spring-mvc-3.0.xsd">
```

```
<context:annotation-config />
<context:component-scan base-package="com.springdemo" />
<mvc:annotation-driven />

<bean id="tilesviewResolver"
  class="org.springframework.web.servlet.view.tiles3.TilesViewResolver"
  p:order="0" />

<bean id="tilesConfigurer"
  class="org.springframework.web.servlet.view.tiles3.TilesConfigurer">
 <property name="definitions">
  <list>
   <value>/WEB-INF/tiles.xml</value>
  </list>
 </property>
</bean>
</beans>
```

Tiles Configuration:

Store the following "tiles.xml" which is specified in Spring Configuration, under `SpringWebDemo/src/main/webapp/WEB-INF`.

```
<?xml version="1.0" encoding="UTF-8"?>

<!DOCTYPE tiles-definitions PUBLIC
    "-//Apache Software Foundation//DTD Tiles Configuration 3.0//EN"
    "http://tiles.apache.org/dtds/tiles-config_3_0.dtd">
<tiles-definitions>

 <definition name="baseLayout"
          template="/WEB-INF/jsp/layout/baseLayout.jsp">
  <put-attribute name="title" value="Employee Payroll Management System" />
  <put-attribute name="header" value="/WEB-INF/jsp/header.jsp" />
  <put-attribute name="menu" value="/WEB-INF/jsp/menu.jsp" />
  <put-attribute name="body" value="" />
  <put-attribute name="footer" value="/WEB-INF/jsp/footer.jsp" />
 </definition>

 <definition name="loginLayout"
          template="/WEB-INF/jsp/layout/loginLayout.jsp">
```

```
  <put-attribute name="title" value="Login" />
  <put-attribute name="header" value="/WEB-INF/jsp/header.jsp" />
  <put-attribute name="body" value="" />
  <put-attribute name="footer" value="/WEB-INF/jsp/footer.jsp" />
 </definition>

 <definition name="login" extends="loginLayout">
  <put-attribute name="body" value="/WEB-INF/jsp/login.jsp" />
 </definition>

 <definition name="main" extends="baseLayout">
  <put-attribute name="body" value="/WEB-INF/jsp/welcome.jsp" />
 </definition>

 <definition name="create" extends="baseLayout">
  <put-attribute name="body" value="/WEB-INF/jsp/create.jsp" />
 </definition>

 <definition name="edit" extends="baseLayout">
  <put-attribute name="body" value="/WEB-INF/jsp/edit.jsp" />
 </definition>

 <definition name="list" extends="baseLayout">
  <put-attribute name="body" value="/WEB-INF/jsp/list.jsp" />
 </definition>

</tiles-definitions>
```

Java Files:

Create necessary packages to store the following Java source files.

```
//FileName: Employee.java
package com.springdemo.entity;

import java.util.UUID;

public class Employee {

 private String id;
 private String empNumber;
 private String empName;
 private double salary;

 public Employee() {
 }
```

```
public Employee(String empNumber, String empName, double salary) {
 id = UUID.randomUUID().toString();
 this.empNumber = empNumber;
 this.empName = empName;
 this.salary = salary;
}

public String getId() {
 return id;
}

public void setId(String id) {
 this.id = id;
}

public String getEmpNumber() {
 return empNumber;
}

public void setEmpNumber(String empNumber) {
 this.empNumber = empNumber;
}

public String getEmpName() {
 return empName;
}

public void setEmpName(String empName) {
 this.empName = empName;
}

public double getSalary() {
 return salary;
}

public void setSalary(double salary) {
 this.salary = salary;
}

}
```

```
//FileName: EmployeeValidator.java
package com.springdemo.validator;

import org.springframework.validation.Errors;
import org.springframework.validation.ValidationUtils;
import org.springframework.validation.Validator;

import com.springdemo.entity.Employee;

public class EmployeeValidator implements Validator {

 public void validate(Object object, Errors errors) {
  ValidationUtils.rejectIfEmptyOrWhitespace(errors, "empNumber",
          "empNumber.required", "Employee Number is required");

  ValidationUtils.rejectIfEmptyOrWhitespace(errors, "empName",
          "empName.required", "Employee Name is required");

  ValidationUtils.rejectIfEmptyOrWhitespace(errors, "salary",
          "salary.required", "Salary is required");
 }

 @SuppressWarnings("rawtypes")
 public boolean supports(Class clazz) {
  return Employee.class.isAssignableFrom(clazz);
 }
}
```

```
//FileName: EmployeeData.java
package com.springdemo.controller;

import java.util.ArrayList;
import java.util.List;

import com.springdemo.entity.Employee;

public class EmployeeData {
  static List<Employee> employeeList = new ArrayList<Employee>();
}
```

```
//FileName: LoginController.java
package com.springdemo.controller;

import org.springframework.stereotype.Controller;
import org.springframework.web.bind.annotation.RequestMapping;
import org.springframework.web.bind.annotation.RequestParam;
import org.springframework.web.context.request.WebRequest;

@Controller
public class LoginController {

 @RequestMapping("/login")
 public String login() {
  return "login";
 }

 @RequestMapping("/doLogin")
 public String doLogin(
   @RequestParam(value = "loginId", defaultValue = "") String loginId,
   @RequestParam(value = "password", defaultValue = "") String password,
   WebRequest request) {

  // Write you code for login operation
  if ((loginId.length() == 0) || (password.length() == 0)) {
  request.setAttribute("MSG", "Please enter both Login Id and Password",
                  WebRequest.SCOPE_REQUEST);
   return "login";
  }

  return "main";
 }

 @RequestMapping("/logout")
 public String logout(WebRequest request) {
  // Write your code for logout operation
  request.setAttribute("MSG", "Logged out successfully",
                  WebRequest.SCOPE_REQUEST);
  return "login";
 }
}
```

```
//FileName: EmployeeController.java
package com.springdemo.controller;

import java.util.UUID;

import org.springframework.stereotype.Controller;
import org.springframework.ui.ModelMap;
import org.springframework.validation.BindingResult;
import org.springframework.validation.ObjectError;
import org.springframework.web.bind.annotation.ModelAttribute;
import org.springframework.web.bind.annotation.RequestMapping;
import org.springframework.web.bind.annotation.RequestParam;
import org.springframework.web.context.request.WebRequest;
import org.springframework.web.servlet.ModelAndView;

import com.springdemo.entity.Employee;
import com.springdemo.validator.EmployeeValidator;

/*
 * This application uses an List for storing employee objects.
 * Write your code to persist them into database / file
 * for permanent storage.
 */

@Controller
public class EmployeeController {

 @RequestMapping("/create")
 public ModelMap create(ModelMap modelMap) {
  modelMap.addAttribute("employee", new Employee());
  return modelMap;
 }

 @RequestMapping("/save")
 public String save(@ModelAttribute("employee") Employee employee,
                BindingResult result, WebRequest request) {
  new EmployeeValidator().validate(employee, result);
  if (result.hasErrors()) {
   return "create";
  }

  for (Employee emp : EmployeeData.employeeList) {
```

```
        if (emp.getEmpNumber().equals(employee.getEmpNumber())) {
            result.addError(new ObjectError("employee",
                    "Employee Number already exists"));
            return "create";
        }
    }
    employee.setId(UUID.randomUUID().toString());
    EmployeeData.employeeList.add(employee);
    request.setAttribute("MSG", "Employee record is saved successfully",
                    WebRequest.SCOPE_REQUEST);
    request.setAttribute("employeeList", EmployeeData.employeeList,
                    WebRequest.SCOPE_REQUEST);
    return "list";
}

@RequestMapping("/edit")
public ModelAndView edit(@RequestParam("employeeId") String employeeId,
                    ModelAndView modelAndView) {
    Employee employee = null;

    for (Employee emp : EmployeeData.employeeList) {
        if (emp.getId().equals(employeeId)) {
            employee = emp;
        }
    }

    if (employee == null) {
        modelAndView.addObject("MSG",
                    "Error occurred. Employee record not found");
        modelAndView.setViewName("list");
    }

    modelAndView.addObject("employee", employee);
    return modelAndView;
}

@RequestMapping(value = "/update")
public String update(@ModelAttribute("employee") Employee employee,
                    BindingResult result, WebRequest request) {
    new EmployeeValidator().validate(employee, result);
    if (result.hasErrors()) {
        return "edit";
    }
```

```
  for (int i=0; i < EmployeeData.employeeList.size(); i++) {
   Employee emp = EmployeeData.employeeList.get(i);
   if (emp.getId().equals(employee.getId())) {
    EmployeeData.employeeList.set(i, employee);
    break;
   }
  }

 request.setAttribute("MSG", "Employee record is updated successfully",
                    WebRequest.SCOPE_REQUEST);
  request.setAttribute("employeeList", EmployeeData.employeeList,
                    WebRequest.SCOPE_REQUEST);
  return "list";
 }

 @RequestMapping("/delete")
 public String delete(@RequestParam("employeeId") String employeeId,
                   WebRequest request) {
  for (int i=0; i < EmployeeData.employeeList.size(); i++) {
   Employee emp = EmployeeData.employeeList.get(i);
   if (emp.getId().equals(employeeId)) {
    EmployeeData.employeeList.remove(i);
    break;
   }
  }

 request.setAttribute("MSG", "Employee record is deleted successfully",
                    WebRequest.SCOPE_REQUEST);
  request.setAttribute("employeeList", EmployeeData.employeeList,
                    WebRequest.SCOPE_REQUEST);
  return "list";
 }

 @RequestMapping("/list")
 public ModelMap list(ModelMap modelMap, WebRequest request) {
  String MSG = (String) request.getAttribute("MSG",
                                  WebRequest.SCOPE_REQUEST);
  modelMap.addAttribute("MSG", MSG);
  System.out.println("EmployeeData.employeeList[" +
                   EmployeeData.employeeList +"]");
```

```
  modelMap.addAttribute("employeeList", EmployeeData.employeeList);
  return modelMap;
 }
}
```

JSP Files:

Store the following JSP files under the specified directory of the project.

Place the following "baseLayout.jsp" under SpringDemoWeb/src/main/webapp/WEB-INF/jsp/layout direcory.

```
<%@ taglib uri="http://tiles.apache.org/tags-tiles" prefix="tiles"%>

<html>
 <head>
 <title><tiles:insertAttribute name="title" ignore="true" /></title>
 </head>
 <body>
   <table border="1" cellpadding="0" cellspacing="0"
        width="100%" height="100%">
     <tr>
       <td height="10%" colspan="2" width="100%">
         <tiles:insertAttribute name="header" />
       </td>
     </tr>
     <tr valign="top">
       <td height="85%" width="10%">
         <tiles:insertAttribute name="menu" />
       </td>
       <td height="85%" width="70%">
         <tiles:insertAttribute name="body" />
       </td>
     </tr>
     <tr>
       <td height="5%" colspan="2" width="100%">
         <tiles:insertAttribute name="footer" />
       </td>
     </tr>
   </table>
 </body>
 </html>
```

Place the following "loginLayout.jsp" under SpringDemoWeb/src/main/webapp/WEB-INF/jsp/layout direcory.

```
<%@ taglib uri="http://tiles.apache.org/tags-tiles" prefix="tiles"%>

<html>
 <head>
  <title><tiles:insertAttribute name="title" ignore="true" /></title>
 </head>
<body>
 <table border="1" cellpadding="20" cellspacing="0"
       width="100%" height="100%">
  <tr>
   <td height="10%" colspan="2" width="100%">
     <tiles:insertAttribute name="header" />
   </td>
  </tr>
  <tr>
   <td height="85%" width="70%">
    <tiles:insertAttribute name="body" />
   </td>
  </tr>
  <tr>
   <td height="5%" colspan="2" width="100%">
    <tiles:insertAttribute name="footer" />
   </td>
  </tr>
 </table>
</body>
</html>
```

Place the following "login.jsp" under SpringDemoWeb/src/main/webapp/WEB-INF/jsp direcory.

```
<html>
<body>
 <center>
  <form name="form" action="/SpringDemoWeb/doLogin">
   <table border="0">
    <tr>
     <td colspan="2">${MSG}</td>
    </tr>
    <tr>
     <td>Login ID:</td>
```

```
      <td><input type="text" name="loginId" size="20"></td>
     </tr>
     <tr>
      <td>Password:</td>
      <td><input type="password" name="password" size="20"></td>
     </tr>
     <tr>
      <td colspan="2" align="center">
        <input type="submit" value="Login"></td>
     </tr>
    </table>
   </form>
  </center>
 </body>
 </html>
```

Place the following "welcome.jsp" under SpringDemoWeb/src/main/webapp/WEB-INF/jsp direcory.

```
<h2 align="center">Welcome to Employee Payroll Management System</h2>
```

Place the following "menu.jsp" under SpringDemoWeb/src/main/webapp/WEB-INF/jsp direcory.

```
<table>
 <tr>
  <td><a href="create">Create Employee</a></td>
 </tr>
 <tr>
  <td><a href="list">List Employees</a></td>
 </tr>
 <tr>
  <td><a href="logout">Logout</a></td>
 </tr>
</table>
```

Place the following "header.jsp" under SpringDemoWeb/src/main/webapp/WEB-INF/jsp direcory.

```
<h2 align="right">Employee Payroll Management System</h2>
```

Place the following "footer.jsp" under SpringDemoWeb/src/main/webapp/WEB-INF/jsp direcory.

```
<p align="right">&copy; XYZ Co. All Rights Reserved</p>
```

Place the following "include.jsp" under SpringDemoWeb/src/main/webapp/WEB-INF/jsp direcory.

```
<%@ taglib prefix="c" uri="http://java.sun.com/jsp/jstl/core"%>
<%@ taglib prefix="fmt" uri="http://java.sun.com/jsp/jstl/fmt"%>
<%@ taglib prefix="spring" uri="http://www.springframework.org/tags"%>
<%@ taglib prefix="form" uri="http://www.springframework.org/tags/
form"%>
<%@ taglib prefix="fn" uri="http://java.sun.com/jsp/jstl/functions"%>
```

Place the following "list.jsp" under SpringDemoWeb/src/main/webapp/WEB-INF/jsp direcory.

```
<%@ include file="/WEB-INF/jsp/include.jsp"%>

<head>
<title>List of Employee Records</title>

<script type="text/javascript">
 function callAddNew() {
  form.action = '/SpringDemoWeb/create';
  form.submit();
 }
</script>

</head>

<body>
 <form:form name="form" action="" method="post">
  <br>
  <table border="0" cellspacing="0" cellpadding="0" width="100%">
   <tr>
    <td width="20"> </td>
    <td>
      <table border="0" cellspacing="0" cellpadding="0" width="100%">
      <tr>
        <td height=50><h2>Employee List</h2></td>
      </tr>
```

```
<tr>
 <td height=50>
  <c:if test="${fn:length(MSG) > 0}">
   <div>${MSG}</div>
  </c:if></td>
</tr>
<tr>
 <td>
  <table border="1" cellspacing="0" cellpadding="0" width="100%">
   <tbody>
    <tr align="left">
     <th>Emp Number</th>
     <th>Emp Name</th>
     <th>Salary</th>
    </tr>

    <c:forEach var="employee" items="${employeeList}"
    varStatus="i">
     <tr onclick="document.location.href=
               '/SpringDemoWeb/edit?employeeId=${employee.id}';">
      <td>${employee.empNumber}</td>
      <td>${employee.empName}</td>
      <td>${employee.salary}</td>
     </tr>
    </c:forEach>
   </tbody>
  </table>
 </td>
</tr>

<tr>
 <td height=50 align="center"><input value="Add New"
  type="button" name="butNew" onclick="callAddNew();"></td>
</tr>
</table>
</td>
<td width="20"> </td>
</tr>
</table>
</form:form>
</body>
</html>
```

Place the following "create.jsp" under SpringDemoWeb/src/main/webapp/WEB-INF/jsp direcory.

```
<%@ include file="/WEB-INF/jsp/include.jsp"%>

<html>
<head>
<title>Create Employee Record</title>
</head>

<body>
 <form:form name="form" action="/SpringDemoWeb/save"
          method="post"
  modelAttribute="employee">
  <br>
  <table border="0" cellspacing="0" cellpadding="0" width="100%">
   <tr>
    <td width="20"> </td>
    <td>
     <table border="0" cellspacing="0" cellpadding="0" width="100%">
      <tr>
       <td height=50><h2>Create Employee Record</h2></td>
      </tr>
      <tr>
       <td>
        <spring:hasBindErrors name="employee">
         <div class="errors">
          <ul>
           <c:forEach var="err" items="${errors.allErrors}">
            <li><c:out value="${err.defaultMessage}" /></li>
           </c:forEach>
          </ul>
         </div>
        </spring:hasBindErrors>
       </td>
      </tr>
      <tr>
       <td height=20></td>
      </tr>
      <tr>
       <td>
        <table border="0" cellspacing="0" cellpadding="5">
```

```
        <tr>
         <td>Emp Number :</td>
          <td><form:input path="empNumber" maxlength="10" /></td>
        </tr>

        <tr>
         <td>Emp Name :</td>
          <td><form:input path="empName" maxlength="50" /></td>
        </tr>

        <tr>
         <td>Salary :</td>
          <td><form:input path="salary" maxlength="10" /></td>
        </tr>
       </table>
      </td>
     </tr>
     <tr>
      <td><input type="submit" value="Save"></td>
     </tr>
    </table>
   </td>
   <td width="20"> </td>
  </tr>
 </table>
</form:form>
</body>
</html>
```

Place the following “edit.jsp” under SpringDemoWeb/src/main/webapp/WEB-INF/jsp direcory.

```
<%@ include file="/WEB-INF/jsp/include.jsp"%>

<html>
<head>
<title>Edit Employee Record</title>

<script type="text/javascript">
 function callUpdate() {
  form.action = '/SpringDemoWeb/update';
  form.submit();
 }
```

```
</script>

</head>

<body>
 <form:form name="form" action="" method="post"
          modelAttribute="employee">
  <form:hidden path="id"/>
  <br>
  <table border="0" cellspacing="0" cellpadding="0" width="100%">
   <tr>
    <td width="20"> </td>
    <td>
     <table border="0" cellspacing="0" cellpadding="0" width="100%">
      <tr>
       <td height=50><h2>Edit Employee Record</h2></td>
      </tr>
      <tr>
       <td>
        <spring:hasBindErrors name="employee">
         <div class="errors">
          <ul>
           <c:forEach var="err" items="${errors.allErrors}">
            <li><c:out value="${err.defaultMessage}" /></li>
           </c:forEach>
          </ul>
         </div>
        </spring:hasBindErrors>
       </td>
      </tr>
      <tr>
       <td height=20></td>
      </tr>
      <tr>
       <td>
        <table border="0" cellspacing="0" cellpadding="5">
         <tr>
          <td>Emp Number :</td>
          <td>
           <form:input path="empNumber" maxlength="10" readonly="true" />
          </td>
         </tr>
```

```
        <tr>
         <td>Emp Name :</td>
         <td><form:input path="empName" maxlength="50" /></td>
        </tr>

        <tr>
         <td>Salary :</td>
         <td><form:input path="salary" maxlength="10" /></td>
        </tr>
       </table>
      </td>
     </tr>
     <tr>
      <td>
       <input class="hand" onclick="callUpdate();"
              value="Update" type="button">
         
       <input class="hand" value="Delete" type="button"
        onclick="javascript: if (confirm(
        'Are you sure you want to delete this record?',
        'Delete Employee')) {
          document.form.action= '/SpringDemoWeb/delete
                          ?employeeId=${employee.id}';
          document.form.submit(); }">
      </td>
     </tr>
    </table>
   </td>
   <td width="20"> </td>
  </tr>
 </table>
</form:form>
</body>
</html>
```

Run the applciation:

Package the project using Maven to generate war file and deploy it in any application server. In our demonstation, the applciation is deployed on Jetty server using Jetty Maven plug-in which is defined in pom.xml.

Use "`mvn eclipse:eclipse`" to download dependencies and generate Eclipse IDE configuration files for the project.

```
C:\Development\Install\eclipse-juno\workspace\SpringDemoWeb> mvn
                                                  eclipse:eclipse
[INFO] ------------------------------------------------------------------------
[INFO] Building SpringDemoWeb Maven Webapp 1.0-SNAPSHOT
[INFO] ------------------------------------------------------------------------
[INFO]
...
...
[INFO] ------------------------------------------------------------------------
[INFO] BUILD SUCCESS
[INFO] ------------------------------------------------------------------------
```

Use "mvn clean compile package" to compile and generate war file of the project.

```
C:\Development\Install\eclipse-juno\workspace\SpringDemoWeb>mvn clean
                                                  compile package
[INFO] ------------------------------------------------------------------------
[INFO] Building SpringDemoWeb Maven Webapp 1.0-SNAPSHOT
[INFO] ------------------------------------------------------------------------
[INFO] Compiling 6 source files to C:\Development\Install\eclipse-
juno\workspace\SpringDemoWeb\target\classes
[INFO] Packaging webapp
[INFO] Assembling webapp
[SpringDemoWeb] in [C:\Development\Install\eclipse juno\workspace\SpringDemoWeb
\target\SpringDemoWeb]
[INFO] Processing war project
[INFO] Copying webapp resources [C:\Development\Install\eclipse-
juno\workspace\SpringDemoWeb\src\main\webapp]
[INFO] Webapp assembled in [5984 msecs]
[INFO] Building war: C:\Development\Install\eclipse
juno\workspace\SpringDemoWeb\target\SpringDemoWeb.war
[INFO] ------------------------------------------------------------------------
[INFO] BUILD SUCCESS
[INFO] ------------------------------------------------------------------------
```

Use "mvn jetty:run" to deploy the web application.

```
C:\Development\Install\eclipse-juno\workspace\SpringDemoWeb>mvn
jetty:run
...
...
```

```
[main] INFO org.apache.tiles.access.TilesAccess - Publishing TilesContext
for context:
org.springframework.web.servlet.view.tiles3.SpringWildcardServlet
TilesApplicationContext
[main] INFO org.springframework.web.servlet.DispatcherServlet
FrameworkServlet 'SpringDemoWeb': initialization completed in 468 ms
2013-05-17 18:13:57.364:INFO::Started SelectChannel Connector@
                                                            0.0.0.0:8080
```

Invoke the browser with the URL: http://localhost:8080/SpringDemoWeb/login

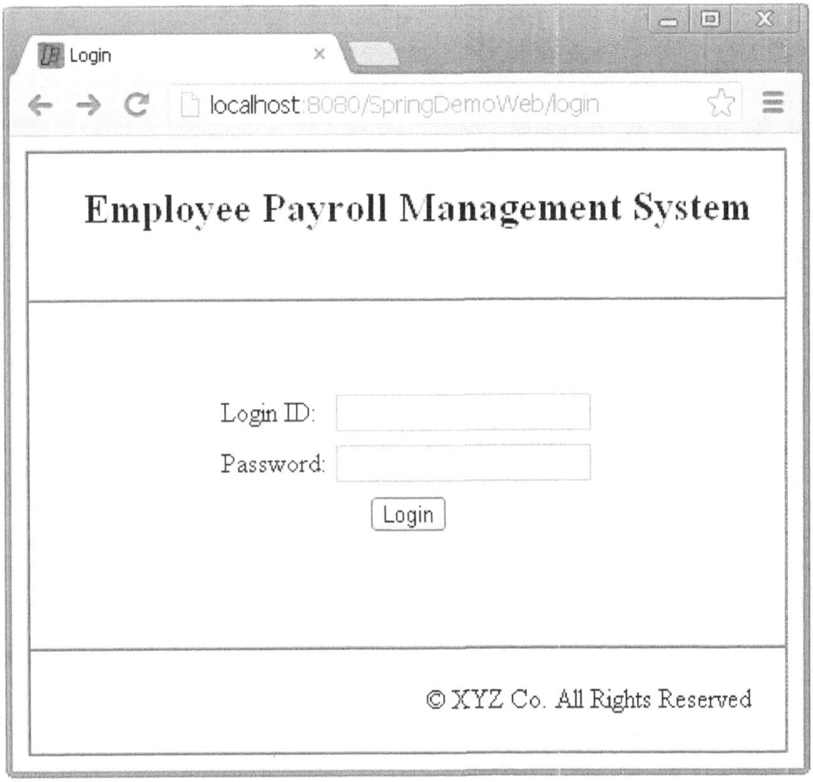

Click on "Login" button without entering login details.

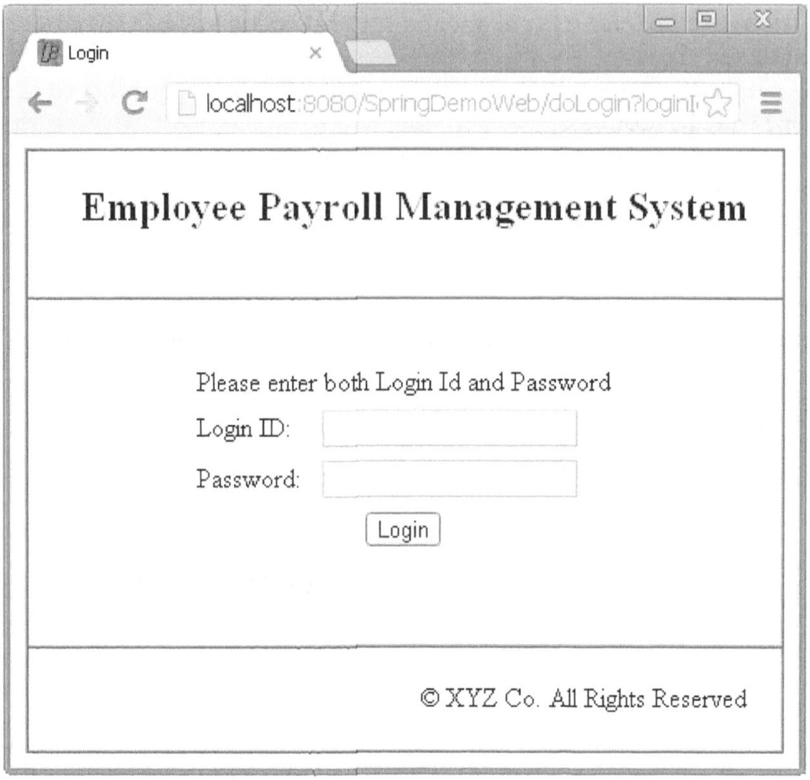

Enter some data (as this applciation will check only both Login ID and password are entered, not check the actual validation) form LoginID and Password, then click on "Login" button.

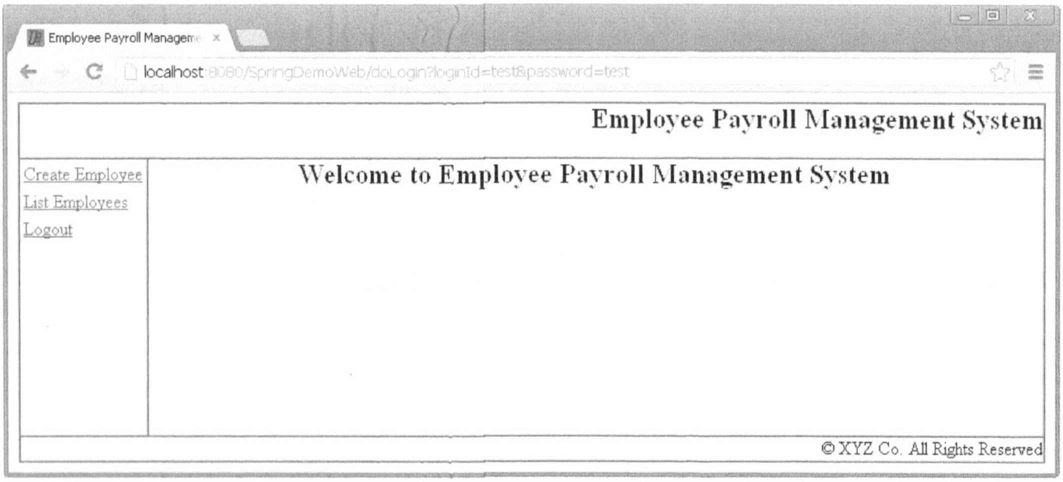

Click on "Create Employee" hyperlink.

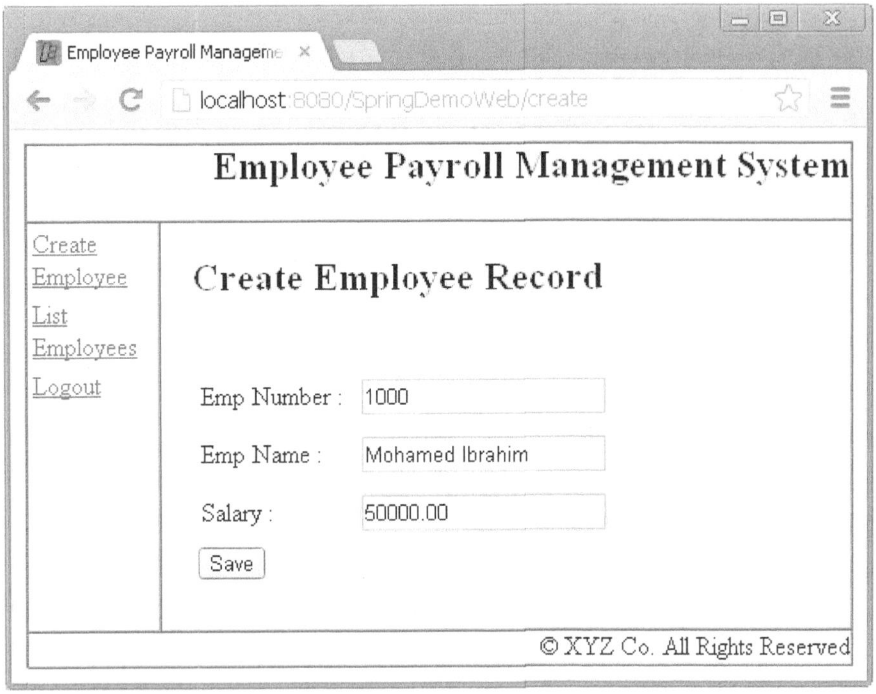

Click on "Save"

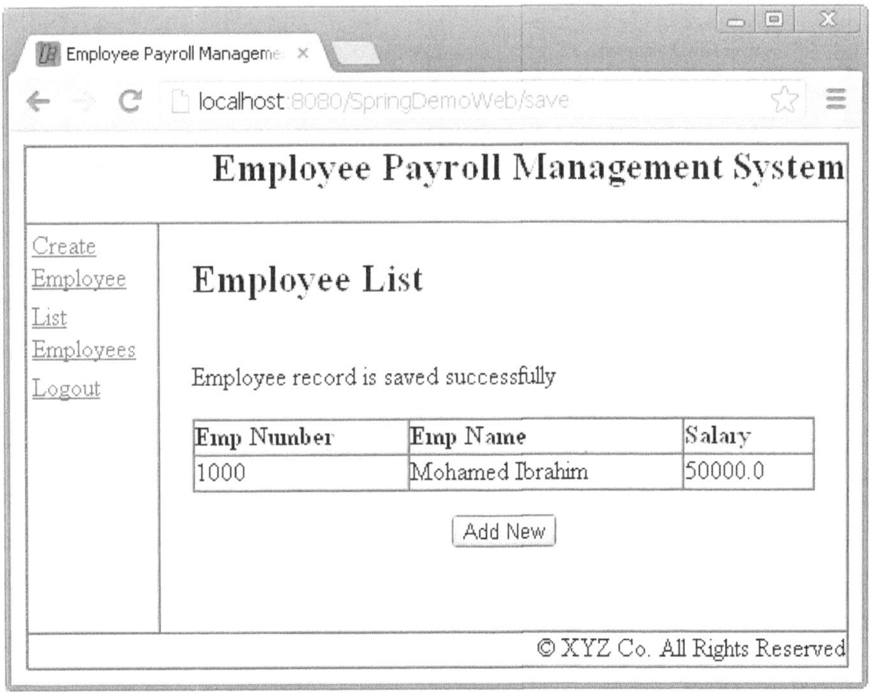

Click on "Add New", it will do the same operation of "Create Employee" link.

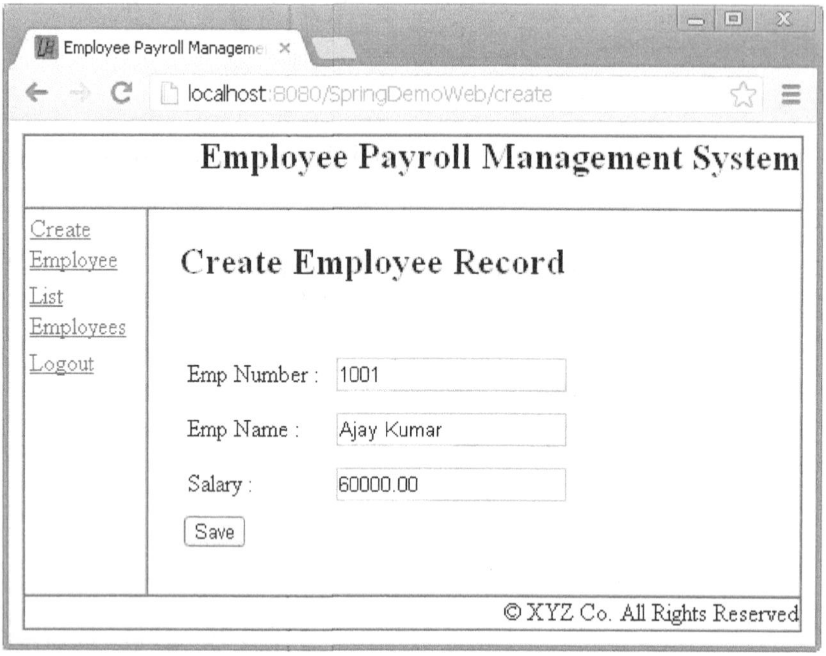

Click on "Save" to add the record. Click on "List Employees" link from the left-side menu.

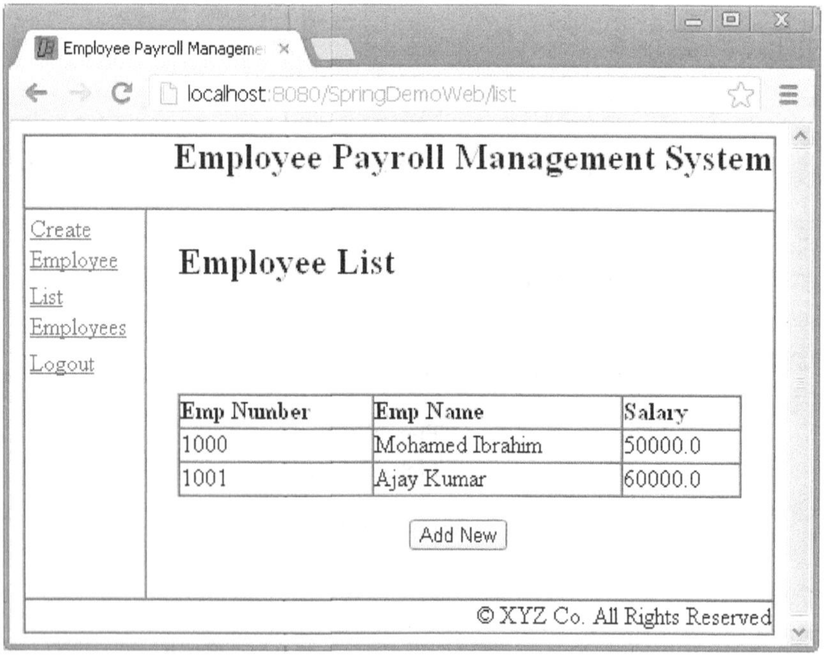

Click on "Logout".

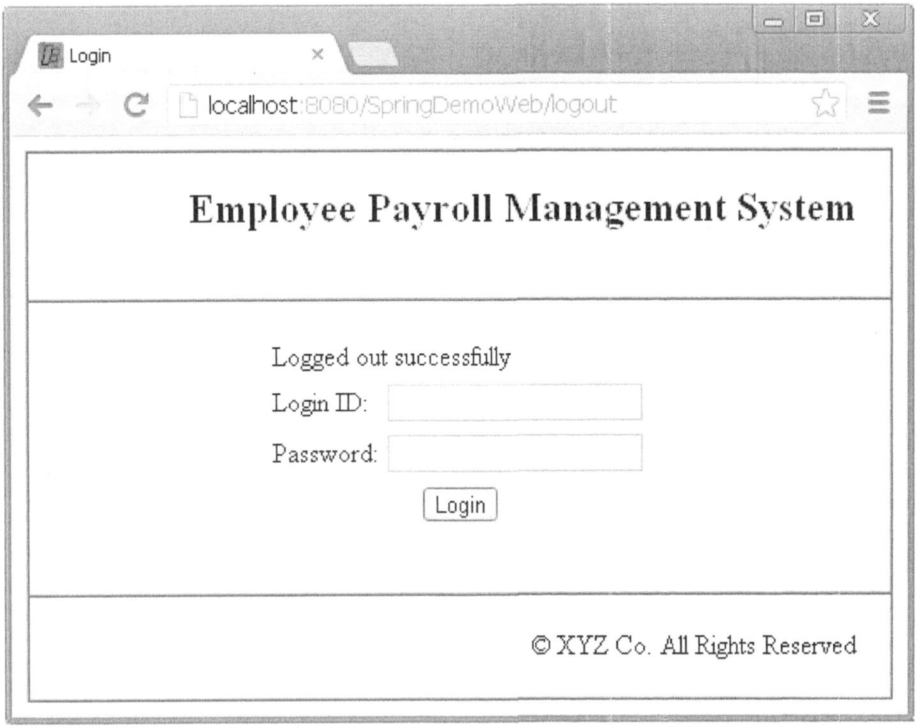

11.14.5 Generating PDF and Excel Output

This application generates PDF content and Excel content as output, along with the usual HTML rendering.

pom.xml

```
<project xmlns="http://maven.apache.org/POM/4.0.0"
       xmlns:xsi="http://www.w3.org/2001/XMLSchema-instance"
       xsi:schemaLocation="http://maven.apache.org/POM/4.0.0
       http://maven.apache.org/maven-v4_0_0.xsd">
  <modelVersion>4.0.0</modelVersion>
  <groupId>SpringDemo</groupId>
  <artifactId>SpringDemoWeb</artifactId>
  <packaging>war</packaging>
  <version>1.0-SNAPSHOT</version>
  <name>SpringDemoWeb Maven Webapp</name>

  <properties>
   <spring.version>3.2.2.RELEASE</spring.version>
   <jdk.version>1.6</jdk.version>
  </properties>
```

```
<dependencies>
 <dependency>
  <groupId>org.springframework</groupId>
  <artifactId>spring-core</artifactId>
  <version>${spring.version}</version>
 </dependency>

 <dependency>
  <groupId>org.springframework</groupId>
  <artifactId>spring-web</artifactId>
  <version>${spring.version}</version>
 </dependency>

 <dependency>
  <groupId>org.springframework</groupId>
  <artifactId>spring-webmvc</artifactId>
  <version>${spring.version}</version>
 </dependency>

 <dependency>
  <groupId>javax.servlet</groupId>
  <artifactId>javax.servlet-api</artifactId>
  <version>3.0.1</version>
 </dependency>

 <dependency>
  <groupId>taglibs</groupId>
  <artifactId>standard</artifactId>
  <version>1.1.2</version>
 </dependency>

 <dependency>
  <groupId>com.lowagie</groupId>
  <artifactId>itext</artifactId>
  <version>2.1.7</version>
 </dependency>

 <dependency>
  <groupId>org.apache.poi</groupId>
  <artifactId>poi</artifactId>
```

```
  <version>3.6</version>
 </dependency>

</dependencies>

<build>
 <finalName>SpringDemoWeb</finalName>
 <plugins>
  <plugin>
   <groupId>org.apache.maven.plugins</groupId>
   <artifactId>maven-compiler-plugin</artifactId>
   <version>3.0</version>
   <configuration>
    <source>${jdk.version}</source>
    <target>${jdk.version}</target>
   </configuration>
  </plugin>

  <plugin>
   <groupId>org.mortbay.jetty</groupId>
   <artifactId>maven-jetty-plugin</artifactId>
   <version>6.1.26</version>
   <configuration>
    <scanIntervalSeconds>10</scanIntervalSeconds>
    <connectors>
     <connector implementation=
         "org.mortbay.jetty.nio.SelectChannelConnector">
      <port>8080</port>
     </connector>
    </connectors>
   </configuration>
  </plugin>
 </plugins>
</build>
</project>
```

Web Configuration File (web.xml) under SpringDemoWeb/src/main/webapp/WEB-INF/

```
<web-app xmlns:xsi="http://www.w3.org/2001/XMLSchema-instance"
        xmlns="http://java.sun.com/xml/ns/javaee"
        xmlns:web="http://java.sun.com/xml/ns/javaee/web-app_2_5.xsd"
        xsi:schemaLocation="http://java.sun.com/xml/ns/javaee
```

```
        http://java.sun.com/xml/ns/javaee/web-app_3_0.xsd"
        id="WebApp_ID" version="3.0">

  <display-name>Spring Demo Web Application</display-name>

  <servlet>
   <servlet-name>SpringDemoWeb</servlet-name>
   <servlet-class>
     org.springframework.web.servlet.DispatcherServlet
   </servlet-class>
   <load-on-startup>1</load-on-startup>
  </servlet>

  <servlet-mapping>
   <servlet-name>SpringDemoWeb</servlet-name>
   <url-pattern>/</url-pattern>
  </servlet-mapping>

  <context-param>
   <param-name>contextConfigLocation</param-name>
   <param-value>/WEB-INF/SpringDemoWeb-servlet.xml</param-value>
  </context-param>

  <listener>
   <listener-class>
    org.springframework.web.context.ContextLoaderListener
   </listener-class>
  </listener>


</web-app>
```

Spring Configuration File (SpringDemoWeb-servlet.xml) under SpringDemoWeb/src/main/webapp/WEB-INF/

```
<?xml version="1.0" encoding="UTF-8"?>
<beans xmlns="http://www.springframework.org/schema/beans"
      xmlns:xsi="http://www.w3.org/2001/XMLSchema-instance"
      xmlns:p="http://www.springframework.org/schema/p"
      xmlns:context="http://www.springframework.org/schema/context"
```

```
    xmlns:mvc="http://www.springframework.org/schema/mvc"
    xsi:schemaLocation="http://www.springframework.org/schema/beans
   http://www.springframework.org/schema/beans/spring-beans-3.0.xsd
    http://www.springframework.org/schema/context
   http://www.springframework.org/schema/context/spring-context-
   3.0.xsd
    http://www.springframework.org/schema/mvc
    http://www.springframework.org/schema/mvc/spring-mvc-3.0.xsd">

  <context:annotation-config />
  <context:component-scan base-package="com.springdemo" />

  <bean class="org.springframework.web.servlet.view.XmlViewResolver">
   <property name="location">
    <value>/WEB-INF/SpringDemoWeb-views.xml</value>
   </property>
  </bean>

 </beans>
```

View Resolutions Dependency File (SpringDemoWeb-views.xml) under SpringDemoWeb/src/main/webapp/WEB-INF/

```
 <beans xmlns="http://www.springframework.org/schema/beans"
      xmlns:xsi="http://www.w3.org/2001/XMLSchema-instance"
      xsi:schemaLocation="http://www.springframework.org/schema/beans
     http://www.springframework.org/schema/beans/spring-beans-2.5.xsd">

  <bean id="employeeView"
       class="org.springframework.web.servlet.view.JstlView">
   <property name="url" value="/WEB-INF/jsp/employeeList.jsp" />
  </bean>

  <bean id="employeePDFView" class="com.springdemo.view. Employee
   PDFView" />

  <bean id="employeeExcelView"
       class="com.springdemo.view.EmployeeExcelView" />

 </beans>
```

Controller class: EmployeeController.java

```
//File Name: EmployeeController.java
package com.springdemo.controller;

import java.util.ArrayList;
import java.util.List;

import org.springframework.stereotype.Controller;
import org.springframework.ui.Model;
import org.springframework.web.bind.annotation.RequestMapping;

import com.springdemo.entity.Employee;

@Controller
public class EmployeeController {

 List<Employee> employeeList = new ArrayList<Employee>();

 public EmployeeController() {
  // Populate Employee data
    employeeList.add(new Employee("1001", "Mohamed Ibrahim", 50000.00));
    employeeList.add(new Employee("1002", "Ajay Kumar", 55000.00));
    employeeList.add(new Employee("1003", "John Peter", 60000.00));
    employeeList.add(new Employee("1004", "Anwar", 65000.00));
    employeeList.add(new Employee("1005", "Mariyana", 70000.00));
 }

 @RequestMapping("/list")
 public String list(Model model) {
  model.addAttribute("employeeList", employeeList);
  return "employeeView";
 }

 @RequestMapping("/listPDF")
 public String listPDF(Model model) {
  model.addAttribute("employeeList", employeeList);
  return "employeePDFView";
 }

 @RequestMapping("/listExcel")
 public String listExcel(Model model) {
```

```
    model.addAttribute("employeeList", employeeList);
    return "employeeExcelView";
  }

}
```

Entity class: Employee.java

```
//FileName: Employee.java
package com.springdemo.entity;

import java.util.UUID;

public class Employee {

 private String id;
 private String empNumber;
 private String empName;
 private double salary;

 public Employee() {
 }

 public Employee(String empNumber, String empName, double salary) {
  id = UUID.randomUUID().toString();
  this.empNumber = empNumber;
  this.empName = empName;
  this.salary = salary;
 }

 public String getId() {
  return id;
 }

 public void setId(String id) {
  this.id = id;
 }

 public String getEmpNumber() {
  return empNumber;
```

```
    }

    public void setEmpNumber(String empNumber) {
     this.empNumber = empNumber;
    }

    public String getEmpName() {
     return empName;
    }

    public void setEmpName(String empName) {
     this.empName = empName;
    }

    public double getSalary() {
     return salary;
    }

    public void setSalary(double salary) {
     this.salary = salary;
    }

}
```

EmployeePDFView.java

```
//File Name: EmployeePDFView.java
package com.springdemo.view;

import java.util.List;
import java.util.Map;

import javax.servlet.http.HttpServletRequest;
import javax.servlet.http.HttpServletResponse;

import org.springframework.web.servlet.view.document.AbstractPdfView;

import com.lowagie.text.Document;
import com.lowagie.text.Paragraph;
import com.lowagie.text.Table;
```

```
import com.lowagie.text.pdf.PdfWriter;
import com.springdemo.entity.Employee;

public class EmployeePDFView extends AbstractPdfView {

 @SuppressWarnings({"unchecked", "rawtypes"})
 @Override
 protected void buildPdfDocument(Map model, Document document,
      PdfWriter writer, HttpServletRequest request,
      HttpServletResponse response) throws Exception {

  List<Employee> employeeList =
           (List<Employee>) model.get("employeeList");
  Paragraph titlePara = new Paragraph("Employee Records");

  Table table = new Table(3);
  table.addCell("Emp. Number");
  table.addCell("Emp. Name");
  table.addCell("Salary");

  for (Employee employee : employeeList) {
   table.addCell(employee.getEmpNumber());
   table.addCell(employee.getEmpName());
   table.addCell(String.valueOf(employee.getSalary()));
  }

  document.add(titlePara);
  document.add(table);
 }
}
```

EmployeeExcelView.java

```
//File Name: EmployeeExcelView.java
package com.springdemo.view;

import java.util.List;
import java.util.Map;

import javax.servlet.http.HttpServletRequest;
import javax.servlet.http.HttpServletResponse;
```

```
import org.apache.poi.hssf.usermodel.HSSFRow;
import org.apache.poi.hssf.usermodel.HSSFSheet;
import org.apache.poi.hssf.usermodel.HSSFWorkbook;
import org.springframework.web.servlet.view.document.AbstractExcelView;

import com.springdemo.entity.Employee;

public class EmployeeExcelView extends AbstractExcelView {

 @SuppressWarnings({"unchecked", "rawtypes"})
 @Override
 protected void buildExcelDocument(Map model, HSSFWorkbook workbook,
                         HttpServletRequest request,
                         HttpServletResponse response)
                         throws Exception {

  List<Employee> employeeList =
            (List<Employee>) model.get("employeeList");
  HSSFSheet sheet = workbook.createSheet("Employees");

  int rowNum = 0;
  HSSFRow header = sheet.createRow(rowNum++);
  header.createCell(0).setCellValue("Emp. Number");
  header.createCell(1).setCellValue("Emp. Name");
  header.createCell(2).setCellValue("Salary");

  for (Employee employee : employeeList) {

   HSSFRow row = sheet.createRow(rowNum++);
   row.createCell(0).setCellValue(employee.getEmpNumber());
   row.createCell(1).setCellValue(employee.getEmpName());
  row.createCell(2).setCellValue(String.valueOf(employee.getSalary()));
  }
 }
}
```

The employeeList.jsp under SpringDemoWeb\src\main\webapp\WEB-INF\jsp directory

```
<%@ include file="/WEB-INF/jsp/include.jsp"%>
```

```
<head>
<title>List of Employee Records</title>
</head>

<body>
 <br>
 <table border="0" cellspacing="0" cellpadding="0" width="100%">
  <tr>
   <td width="20"> </td>
   <td>
    <table border="0" cellspacing="0" cellpadding="0" width="100%">
     <tr>
      <td height=50><h2>Employee List</h2></td>
     </tr>
     <tr>
      <td>
       <table border="1" cellspacing="0" cellpadding="0" width="100%">
        <tbody>
         <tr align="left">
          <th>Emp Number</th>
          <th>Emp Name</th>
          <th>Salary</th>
         </tr>

       <c:forEach var="employee" items="${employeeList}" varStatus="i">
          <tr>
           <td>${employee.empNumber}</td>
           <td>${employee.empName}</td>
           <td>${employee.salary}</td>
          </tr>
         </c:forEach>
        </tbody>
       </table>
      </td>
     </tr>
    </table>
   </td>
   <td width="20"> </td>
  </tr>
 </table>
</body>
</html>
```

The include.jsp under SpringDemoWeb\src\main\webapp\WEB-INF\jsp directory

```
<%@ taglib prefix="c" uri="http://java.sun.com/jsp/jstl/core"%>
<%@ taglib prefix="fmt" uri="http://java.sun.com/jsp/jstl/fmt"%>
<%@ taglib prefix="spring" uri="http://www.springframework.org/tags"%>
<%@ taglib prefix="form" uri="http://www.springframework.org/tags/
form"%>
<%@ taglib prefix="fn" uri="http://java.sun.com/jsp/jstl/functions"%>
```

Configure the project in Eclipse IDE:

```
C:\Development\Install\eclipse-juno\workspace\SpringDemoWeb> mvn
                                                    eclipse:eclipse
[INFO] Scanning for projects...
[INFO]
[INFO] ------------------------------------------------------------------------
[INFO] Building SpringDemoWeb Maven Webapp 1.0-SNAPSHOT
[INFO] ------------------------------------------------------------------------
...
...
[INFO] BUILD SUCCESS
```

Compile, package, and deploy the project on Jetty Server:

```
C:\Development\Install\eclipse-juno\workspace\SpringDemoWeb> mvn clean
                              compile package jetty:run
[INFO] Scanning for projects...
[INFO]
[INFO] ------------------------------------------------------------------------
[INFO] Building SpringDemoWeb Maven Webapp 1.0-SNAPSHOT
[INFO] ------------------------------------------------------------------------
...
...
INFO::Started SelectChannelConnector@0.0.0.0:8080
[INFO] Started Jetty Server
[INFO] Starting scanner at interval of 10 seconds.
```

The URL http://localhost:8080/SpringDemoWeb/list brings normal JSTL view.

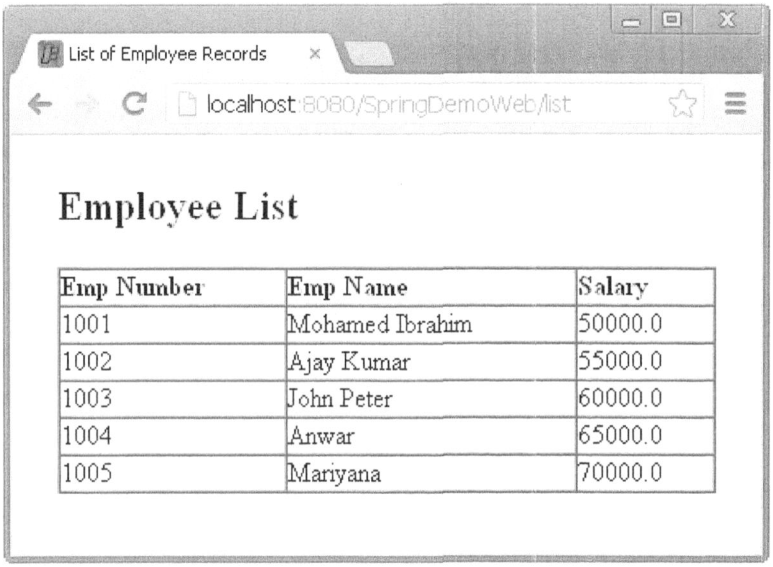

The URL http://localhost:8080/SpringDemoWeb/listPDF brings PDF view; you can save the PDF file also from the browser.

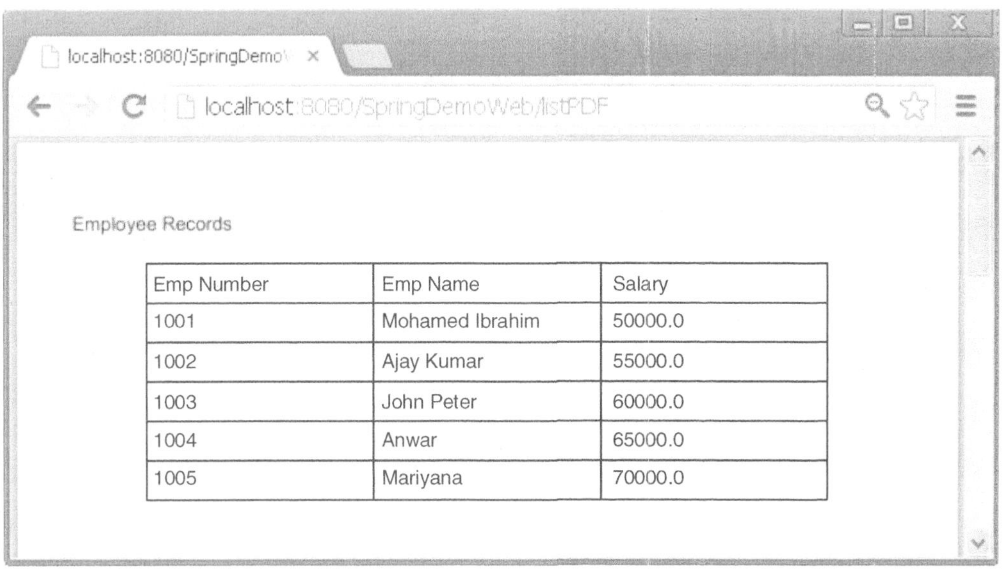

The URL http://localhost:8080/SpringDemoWeb/listExcel brings Excel view; you can save the Excel file also from the browser.

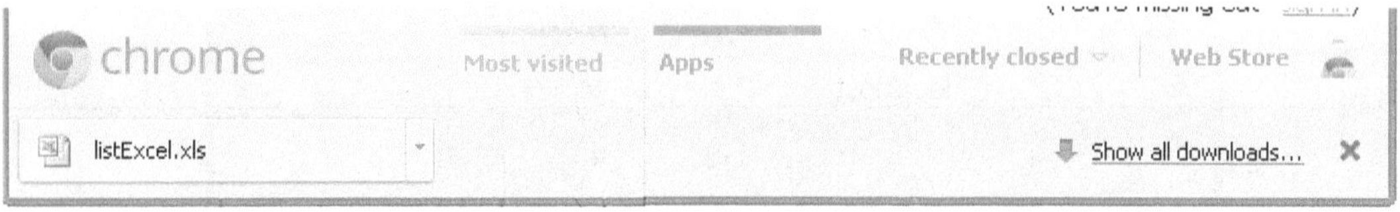

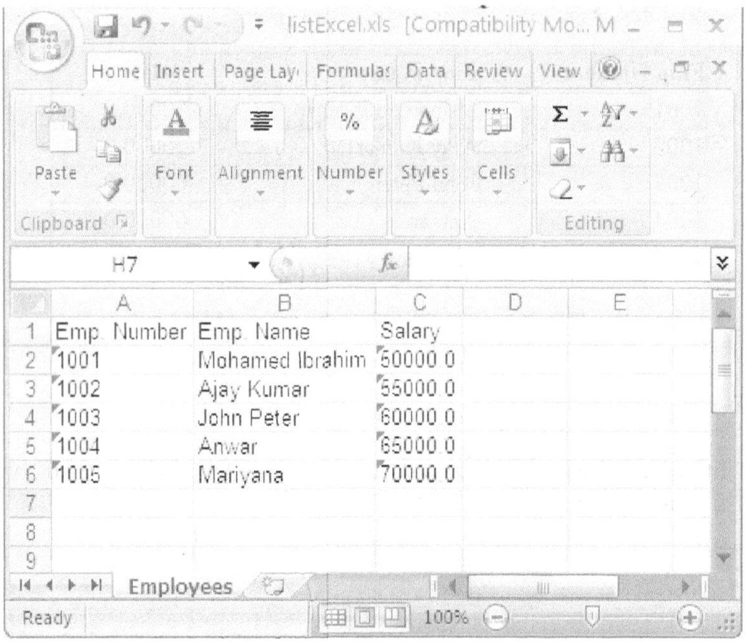

CHAPTER 12

WEB SERVICES

A Web Service is an application functionality service that can be accessed by any application via standard Internet Protocols such as HTTP. In a simple term, any procedures (methods in Java) in a web application can be accessed by any other application, which is developed on any programming tool and running on any platform, via web using Web Services. Web Services are using XML as data exchange format, and the XML format is supported by all modern programming languages. Here, the word "service" refers the endpoint of a connection of web applications (programming functionality).

12.1 COMPONENTS OF WEB SERVICES

The following are the main components of Web Services:

- **XML (eXtensible Mark-up Language):** In Web Service, request and response data will be exchanged between applications in this XML format.
- **WSDL (Web Services Description Language):** It is used to describe a web service, and it uses XML format to describe.
- **SOAP (Simple Object Access Protocol):** It is XML based protocol, which is used to define requests / responses for a Web Service (mandatory, optional, minimum / maximum occurrences of elements for defining data in requests / responses). HTTP (Hyper-Text Transport Protocol) is used to deliver web service requests and responses.

12.2 WEB SERVICE DEVELOPMENT WITH JAX-WS

The annotation based features for JAX-WS (Java API for XML Web Services) simplifies web-service development process.

The annotation `@WebService` declares a class as Web Service (End-point class), `@WebMethod` annotation declares a method in an endpoint class as a web method (exposes as a web-service operation), and `@WebParam` customizes the mapping of individual parameter(s) to a web-method.

General formats of these annotations with important parameters:

```
@WebService(serviceName=service_name_of_web_service,
        endpointInterface=service_endpoint_interface)
```

`@WebMethod(exclude=boolean_value)` -A value `'true'` as value for `exclude` makes a method in a `@WebService` class to not be exposed as a web method.

`@WebParam(name=name_of_the_parameter)` -Defines the parameters for a web method.

12.2.1 Creating a Simple Web Service

In this section, we will see how to create a Web Service and how to access it via a Java application. We will use JAX-WS with Spring Framework for the creation of Web Service. Apache Maven is used for managing our project, and Jetty Application Server is used for the deployment of the web application.

Install Maven: Download the latest version of Maven, a Project Management Tool, from its official web site (http://maven.apache.org/download.cgi) in Zip format. I downloaded Maven version 3.0.5; unzip the file and include its bin directory in to the PATH variable so that you can access "mvn" in any command prompt/shell window.

Create a Web Project: Go to your workspace directory in the command prompt/shell window and invoke "mvn" command as shown below.

```
C:\Development\Install\eclipse-juno\workspace> mvn archetype:generate
-DgroupId=SpringDemo -DartifactId=SpringDemoWS
-DarchetypeArtifactId=maven-archetype-webapp -DinteractiveMode=false

[INFO] Scanning for projects...
[INFO] Building Maven Stub Project (No POM) 1
[INFO] >>> maven-archetype-plugin:2.2:generate (default-cli)
@ standalone-pom
[INFO] Using following parameters for creating project from Old (1.x)
    Archetype: maven-archetype-webapp:1.0
[INFO] Parameter: groupId, Value: SpringDemo
[INFO] Parameter: packageName, Value: SpringDemo
[INFO] Parameter: package, Value: SpringDemo
[INFO] Parameter: artifactId, Value: SpringDemoWS
[INFO]Parameter: basedir,
    Value: C:\Development\Install\eclipse-juno\workspace
[INFO] Parameter: version, Value: 1.0-SNAPSHOT
[INFO] project created from Old (1.x) Archetype in dir:
    C:\Development\Install\eclipse-juno\workspace\SpringDemoWS
[INFO] -------------------------------------------------------------
[INFO] BUILD SUCCESS
[INFO] -------------------------------------------------------------
```

Then, a directory named "SpringDemoWeb" will be created with "src" directory and "pom.xml" file.

```
C:\Development\Install\eclipse-juno\workspace>
C:\Development\Install\eclipse-juno\workspace> cd SpringDemoWS

C:\Development\Install\eclipse-juno\workspace\SpringDemoWS> dir
 Volume in drive C has no label.
 Volume Serial Number is EC82-6ECD

 Directory of C:\Development\Install\eclipse-juno\workspace\SpringDemoWS

07/29/2013  11:11 AM    <DIR>          .
07/29/2013  11:11 AM    <DIR>          ..
07/29/2013  11:11 AM               742 pom.xml
07/29/2013  11:11 AM    <DIR>          src
               1 File(s)            742 bytes
               3 Dir(s)  23,018,373,120 bytes free
```

Add the project to Eclipse IDE: I am using Eclipse IDE (Eclipse Juno / 4.2) for application development; we need to add the created Maven project into Eclipse, this can be done using Eclipse Maven plug-in or through the following command at command prompt.

Go to the project directory and issue the `"mvn eclipse:eclipse"` command to convert the project as Eclipse Java project, add `"-Dwtpversion=2.0"` to specify Web Tools Platform (WTP) version that converts the project as Eclipse Web project.

```
C:\Development\Install\eclipse-juno\workspace\SpringDemoWS> mvn
eclipse:eclipse -Dwtpversion=2.0

 [INFO] Scanning for projects...
 [INFO] Building SpringDemoWS Maven Webapp 1.0-SNAPSHOT
 [INFO] >>> maven-eclipse-plugin:2.9:eclipse (default-cli) @ SpringDemoWS
 >>>
 [INFO] Adding support for WTP version 2.0.
 [INFO]Using Eclipse Workspace: C:\Development\Install\eclipse-
juno\workspace
 [INFO] Wrote Eclipse project for "SpringDemoWS" to
        C:\Development\Install\eclipse-juno\workspace\SpringDemoWS.
 [INFO] ------------------------------------------------------------------------
 [INFO] BUILD SUCCESS
 [INFO] ------------------------------------------------------------------------
```

Invoke Eclipse IDE, File → Import → Existing Projects into Workspace → Select the "SpringDemoWeb" directory for "Select root directory" → Finish.

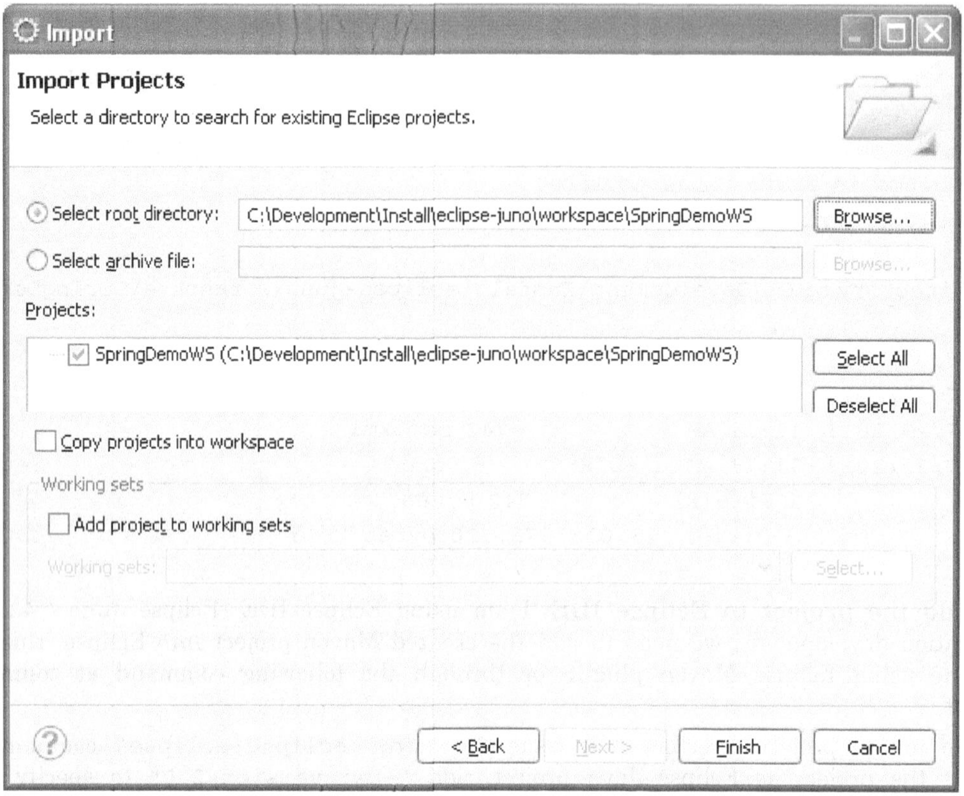

Edit pom.xml: POM stands for "Project Object Model". This pom.xml file in a Maven project specifies all the configurations in order to build the project.

Open the pom.xml in Eclipse IDE and update it content as given below.

```
<project xmlns="http://maven.apache.org/POM/4.0.0"
        xmlns:xsi="http://www.w3.org/2001/XMLSchema-instance"
        xsi:schemaLocation="http://maven.apache.org/POM/4.0.0
        http://maven.apache.org/maven-v4_0_0.xsd">
  <modelVersion>4.0.0</modelVersion>
  <groupId>SpringDemo</groupId>
  <artifactId>SpringDemoWS</artifactId>
  <packaging>war</packaging>
  <version>1.0-SNAPSHOT</version>
  <name>SpringDemoWS Maven Webapp</name>

  <properties>
   <spring.version>3.2.2.RELEASE</spring.version>
   <java.version>1.6</java.version>
  </properties>
```

```
<dependencies>
  <dependency>
    <groupId>org.springframework</groupId>
    <artifactId>spring-core</artifactId>
    <version>${spring.version}</version>
  </dependency>

  <dependency>
    <groupId>org.springframework</groupId>
    <artifactId>spring-web</artifactId>
    <version>${spring.version}</version>
  </dependency>

  <dependency>
    <groupId>org.springframework</groupId>
    <artifactId>spring-webmvc</artifactId>
    <version>${spring.version}</version>
  </dependency>

  <dependency>
    <groupId>javax.servlet</groupId>
    <artifactId>javax.servlet-api</artifactId>
    <version>3.0.1</version>
  </dependency>

  <dependency>
    <groupId>com.sun.xml.ws</groupId>
    <artifactId>jaxws-rt</artifactId>
    <version>2.2.8</version>
  </dependency>

  <!-- Library from java.net, integrate Spring with JAX-WS -->
  <dependency>
    <groupId>org.jvnet.jax-ws-commons.spring</groupId>
    <artifactId>jaxws-spring</artifactId>
    <version>1.8</version>
    <exclusions>
     <exclusion>
       <groupId>org.springframework</groupId>
       <artifactId>spring-core</artifactId>
     </exclusion>
     <exclusion>
       <groupId>org.springframework</groupId>
```

```
      <artifactId>spring-context</artifactId>
    </exclusion>
    <exclusion>
      <groupId>com.sun.xml.stream.buffer</groupId>
      <artifactId>streambuffer</artifactId>
    </exclusion>
    <exclusion>
      <groupId>org.jvnet.staxex</groupId>
      <artifactId>stax-ex</artifactId>
    </exclusion>
   </exclusions>
  </dependency>

 </dependencies>
 <build>
  <finalName>SpringDemoWS</finalName>
  <plugins>
   <plugin>
    <groupId>org.apache.maven.plugins</groupId>
    <artifactId>maven-compiler-plugin</artifactId>
    <version>3.0</version>
    <configuration>
     <source>${java.version}</source>
     <target>${java.version}</target>
    </configuration>
   </plugin>

   <plugin>
    <groupId>org.mortbay.jetty</groupId>
    <artifactId>maven-jetty-plugin</artifactId>
    <version>6.1.26</version>
    <configuration>
     <connectors>
      <connector implementation=
                "org.mortbay.jetty.nio.SelectChannelConnector">
       <port>9090</port>
      </connector>
     </connectors>
    </configuration>
   </plugin>
  </plugins>
 </build>
</project>
```

Spring Configuration File: Create the following "SpringDemoWS-context.xml" file under `src/main/webapp/WEB-INF` directory of the project.

```
<?xml version="1.0" encoding="UTF-8"?>
<beans xmlns="http://www.springframework.org/schema/beans"
 xmlns:xsi="http://www.w3.org/2001/XMLSchema-instance"
 xmlns:ws="http://jax-ws.dev.java.net/spring/core"
 xmlns:wss="http://jax-ws.dev.java.net/spring/servlet"
 xsi:schemaLocation="http://www.springframework.org/schema/beans
 http://www.springframework.org/schema/beans/spring-beans-2.5.xsd
 http://jax-ws.dev.java.net/spring/core
 http://jax-ws.dev.java.net/spring/core.xsd
 http://jax-ws.dev.java.net/spring/servlet
 http://jax-ws.dev.java.net/spring/servlet.xsd">

 <bean id="arithmeticWebService"
      class="com.springdemo.ws.ArithmeticWebService" />

 <wss:binding url="/arithWebService">
  <wss:service>
   <ws:service bean="#arithmeticWebService" />
  </wss:service>
 </wss:binding>

</beans>
```

Update web.xml: Update the "web.xml" file under `src/main/webapp/WEB-INF` as shown below.

```
<web-app xmlns:xsi="http://www.w3.org/2001/XMLSchema-instance"
 xmlns="http://java.sun.com/xml/ns/javaee"
 xmlns:web="http://java.sun.com/xml/ns/javaee/web-app_2_5.xsd"
 xsi:schemaLocation="http://java.sun.com/xml/ns/javaee
 http://java.sun.com/xml/ns/javaee/web-app_3_0.xsd"
 id="WebApp_ID" version="3.0">

 <display-name>Spring Demo WS Application</display-name>

 <servlet>
  <servlet-name>SpringDemoWS</servlet-name>
  <servlet-class>
      com.sun.xml.ws.transport.http.servlet.WSSpringServlet
```

```
    </servlet-class>
    <load-on-startup>1</load-on-startup>
  </servlet>

  <servlet-mapping>
    <servlet-name>SpringDemoWS</servlet-name>
    <url-pattern>/</url-pattern>
  </servlet-mapping>

  <context-param>
    <param-name>contextConfigLocation</param-name>
    <param-value>/WEB-INF/SpringDemoWS-context.xml</param-value>
  </context-param>

  <listener>
    <listener-class>
        org.springframework.web.context.ContextLoaderListener
    </listener-class>
  </listener>
</web-app>
```

Create Java Files: Create a directory named "java" under "src/main" and then crate a package named "com.springdemo.ws" under "src/main/java". Add the following web-service class.

```
//File Name: ArithmeticWebService.java
package com.springdemo.ws;

import javax.jws.WebMethod;
import javax.jws.WebParam;
import javax.jws.WebService;

@WebService
public class ArithmeticWebService {

 @WebMethod
 public int add(@WebParam(name = "value1") int value1,
             @WebParam(name = "value2") int value2) {
  return value1 + value2;
 }

 @WebMethod
```

```
public int subtract(@WebParam(name = "value1") int value1,
                    @WebParam(name = "value2") int value2) {
  return value1 - value2;
}

@WebMethod
public double multiply(@WebParam(name = "multiplicand") double value1,
                       @WebParam(name = "multiplier") double value2) {
  return value1 * value2;
}

@WebMethod
public double divide(@WebParam(name = "dividend") double value1,
                     @WebParam(name = "divisor") double value2) {
  return value1 / value2;
}
}
```

Compile and Package the Project: Use Maven to compile and package the project. Then the project will be compiled and the ".war" file will be generated in the "target" directory of the project.

Note: Internet connection will be required at least first time to import the libraries and plug-ins used in the pom.xml file.

```
C:\Development\Install\eclipse-juno\workspace\SpringDemoWS> mvn
eclipse:eclipse -Dwtpversion=2.0

[INFO] Scanning for projects...
[INFO] Building SpringDemoWS Maven Webapp 1.0-SNAPSHOT
[INFO] >>> maven-eclipse-plugin:2.9:eclipse (default-cli) @ SpringDemoWS
>>>
[INFO] Using Eclipse Workspace: C:\Development\Install\eclipse-
juno\workspace
[INFO] ------------------------------------------------------------
[INFO] BUILD SUCCESS
[INFO] ------------------------------------------------------------

C:\Development\Install\eclipse-juno\workspace\SpringDemoWS> mvn clean
compile package

[INFO] Scanning for projects...
[INFO] Building SpringDemoWS Maven Webapp 1.0-SNAPSHOT
```

```
[INFO] maven-clean-plugin:2.4.1:clean (default-clean) @ SpringDemoWS
[INFO] Deleting
    C:\Development\Install\eclipse-juno\workspace\SpringDemoWS\target
[INFO] maven-compiler-plugin:3.0:compile (default-compile)
@ SpringDemoWS
[INFO] Compiling 1 source file to C:\Development\Install\
        eclipse-juno\workspace\SpringDemoWS\target\classes
[INFO] maven-compiler-plugin:3.0:compile (default-compile)
@ SpringDemoWS
[INFO] Compiling 1 source file to C:\Development\Install\
        eclipse-juno\workspace\SpringDemoWS\target\classes
[INFO] maven-war-plugin:2.1.1:war (default-war) @ SpringDemoWS
[INFO] Packaging webapp
[INFO] Assembling webapp [SpringDemoWS] in [C:\Development\Install
        \eclipse-juno\workspace\SpringDemoWS\target\SpringDemoWS]
[INFO] Processing war project
[INFO] Copying webapp resources [C:\Development\Install
        \eclipse-juno\workspace\SpringDemoWS\src\main\webapp]
[INFO] Webapp assembled in [4736 msecs]
[INFO] Building war: C:\Development\Install
        \eclipse-juno\workspace\SpringDemoWS\target\SpringDemoWS.war
[INFO] ------------------------------------------------------------------------
[INFO] BUILD SUCCESS
[INFO] ------------------------------------------------------------------------
```

Deploying Application on Application Server: Observe that a war file named "SpringDemoWS.war" is created in the "target" folder of the application. You can deploy this war file in any Servlet-enabled application server / Servlet container.

I planned to use Jetty Servlet container to test our application; to do so I am using Maven Jetty Plug-in which is already configured in the pom.xml file of our project.

Invoke the `"mvn jetty:run"` command to invoke the Jetty server.

```
C:\Development\Install\eclipse-juno\workspace\SpringDemoWS> mvn
jetty:run
[INFO] Scanning for projects...
[INFO] >>> maven-jetty-plugin:6.1.10:run (default-cli) @ SpringDemoWS
>>>
[INFO] maven-resources-plugin:2.5:resources @ SpringDemoWS
...
[INFO] Context path = /SpringDemoWS
...
INFO: WSSERVLET14: JAX-WS servlet initializing
```

```
INFO:  Started SelectChannelConnector@0.0.0.0:9090
[INFO] Started Jetty Server
```

Jetty is listening requests on the port 9090 as specified in the pom.xml plug-in configuration. Invoke a browser with the URL: http://localhost:9090/SpringDemoWS/arithWebService?wsdl

As mentioned earlier, in alternate to deploy the web application on Jetty server as shown above, we can deploy it on any application server/Servlet container. The procedure for the installing the web application under Tomcat is given below.

Download the Tomcat from its home page (http://tomcat.apache.org/) in .zip format. Unzip it (installation) and check that Java is installed and configurations are set properly. Place our web application file SpringDemoWS.war under "webapps" directory. Start up the Tomcat server by invoking "startup.bat" under "bin" directory of the installation. Once Tomcat is started-up, we can check the WSDL of the deployed Web Service using the URL: http://localhost:8080/SpringDemoWS/arithWebService?wsdl. Note that Tomcat is running on the port 8080 as per the default configuration of Tomcat installation.

Web Service Client: To invoke a particular Web Service, we can use any Web Service Client tools such as SOAP UI, or we can call the required web methods through our code.

The procedure for invoking Web Services through SOAP UI Tool is given below.

Download latest SOAP UI Tool (A web-service client testing tool) from http://www.soapui.org/ and install.

File → New soapUI Project → Project Name: ArithWS →

Initial WSDL: http://localhost:9090/SpringDemoWS/arithWebService?wsdl

And click on "OK".

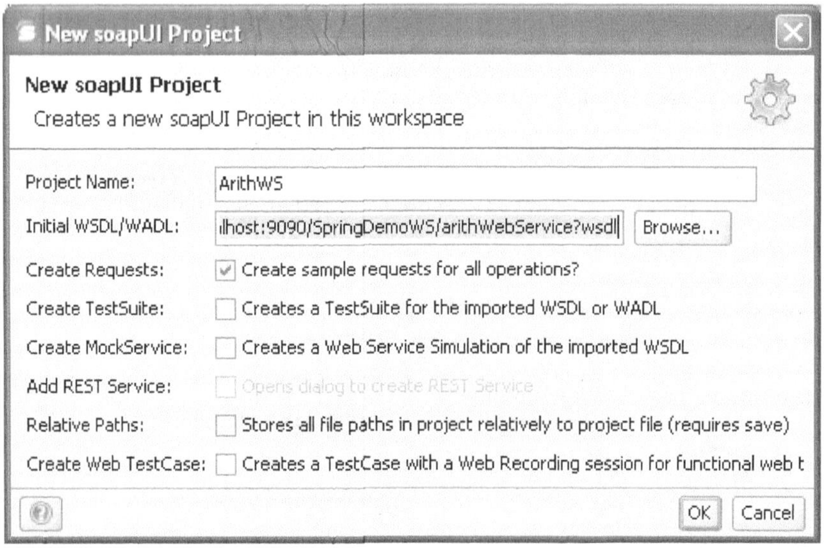

Collapse the tree, and click on "Request1" under "add". Update the input values and click on "run" (green color button) button. Observe that the result.

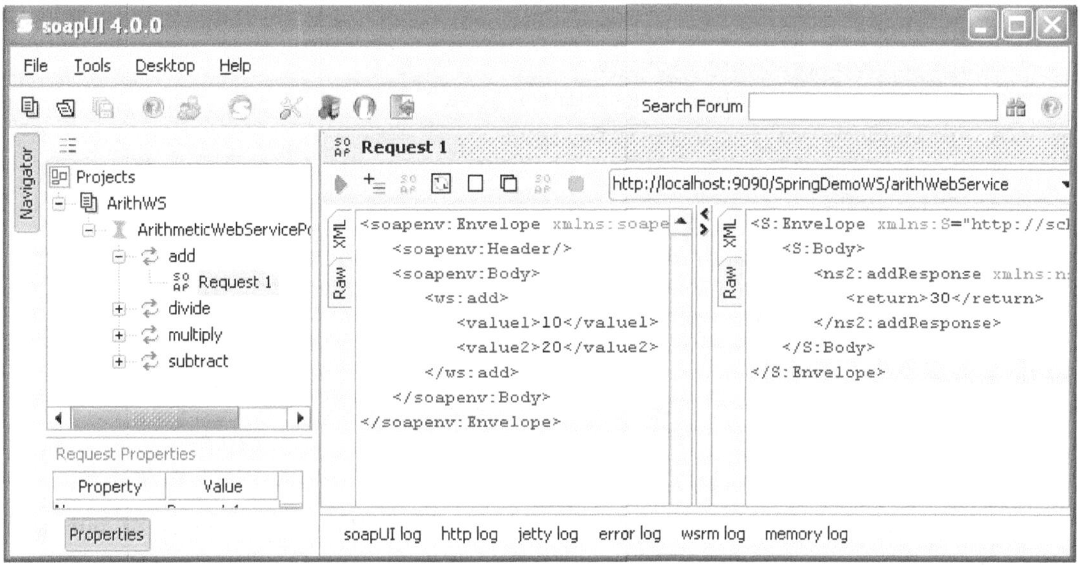

The below section explains how to invoke the Web Service using a Java application program.

The "wsimport" tool (which is available in the "bin" directory of JDK installation) is used to parse the published WSDL file, and generate necessary client files (stub) to access the published web service.

The following command parses and generates the stubs and supported files of the WSDL-http://localhost:9090/SpringDemoWS/arithWebService?wsdl

Make sure your JDK installation "bin" directory is set in the Windows PATH variable.

```
C:\WSClient> wsimport -keep -verbose
        http://localhost:9090/SpringDemoWS/arithWebService?wsdl

parsing WSDL...

generating code...

com\springdemo\ws\Add.java
com\springdemo\ws\AddResponse.java
com\springdemo\ws\ArithmeticWebService.java
com\springdemo\ws\ArithmeticWebServiceService.java
com\springdemo\ws\Divide.java
com\springdemo\ws\DivideResponse.java
com\springdemo\ws\Multiply.java
com\springdemo\ws\MultiplyResponse.java
```

```
com\springdemo\ws\ObjectFactory.java
com\springdemo\ws\Subtract.java
com\springdemo\ws\SubtractResponse.java
com\springdemo\ws\package-info.java

compiling code...

C:\WSClient>tree
Folder PATH listing
C:.
└───com
    └─── springdemo
        └───ws
```

Create a Java Project in Eclipse IDE for invoking the web-methods of our web service.

File → New → Java Project → Project Name: SpringDemoWSClient → Finish.

Copy the generated "com" folder (which was generated earlier using `wsimport` tool and available under `C:\WSClient`) to "src" folder of the project.

Note: We can also use Eclipse IDE's Web Service Client (Select the project → File → New → Other → Web Service Client) tool for generating the stubs for a particular WSDL file.

Store the following Web Service Client program (`ArithmeticWSClient.java`) under `com/springdemo` package of our project (SpringDemoWSClient).

```
//File Name: ArithmeticWSClient.java
package com.springdemo;

import java.net.MalformedURLException;
import java.net.URL;

import javax.xml.namespace.QName;

import com.springdemo.ws.ArithmeticWebService;
import com.springdemo.ws.ArithmeticWebServiceService;

public class ArithmeticWSClient {

 public static void main(String[] args) throws MalformedURLException {

  ArithmeticWebServiceService arithmeticWebService =
   new ArithmeticWebServiceService(
```

```
      new URL("http://localhost:9090/SpringDemoWS/arithWebService"),
      new QName("http://ws.springdemo.com/",
     "ArithmeticWebServiceService"));

   ArithmeticWebService arithWS =
     arithmeticWebService.getArithmeticWebServicePort();


   System.out.println("Addition Result[" +
                 arithWS.add(10, 20) + "]");

   System.out.println("Subtraction Result[" +
                 arithWS.subtract(10, 20) + "]");

   System.out.println("Multiplication Result[" +
                 arithWS.multiply(10, 20) + "]");

   System.out.println("Division Result[" +
                 arithWS.divide(10, 20) + "]");
  }
}
```

Execute the above application, which results as below. (Assumed that the web-service-`arithWebService` is up and running on 8080 port of localhost).

```
Addition Result[30]
Subtraction Result[-10]
Multiplication Result[200.0]
Division Result[0.5]
```

12.2.2 Web Methods with Value Objects as Parameters

This section demonstrates how to pass/receive value objects as parameters/return value. All the steps that should be followed are the same as of the above example, the only additional step needed is, that we need to generate JAX-WS portable artifacts (Java files) of value objects for web service deployment. This can be done using "wsgen" tool provided by JDK.

As an alternate to command-line "wsgen" utility, we used "jaxws-maven-plugin" Maven plug-in to achieve the wsgen goal (configured in the pom.xml of our project).

The "Employee" object is passed/returned as value object to/from web methods of our demonstration application. We are using the same "SpringDemoWS" project (which is created earlier) for Web Service development, and the same project "SpringDemoWSClient" for testing Web Service.

Do the following changes in the "SpringDemoWS" project.

<u>**Add Java Source Files:**</u> Add the following files under "com.springdemo.ws" package.

```
//File Name: Employee.java
package com.springdemo.ws;

import java.io.Serializable;

public class Employee implements Serializable {

 private static final long serialVersionUID = 1L;

 private int empNumber;
 private String empName;
 private double basicPay;
 private double allowances;
 private double deductions;
 private double netpay;

 public int getEmpNumber() {
  return empNumber;
 }

 public void setEmpNumber(int empNumber) {
  this.empNumber = empNumber;
 }

 public String getEmpName() {
  return empName;
 }

 public void setEmpName(String empName) {
  this.empName = empName;
 }

 public double getBasicPay() {
  return basicPay;
 }

 public void setBasicPay(double basicPay) {
  this.basicPay = basicPay;
 }

 public double getAllowances() {
```

```
    return allowances;
   }

   public void setAllowances(double allowances) {
    this.allowances = allowances;
   }

   public double getDeductions() {
    return deductions;
   }

   public void setDeductions(double deductions) {
    this.deductions = deductions;
   }

   public double getNetpay() {
    return netpay;
   }

   public void setNetpay(double netpay) {
    this.netpay = netpay;
   }

  }
```

```
//File Name: EmployeeWS.java
package com.springdemo.ws;

import java.util.HashMap;
import java.util.Map;

import javax.jws.WebMethod;
import javax.jws.WebService;

@WebService
public class EmployeeWS {

 // You may add persistence logic code to access employee data
 Map<Integer, Employee> mapEmployee = new HashMap<Integer, Employee>();

 @WebMethod
 public String addEmployee(Employee emp) {
```

```
  emp.setNetpay(emp.getBasicPay()
            + emp.getAllowances()
            - emp.getDeductions());
  mapEmployee.put(emp.getEmpNumber(), emp);
 return "Employee record is added";
}

@WebMethod
public Employee retrieveEmployee(int empNumber) {
 return mapEmployee.get(empNumber);
}

@WebMethod
public String updateEmployee(Employee emp) {
 mapEmployee.put(emp.getEmpNumber(), emp);
 return "Employee record is updated";
}

@WebMethod
public String deleteEmployee(int empNumber) {
 if (mapEmployee.containsKey(empNumber)) {
  mapEmployee.remove(empNumber);
  return "Employee record is deleted";
 }
 else {
  return "Employee record does not exist";
 }
}
}
```

Update the SpringDemoWS-context.xml file under SpringDemoWS\src\main\webapp\WEB-INF as below.

```
<?xml version="1.0" encoding="UTF-8"?>
<beans xmlns="http://www.springframework.org/schema/beans"
 xmlns:xsi="http://www.w3.org/2001/XMLSchema-instance"
 xmlns:ws="http://jax-ws.dev.java.net/spring/core"
 xmlns:wss="http://jax-ws.dev.java.net/spring/servlet"
 xsi:schemaLocation="http://www.springframework.org/schema/beans
 http://www.springframework.org/schema/beans/spring-beans-2.5.xsd
 http://jax-ws.dev.java.net/spring/core
```

```
  http://jax-ws.dev.java.net/spring/core.xsd
  http://jax-ws.dev.java.net/spring/servlet
  http://jax-ws.dev.java.net/spring/servlet.xsd">

  <bean id="employeeWebService" class="com.springdemo.ws.EmployeeWS" />

  <wss:binding url="/empWebService">
   <wss:service>
    <ws:service bean="#employeeWebService" />
   </wss:service>
  </wss:binding>

</beans>
```

Update the pom.xml under SpringDemoWS as below.

```
<project xmlns="http://maven.apache.org/POM/4.0.0"
    xmlns:xsi="http://www.w3.org/2001/XMLSchema-instance"
    xsi:schemaLocation="http://maven.apache.org/POM/4.0.0
    http://maven.apache.org/maven-v4_0_0.xsd">

  <modelVersion>4.0.0</modelVersion>
  <groupId>SpringDemo</groupId>
  <artifactId>SpringDemoWS</artifactId>
  <packaging>war</packaging>
  <version>1.0-SNAPSHOT</version>
  <name>SpringDemoWS Maven Webapp</name>

  <properties>
   <spring.version>3.2.2.RELEASE</spring.version>
   <java.version>1.6</java.version>
  </properties>

  <dependencies>
   <dependency>
    <groupId>org.springframework</groupId>
    <artifactId>spring-core</artifactId>
    <version>${spring.version}</version>
   </dependency>

   <dependency>
```

```
  <groupId>org.springframework</groupId>
  <artifactId>spring-web</artifactId>
  <version>${spring.version}</version>
</dependency>

<dependency>
  <groupId>org.springframework</groupId>
  <artifactId>spring-webmvc</artifactId>
  <version>${spring.version}</version>
</dependency>

<dependency>
  <groupId>javax.servlet</groupId>
  <artifactId>javax.servlet-api</artifactId>
  <version>3.0.1</version>
</dependency>

<dependency>
  <groupId>com.sun.xml.ws</groupId>
  <artifactId>jaxws-rt</artifactId>
  <version>2.2.8</version>
</dependency>

<dependency>
  <groupId>org.jvnet.jax-ws-commons.spring</groupId>
  <artifactId>jaxws-spring</artifactId>
  <version>1.8</version>
  <exclusions>
   <exclusion>
     <groupId>org.springframework</groupId>
     <artifactId>spring-core</artifactId>
   </exclusion>
   <exclusion>
     <groupId>org.springframework</groupId>
     <artifactId>spring-context</artifactId>
   </exclusion>
   <exclusion>
     <groupId>com.sun.xml.stream.buffer</groupId>
     <artifactId>streambuffer</artifactId>
   </exclusion>
   <exclusion>
     <groupId>org.jvnet.staxex</groupId>
```

```
      <artifactId>stax-ex</artifactId>
     </exclusion>
    </exclusions>
   </dependency>

  </dependencies>
  <build>
   <finalName>SpringDemoWS</finalName>
   <plugins>
    <plugin>
      <groupId>org.apache.maven.plugins</groupId>
      <artifactId>maven-compiler-plugin</artifactId>
     <version>3.0</version>
     <configuration>
       <source>${java.version}</source>
       <target>${java.version}</target>
     </configuration>
    </plugin>

    <plugin>
      <groupId>org.codehaus.mojo</groupId>
      <artifactId>jaxws-maven-plugin</artifactId>
     <version>1.10</version>
     <executions>
      <execution>
        <id>EmployeeWebService</id>
       <goals>
         <goal>wsgen</goal>
       </goals>
        <phase>compile</phase>
       <configuration>
         <sei>com.springdemo.ws.EmployeeWS</sei>
         <genWsdl>true</genWsdl>
         <keep>true</keep>
       </configuration>
      </execution>
     </executions>
    </plugin>

    <plugin>
      <groupId>org.mortbay.jetty</groupId>
      <artifactId>maven-jetty-plugin</artifactId>
```

```
            <version>6.1.26</version>
            <configuration>
             <connectors>
               <connector implementation=
                    "org.mortbay.jetty.nio.SelectChannelConnector">
                <port>9090</port>
               </connector>
             </connectors>
            </configuration>
          </plugin>
        </plugins>
      </build>
    </project>
```

Compile and Deploy the Application:

Compile, package the package and invoke Jetty which will automatically deploy the web application (deploy the war at target directory of the project).

```
C:\Development\Install\eclipse-juno\workspace\SpringDemoWS> mvn clean
  compile package install jetty:run
[INFO] Scanning for projects...
...
...
INFO: Root WebApplicationContext: initialization completed in 1374 ms
INFO: WSSERVLET14: JAX-WS servlet initializing
INFO::Started SelectChannelConnector@0.0.0.0:9090
[INFO] Started Jetty Server
```

Check for WSDL: Now, the Web Service is ready for service. You can check for WSDL by invoking the following URL in any browser.

http://localhost:9090/SpringDemoWS/empWebService?wsdl

Do the following changes in the "SpringDemoWSClient" project.

Generate JAX-WS Portable Artifacts for Client: Generate the JAX-WS portable artifacts of the WSDL for our Web Service client application.

```
C:\WSClient> wsimport -keep -verbose
          http://localhost:9090/SpringDemoWS/empWebService?wsdl
parsing WSDL...
```

```
generating code...

com\springdemo\ws\AddEmployee.java
com\springdemo\ws\AddEmployeeResponse.java
com\springdemo\ws\DeleteEmployee.java
com\springdemo\ws\DeleteEmployeeResponse.java
com\springdemo\ws\Employee.java
com\springdemo\ws\EmployeeWS.java
com\springdemo\ws\EmployeeWSService.java
com\springdemo\ws\ObjectFactory.java
com\springdemo\ws\RetrieveEmployee.java
com\springdemo\ws\RetrieveEmployeeResponse.java
com\springdemo\ws\UpdateEmployee.java
com\springdemo\ws\UpdateEmployeeResponse.java
com\springdemo\ws\package-info.java

compiling code...
```

Copy the "com" folder to "src" folder of our client project.

Add the following main program under "com.springdemo" package.

```
//File Name: EmployeeWSClient.java
package com.springdemo;

import java.net.MalformedURLException;
import java.net.URL;

import javax.xml.namespace.QName;

import com.springdemo.ws.Employee;
import com.springdemo.ws.EmployeeWS;
import com.springdemo.ws.EmployeeWSService;

public class EmployeeWSClient {

  public static void main(String[] args) throws MalformedURLException {
   EmployeeWSService employeeWSService =
       new EmployeeWSService(
         new URL("http://localhost:9090/SpringDemoWS/empWebService"),
         new QName("http://ws.springdemo.com/", "EmployeeWSService"));
```

```
    EmployeeWS employeeWS = employeeWSService.getEmployeeWSPort();

    Employee emp = new Employee();
    emp.setEmpNumber(1001);
    emp.setEmpName("Mohamed");
    emp.setBasicPay(50000.0);
    emp.setAllowances(20000.0);
    emp.setDeductions(10000.0);
    String result = employeeWS.addEmployee(emp);
    System.out.println(result);

    Employee empObj = employeeWS.retrieveEmployee(1001);
    if (empObj == null) {
     System.out.println("Employee record does not exist");
    }
    else {
     System.out.println("\nRetrieved Employee object:");
     System.out.println("Employee Number :" + empObj.getEmpNumber());
     System.out.println("Employee Name :" + empObj.getEmpName());
     System.out.println("Basicpay :" + empObj.getBasicPay());
     System.out.println("Allowances :" + empObj.getAllowances());
     System.out.println("Deductions :" + empObj.getDeductions());
     System.out.println("Netpay :" + empObj.getNetpay());
    }

    empObj.setEmpName("Mohamed Ibrahim");
    result = employeeWS.updateEmployee(empObj);
    System.out.println("\n" + result);

    Employee empObj2 = employeeWS.retrieveEmployee(1001);
    System.out.println("Employee Name :" + empObj2.getEmpName());

    result = employeeWS.deleteEmployee(1001);
    System.out.println("\n" + result);

    System.out.println("\nTrying to delete unavailable record");
    result = employeeWS.deleteEmployee(1001);
    System.out.println("\n" + result);
   }
  }
```

Execute the above "EmployeeWSClient.java" application, which will result as shown below.

```
Employee record is added

Retrieved Employee object:
Employee Number :1001
Employee Name :Mohamed
Basicpay :50000.0
Allowances :20000.0
Deductions :10000.0
Netpay :60000.0

Employee record is updated
Employee Name :Mohamed Ibrahim

Employee record is deleted

Trying to delete unavailable record

Employee record does not exist
```

12.3 RESTFUL WEB SERVICES

In the recent years, one more architectural style is employed for building Web services: RESTful services, as a light-weight simple architecture and an alternate to services based on the WS-standards (also known as "SOAP Web services").

For SOAP-based web services, the standard defines envelopes to transmit requests and responses. In contrast, the REST (REpresentational State Transfer) concepts coined by Roy Fielding simplify access to web services by reusing existing and widespread standards instead of adding new layers to the communication stack. In the REST architecture, clients and servers exchange representations of resources using a standardized interface and protocol.

RESTful web services are web applications built upon the REST architecture. They expose resources (data and functionality) through web URIs, and use the four main HTTP methods POST, GET, PUT, and DELETE to create, retrieve, update, and delete resources respectively. RESTful web services typically map these four main HTTP methods to the so-called CRUD actions: create, retrieve, update, and delete.

12.3.1 Creating a Simple RESTful Web Service

Let us create a simple application using RESTful web services.

Create a project: Create a project named "SpringDemoREST" in Eclipse IDE, like the one we created earlier -SpringDemoWeb.

```
C:\Development\Install\eclipse-juno\workspace> mvn archetype:generate
                        -DgroupId=SpringDemo
```

```
                   -DartifactId=SpringDemoREST
                   -DarchetypeArtifactId=maven-archetype-webapp
                  -DinteractiveMode=false
[INFO] Scanning for projects...
[INFO]
[INFO] ------------------------------------------------------------------
[INFO] Building Maven Stub Project (No POM) 1
[INFO] ------------------------------------------------------------------
[INFO] Parameter: groupId, Value: SpringDemo
[INFO] Parameter: packageName, Value: SpringDemo
[INFO] Parameter: package, Value: SpringDemo
[INFO] Parameter: artifactId, Value: SpringDemoREST
[INFO] Parameter: basedir, Value: C:\Development\Install\eclipse-
juno\workspace
[INFO] Parameter: version, Value: 1.0-SNAPSHOT
[INFO] project created from Old (1.x) Archetype in dir:
C:\Development\Install\eclipse-juno\workspace\SpringDemoREST
[INFO] ------------------------------------------------------------------
[INFO] BUILD SUCCESS
[INFO] ------------------------------------------------------------------
```

Configure the Project for Eclipse IDE:

```
C:\Development\Install\eclipse-juno\workspace\SpringDemoREST> mvn
                                   eclipse:eclipse -Dwtpversion=2.0
[INFO] Scanning for projects...
[INFO]
[INFO] ------------------------------------------------------------------
[INFO] Building SpringDemoREST Maven Webapp 1.0-SNAPSHOT
[INFO] ------------------------------------------------------------------
...
...
[INFO] Wrote Eclipse project for "SpringDemoREST" to
C:\Development\Install\eclipse-juno\workspace\SpringDemoREST.
[INFO] BUILD SUCCESS
```

In Eclipse IDE, File → Import → Existing Projects into Workspace → Select "C:\Development\Install\eclipse-juno\workspace\SpringDemoREST" as root directory → Check "SpringDemoREST" and click on Finish.

Update pom.xml: Update the pom.xml as below.

```
<project xmlns="http://maven.apache.org/POM/4.0.0"
      xmlns:xsi="http://www.w3.org/2001/XMLSchema-instance"
```

```
      xsi:schemaLocation="http://maven.apache.org/POM/4.0.0
      http://maven.apache.org/maven-v4_0_0.xsd">
  <modelVersion>4.0.0</modelVersion>
  <groupId>SpringDemo</groupId>
  <artifactId>SpringDemoREST</artifactId>
  <packaging>war</packaging>
  <version>1.0-SNAPSHOT</version>
  <name>SpringDemoREST Maven Webapp</name>

  <properties>
   <spring.version>3.2.2.RELEASE</spring.version>
   <java.version>1.6</java.version>
  </properties>

  <dependencies>
   <dependency>
    <groupId>org.springframework</groupId>
    <artifactId>spring-core</artifactId>
    <version>${spring.version}</version>
   </dependency>

   <dependency>
    <groupId>org.springframework</groupId>
    <artifactId>spring-web</artifactId>
    <version>${spring.version}</version>
   </dependency>

   <dependency>
    <groupId>org.springframework</groupId>
    <artifactId>spring-webmvc</artifactId>
    <version>${spring.version}</version>
   </dependency>
  </dependencies>

  <build>
   <finalName>SpringDemoREST</finalName>
   <plugins>
    <plugin>
     <groupId>org.apache.maven.plugins</groupId>
     <artifactId>maven-compiler-plugin</artifactId>
     <version>3.0</version>
     <configuration>
```

```
            <source>${java.version}</source>
            <target>${java.version}</target>
          </configuration>
        </plugin>

        <plugin>
          <groupId>org.mortbay.jetty</groupId>
          <artifactId>maven-jetty-plugin</artifactId>
          <version>6.1.26</version>
          <configuration>
            <connectors>
              <connector implementation=
                    "org.mortbay.jetty.nio.SelectChannelConnector">
                <port>9090</port>
              </connector>
            </connectors>
          </configuration>
        </plugin>
      </plugins>
    </build>
  </project>
```

Update Web Configuration (web.xml): Update the web.xml, stored under `/webapp/WEB-INF`, as shown below.

```
<web-app xmlns="http://java.sun.com/xml/ns/javaee"
      xmlns:xsi="http://www.w3.org/2001/XMLSchema-instance"
      xsi:schemaLocation="http://java.sun.com/xml/ns/javaee
      http://java.sun.com/xml/ns/javaee/web-app_2_5.xsd"
      version="2.5">

  <display-name>Spring Demo REST Application</display-name>

  <servlet>
    <servlet-name>SpringDemoREST</servlet-name>
    <servlet-class>
      org.springframework.web.servlet.DispatcherServlet
    </servlet-class>
    <load-on-startup>1</load-on-startup>
  </servlet>

  <servlet-mapping>
```

```
  <servlet-name>SpringDemoREST</servlet-name>
  <url-pattern>/</url-pattern>
 </servlet-mapping>

 <context-param>
  <param-name>contextConfigLocation</param-name>
  <param-value>/WEB-INF/SpringDemoREST-servlet.xml</param-value>
 </context-param>

 <listener>
  <listener-class>
   org.springframework.web.context.ContextLoaderListener
  </listener-class>
 </listener>

</web-app>
```

Spring Configuration File: Store the following Spring configuration file (SpringDemoREST-servlet.xml) under /webapp/WEB-INF directory of the project.

```
<beans xmlns="http://www.springframework.org/schema/beans"
  xmlns:context="http://www.springframework.org/schema/context"
  xmlns:p="http://www.springframework.org/schema/p"
  xmlns:mvc="http://www.springframework.org/schema/mvc"
  xmlns:xsi="http://www.w3.org/2001/XMLSchema-instance"
  xsi:schemaLocation="
  http://www.springframework.org/schema/beans
  http://www.springframework.org/schema/beans/spring-beans-3.0.xsd
  http://www.springframework.org/schema/context
  http://www.springframework.org/schema/context/spring-context-3.0.xsd
  http://www.springframework.org/schema/mvc
  http://www.springframework.org/schema/mvc/spring-mvc-3.0.xsd">

 <context:component-scan base-package="com.springdemo.controller" />

 <mvc:annotation-driven />

 <bean
 class="org.springframework.web.servlet.view.InternalResourceViewResolver"
  p:prefix="/WEB-INF/jsp/" p:suffix=".jsp" />

</beans>
```

Controller Class: Store the following Controller class (CountryController.java) under the package "com.springdemo.controller" of the project.

```
//File Name: CountryController.java
package com.springdemo.controller;

import java.util.HashMap;
import java.util.Map;

import org.springframework.stereotype.Controller;
import org.springframework.ui.ModelMap;
import org.springframework.web.bind.annotation.PathVariable;
import org.springframework.web.bind.annotation.RequestMapping;
import org.springframework.web.bind.annotation.RequestMethod;

@Controller
@RequestMapping("/country")
public class CountryController {

  public static Map<String, String> countryMap =
                              new HashMap<String, String>();
  public static Map<String, String> stateMap = new HashMap<String,
String>();

  static {
    // Data representation logic for illustrating REST WS only
    countryMap.put("AF", "AFGHANISTAN");
    countryMap.put("CN", "CHINA");
    countryMap.put("IN", "INDIA");
    countryMap.put("MY", "MALAYSIA");
    countryMap.put("SG", "SINGAPORE");

    // Few states in India
    stateMap.put("AP", "Andhra Pradesh");
    stateMap.put("TN", "TAMIL NADU");
    stateMap.put("UP", "Uttar Pradesh");
  }

  @RequestMapping(value = "/{countryCode}", method = RequestMethod.GET)
  public String getCountryName(@PathVariable String countryCode,
                               ModelMap model) {
    String countryName = countryMap.get(countryCode);
    if (countryName == null)
```

```
        countryName = "Country code is not found";
      model.addAttribute("countryName", countryName);
      return "display";
    }

    @RequestMapping(value = "/{countryCode}/{stateCode}",
                method = RequestMethod.GET)
  public String getCountryAndStateName(@PathVariable String countryCode,
                @PathVariable String stateCode, ModelMap model) {
      String countryName = countryMap.get(countryCode);
      String stateName = null;
      if (countryName == null) {
        countryName = "Country code is not found";
      }
      else {
        stateName = stateMap.get(stateCode);

        if (stateName == null)
          stateName = "State code is not found";
      }
      model.addAttribute("countryName", countryName);
      model.addAttribute("stateName", stateName);
      return "display";
    }
  }
```

JSP File (View):

Store the following "display.jsp" under /webapp/WEB-INF/jsp directory of the project.

```
<html>
 <body>
   <h2>Country Name: ${countryName}</h2>
   <h2>State Name: ${stateName}</h2>
 </body>
</html>
```

Deploy the Application on Jetty Server: Compile, package and deploy our web application for testing. As we already configured Jerry application server in pom.xml, simply use 'mvn jetty:run'.

```
C:\Development\Install\eclipse-juno\workspace\SpringDemoREST> mvn clean
                          compile package install jetty:run
```

```
[INFO] Scanning for projects...
[INFO]
[INFO] ------------------------------------------------------------------------
[INFO] Building SpringDemoREST Maven Webapp 1.0-SNAPSHOT
[INFO] ------------------------------------------------------------------------
...
[INFO] Webapp assembled in [639 msecs]
[INFO] Building war: C:\Development\Install\eclipse-juno\workspace\SpringDemoREST\target\SpringDemoREST.war
...
[INFO] Configuring Jetty for project: SpringDemoREST Maven Webapp
[INFO] Webapp source directory = C:\Development\Install\eclipse-juno\workspace\SpringDemoREST\src\main\webapp
...
[INFO] Context path = /SpringDemoREST
INFO::Started SelectChannelConnector@0.0.0.0:9090
[INFO] Started Jetty Server
```

Test the Application: Invoke the browser with path-variables are substituted with actual values.

URL: http://localhost:9090/SpringDemoREST/country/**IN/TN**

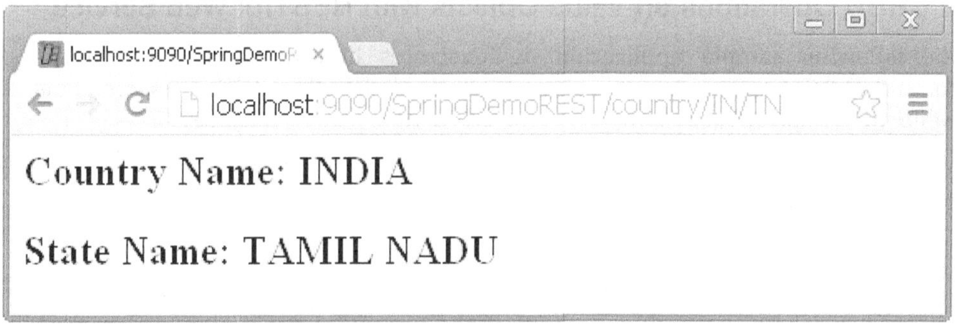

URL: http://localhost:9090/SpringDemoREST/country/IN/MP

URL: http://localhost:9090/SpringDemoREST/country/IN

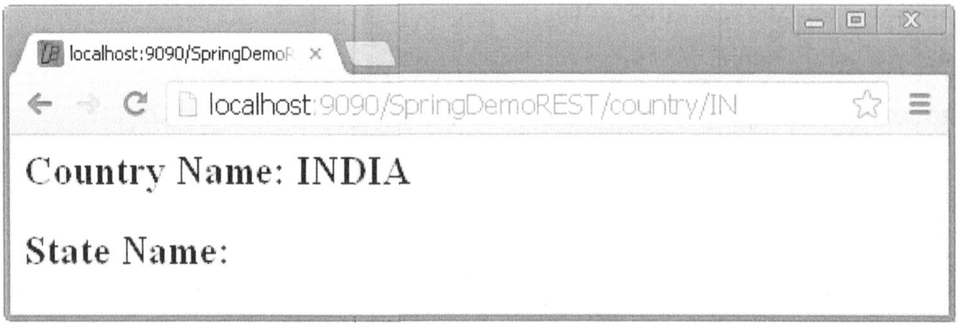

URL: http://localhost:9090/SpringDemoREST/country/AU

12.3.2 CRUD Operations on Value Objects with RESTful Web Service

The following sample application demonstrates how to do CRUD (Create, Read, Update, and Delete) operations on value objects with RESTful Web Services. This service is capable in accepting/responding data in XML and JSON formats.

Java Files: Add the following Employee entity file to the 'com.springdemo.entity' package.

```
//File Name: Employee.java
package com.springdemo.entity;

import java.io.Serializable;

import javax.xml.bind.annotation.XmlRootElement;
import org.codehaus.jackson.annotate.JsonAutoDetect;

@XmlRootElement
@JsonAutoDetect
public class Employee implements Serializable {

  private static final long serialVersionUID = 1L;

  private int empNumber;
```

```
private String empName;
private double basicPay;
private double allowances;
private double deductions;
private double netpay;

public Employee() {}

public Employee(int empNumber, String empName, double basicPay,
             double allowances, double deductions) {
  this.empNumber = empNumber;
  this.empName = empName;
  this.basicPay = basicPay;
  this.allowances = allowances;
  this.deductions = deductions;
  this.netpay = basicPay + allowances - deductions;
}

public int getEmpNumber() {
  return empNumber;
}

public void setEmpNumber(int empNumber) {
  this.empNumber = empNumber;
}

public String getEmpName() {
  return empName;
}

public void setEmpName(String empName) {
  this.empName = empName;
}

public double getBasicPay() {
  return basicPay;
}

public void setBasicPay(double basicPay) {
  this.basicPay = basicPay;
}
```

```
  public double getAllowances() {
    return allowances;
  }

  public void setAllowances(double allowances) {
    this.allowances = allowances;
  }

  public double getDeductions() {
    return deductions;
  }

  public void setDeductions(double deductions) {
    this.deductions = deductions;
  }

  public double getNetpay() {
    return netpay;
  }

  public void setNetpay(double netpay) {
    this.netpay = netpay;
  }

  public String toString() {
    return "\nEmployee No.: \t" + empNumber +
           "\nEmployee Name: \t" + empName +
           "\nBasic Pay: \t" + basicPay +
           "\nAllowances: \t" + allowances +
           "\nDeductions: \t" + deductions +
           "\nNetpay: \t" + netpay;
  }
}
```

Store the following value object file in the package 'com.springdemo.entity'.

```
//EmployeeList.java
package com.springdemo.entity;

import java.util.ArrayList;
import java.util.List;
```

```
import javax.xml.bind.annotation.XmlRootElement;

import org.codehaus.jackson.annotate.JsonAutoDetect;

@XmlRootElement
@JsonAutoDetect
public class EmployeeList {

  List<Employee> employee = new ArrayList<Employee>();

  public List<Employee> getEmployee() {
    return employee;
  }

  public void setEmployee(List<Employee> employee) {
    this.employee = employee;
  }
}
```

Store the following controller class under 'com.springdemo.controller' package.

```
//File Name: EmployeeController.java
package com.springdemo.controller;

import java.util.ArrayList;
import java.util.HashSet;
import java.util.Iterator;
import java.util.Set;

import org.springframework.http.HttpStatus;
import org.springframework.stereotype.Controller;
import org.springframework.web.bind.annotation.PathVariable;
import org.springframework.web.bind.annotation.RequestBody;
import org.springframework.web.bind.annotation.RequestMapping;
import org.springframework.web.bind.annotation.RequestMethod;
import org.springframework.web.bind.annotation.ResponseBody;
import org.springframework.web.bind.annotation.ResponseStatus;

import com.springdemo.entity.Employee;
import com.springdemo.entity.EmployeeList;

@Controller
```

```
@RequestMapping("/employee")
public class EmployeeController {

  static Set<Employee> employeeSet = new HashSet<Employee>();

  static {
    // Populate Employee data
    employeeSet.add(
    new Employee(1001, "Mohamed Ibrahim", 50000.00, 20000.0, 10000.0));
    employeeSet.add(
     new Employee(1002, "Ajay Kumar", 55000.00, 21000.0, 10500.0));
    employeeSet.add(
     new Employee(1003, "John Peter", 60000.00, 22000.0, 11000.0));
    employeeSet.add(
     new Employee(1004, "Anwar", 65000.00, 23000.0, 13500.0));
    employeeSet.add(
     new Employee(1005, "Mariyana", 70000.00, 25000.0, 14000.0));
  }

  @RequestMapping(value = "/{empNumber}",
             method = RequestMethod.GET,
             headers = "Accept=application/xml, application/json",
             produces = {"application/json", "application/xml"})
  @ResponseBody
  public Employee getEmployee(@PathVariable int empNumber) {
    for (Employee employee : employeeSet) {
      if (employee.getEmpNumber() == empNumber) {
        return employee;
      }
    }
    return null;
  }

  @RequestMapping(method = RequestMethod.GET,
             headers = "Accept=application/xml, application/json",
             produces = {"application/json", "application/xml"})
  @ResponseStatus(HttpStatus.OK)
  @ResponseBody
  public EmployeeList getAllEmployees() {
    EmployeeList employeeList = new EmployeeList();
     employeeList.setEmployee(new ArrayList<Employee>(employeeSet));
    return employeeList;
  }
```

```
@RequestMapping(value = "/{empNumber}", method = RequestMethod.PUT,
        headers = "Accept=application/xml, application/json",
        produces = {"application/json", "application/xml"},
        consumes = {"application/json", "application/xml"})
@ResponseBody
public Employee updateEmployee(@RequestBody Employee employee,
                               @PathVariable int empNumber) {
  for (Employee emp : employeeSet) {
    if (emp.getEmpNumber() == empNumber) {
      emp.setEmpName(employee.getEmpName());
      emp.setBasicPay(employee.getBasicPay());
      emp.setAllowances(employee.getAllowances());
      emp.setDeductions(employee.getDeductions());
      emp.setNetpay(employee.getBasicPay()
            + employee.getAllowances()
            - employee.getDeductions());

      return emp;
    }
  }

  return null;
}

@RequestMapping(value = "/{empNumber}", method = RequestMethod.DELETE,
        headers = "Accept=application/xml, application/json",
        produces = {"application/json", "application/xml"})
@ResponseStatus(HttpStatus.ACCEPTED)
@ResponseBody
public String deleteEmployee(@PathVariable int empNumber) {
  Iterator<Employee> employeeIterator = employeeSet.iterator();
  while (employeeIterator.hasNext()) {
    Employee employee = employeeIterator.next();
    if (employee.getEmpNumber() == empNumber) {
      employeeIterator.remove();
      return "Record is deleted";
    }
  }
  return "Record is not found";
}
```

```
  @RequestMapping(method = RequestMethod.POST,
                  headers = "Accept=application/xml, application/json",
                  produces = {"application/json", "application/xml"},
                  consumes = {"application/json", "application/xml"})
  @ResponseBody
  @ResponseStatus(HttpStatus.CREATED)
  public String createEmployee(@RequestBody Employee employee) {
    employeeSet.add(employee);
    return "Employee record is added";
  }
}
```

Compile, Package, and Deploy the project on Jetty Server:

```
C:\Development\Install\eclipse-juno\workspace\SpringDemoREST> mvn clean
                                                compile package jetty:run
[INFO] Scanning for projects...
[INFO] ------------------------------------------------------------------------
[INFO] Building SpringDemoREST Maven Webapp 1.0-SNAPSHOT
[INFO] ------------------------------------------------------------------------
...
...
INFO: FrameworkServlet 'SpringDemoREST': initialization completed in
327 ms
INFO::Started SelectChannelConnector@0.0.0.0:9090
[INFO] Started Jetty Server
```

Web Service Client Application

Create a simple Java project and execute the following client application which invokes the RESTful Web Service which is deployed as shown in the above section.

Create a Java Project in Eclipse IDE: File → New → Other → Java Project → Specify 'SpringDemoRESTWSClient' as Project Name → Finish.

Store the following Employee and EmployeeList value objects under the package 'com.springdemo.entity' (you can copy these classes from the SpringDemoREST project).

```
//File Name: Employee.java
package com.springdemo.entity;

import java.io.Serializable;

import javax.xml.bind.annotation.XmlRootElement;
```

```
@XmlRootElement
public class Employee implements Serializable {

  private static final long serialVersionUID = 1L;

  private int empNumber;
  private String empName;
  private double basicPay;
  private double allowances;
  private double deductions;
  private double netpay;

  public Employee() {
  }

  public Employee(int empNumber, String empName, double basicPay,
              double allowances, double deductions) {
    this.empNumber = empNumber;
    this.empName = empName;
    this.basicPay = basicPay;
    this.allowances = allowances;
    this.deductions = deductions;
    this.netpay = basicPay + allowances - deductions;
  }

  public int getEmpNumber() {
    return empNumber;
  }

  public void setEmpNumber(int empNumber) {
    this.empNumber = empNumber;
  }

  public String getEmpName() {
    return empName;
  }

  public void setEmpName(String empName) {
    this.empName = empName;
  }

  public double getBasicPay() {
```

```
    return basicPay;
  }

  public void setBasicPay(double basicPay) {
    this.basicPay = basicPay;
  }

  public double getAllowances() {
    return allowances;
  }

  public void setAllowances(double allowances) {
    this.allowances = allowances;
  }

  public double getDeductions() {
    return deductions;
  }

  public void setDeductions(double deductions) {
    this.deductions = deductions;
  }

  public double getNetpay() {
    return netpay;
  }

  public void setNetpay(double netpay) {
    this.netpay = netpay;
  }

  public String toString() {
    return "\nEmployee No.: \t" + empNumber +
           "\nEmployee Name: \t" + empName +
           "\nBasic Pay: \t" + basicPay +
           "\nAllowances: \t" + allowances +
           "\nDeductions: \t" + deductions +
           "\nNetpay: \t" + netpay;
  }
}

//File Name: EmployeeList.java
package com.springdemo.entity;

import java.util.ArrayList;
```

```
import java.util.List;

import javax.xml.bind.annotation.XmlRootElement;

@XmlRootElement
public class EmployeeList {

  List<Employee> employee = new ArrayList<Employee>();

  public List<Employee> getEmployee() {
    return employee;
  }

  public void setEmployee(List<Employee> employee) {
    this.employee = employee;
  }
}
```

Store the following client application under the 'com.springdemo' package of our client project. This application uses XML as data exchange format.

```
//File Name: EmployeeWSClient.java
package com.springdemo;

import java.io.BufferedReader;
import java.io.InputStreamReader;
import java.io.OutputStream;
import java.io.OutputStreamWriter;
import java.io.StringReader;
import java.io.StringWriter;
import java.io.Writer;
import java.net.HttpURLConnection;
import java.net.URL;

import javax.xml.bind.JAXBContext;
import javax.xml.bind.Marshaller;
import javax.xml.bind.Unmarshaller;
import javax.xml.transform.OutputKeys;
import javax.xml.transform.Source;
import javax.xml.transform.Transformer;
import javax.xml.transform.TransformerFactory;
import javax.xml.transform.stream.StreamResult;
```

```
import javax.xml.transform.stream.StreamSource;

import com.springdemo.entity.Employee;
import com.springdemo.entity.EmployeeList;

public class EmployeeWSClient {

  HttpURLConnection connection;
  BufferedReader br;
  String result;
  JAXBContext jaxbContext;
  Marshaller jaxbMarshaller;
  Unmarshaller jaxbUnmarshaller;

  public static void main(String[] args) {

    try {
      EmployeeWSClient restClient = new EmployeeWSClient();

      System.out.println("Get the list of All Employees");
      EmployeeList empList = restClient.getAllEmployees();

      System.out.println("\n=====================================\n");
      System.out.println("Get specific employee record
                with empNumber: 1001");
      Employee emp = restClient.getEmployee(1001);

      System.out.println("\n=====================================\n");
      System.out.println("Create an Employee record
                and add it into Employee list");
      Employee empNew = new Employee
              (1006, "Tammam", 75000.0, 28000.0, 16000.0);
      String result = restClient.createEmployee(empNew);

      System.out.println("\n=====================================\n");
      System.out.println("Get the created employee
                record [empNumber: 1006]");
      Employee empCreated = restClient.getEmployee(1006);

      System.out.println("\n=====================================\n");
      System.out.println("Update the employee record [empNumber: 1006]");
      empCreated.setEmpName("Tammam Fadal");
```

```
      empCreated.setBasicPay(76000.0);
      restClient.updateEmployee(1006, empCreated);

      System.out.println("\n=====================================\n");
      System.out.println("Get the updated employee record
                    [empNumber: 1006]");
      restClient.getEmployee(1006);

      System.out.println("\n=====================================\n");
      System.out.println("Delete employee record [empNumber: 1002]");
      restClient.deleteEmployee(1002);

      System.out.println("\n=====================================\n");
      System.out.println("Try to get the deleted employee record
                    [empNumber: 1002]");
      restClient.getEmployee(1002);
    }
    catch (Exception e) {
      System.out.println(e);
    }
  }

  EmployeeList getAllEmployees() throws Exception {
    try {
      // Get All Employees in XML format
      URL url = new URL("http://localhost:9090/SpringDemoREST/employee");
      connection = (HttpURLConnection) url.openConnection();
      connection.setRequestMethod("GET");
      connection.setRequestProperty("Accept", "application/xml");

      if (connection.getResponseCode() != HttpURLConnection.HTTP_OK) {
        throw new RuntimeException("Failed : HTTP error code : " +
                          connection.getResponseCode());
      }

      br = new BufferedReader(new InputStreamReader(
                    (connection.getInputStream())));
      result = br.readLine();
      System.out.println("Result of getAllEmployees:\n");
      printXML(result);
      connection.disconnect();

      // Bind the result into Value Object and display the values
```

```
        jaxbContext = JAXBContext.newInstance(EmployeeList.class);
        jaxbUnmarshaller = jaxbContext.createUnmarshaller();
        EmployeeList employeeList = (EmployeeList)
                                jaxbUnmarshaller.unmarshal(
                                new StringReader(result));

        System.out.println("EMPLOYEE LIST");
        for (Employee emp : employeeList.getEmployee()) {
          System.out.println(emp);
        }

        return employeeList;
      }
      catch (Exception e) {
        System.out.println("Error [" + e.getMessage() + "]");
        throw e;
      }
      finally {
        if (connection != null) {
          connection.disconnect();
        }
      }
    }

    Employee getEmployee(int employeeNumber) throws Exception {
      try {
        // Get specific employee record
        URL url = new URL("http://localhost:9090/SpringDemoREST/employee/
                " + employeeNumber);
        connection = (HttpURLConnection) url.openConnection();
        connection.setRequestMethod("GET");
        connection.setRequestProperty("Accept", "application/xml");

        if (connection.getResponseCode() != HttpURLConnection.HTTP_OK) {
          throw new RuntimeException("Failed : HTTP error code : " +
                                connection.getResponseCode());
        }

        br = new BufferedReader(new InputStreamReader(
                        (connection.getInputStream())));
        result = br.readLine();
```

```
        connection.disconnect();

        if (result != null) {
          System.out.println("Result of retrieving specific record:\n");
          printXML(result);

          // Bind the result into Value Object and display the values
          jaxbContext = JAXBContext.newInstance(Employee.class);
          jaxbUnmarshaller = jaxbContext.createUnmarshaller();
          Employee employee = (Employee)
                          jaxbUnmarshaller.unmarshal(
                          new StringReader(result));
          System.out.println("EMPLOYEE");
          System.out.println(employee);

          return employee;
        }
        else {
         System.out.println("No employee record found with Employee Number: "
                            + employeeNumber);
          return null;
        }
      }
      catch (Exception e) {
        System.out.println("Error [" + e.getMessage() + "]");
        throw e;
      }
      finally {
        if (connection != null) {
          connection.disconnect();
        }
      }
    }

    String createEmployee(Employee empNew) throws Exception {
      try {
      URL url = new URL("http://localhost:9090/SpringDemoREST/employee");
      connection = (HttpURLConnection) url.openConnection();
      connection.setRequestMethod("POST");
      connection.setDoOutput(true);
      connection.setDoInput(true);
      connection.setUseCaches(false);
```

```
      connection.setAllowUserInteraction(false);
     connection.setRequestProperty("Content-Type", "application/xml");

      StringWriter stringWriter = new StringWriter();
      jaxbContext = JAXBContext.newInstance(Employee.class);
      jaxbMarshaller = jaxbContext.createMarshaller();
      jaxbMarshaller.marshal(empNew, stringWriter);
      String empNewXML = stringWriter.getBuffer().toString();

      System.out.println("Given Employee Record in XML format:");
      printXML(empNewXML);

      OutputStream out = connection.getOutputStream();
      Writer writer = new OutputStreamWriter(out, "UTF-8");
      writer.write(empNewXML);
      writer.close();
      out.close();

    if (connection.getResponseCode() != HttpURLConnection.HTTP_CREATED)
  {
        throw new RuntimeException("Failed : HTTP error code : " +
                                connection.getResponseCode());
      }

      br = new BufferedReader(new InputStreamReader(
                            (connection.getInputStream())));
      result = br.readLine();
      connection.disconnect();

      System.out.println(result);

      return result;
    }
    catch (Exception e) {
      System.out.println("Error [" + e.getMessage() + "]");
      throw e;
    }
    finally {
      if (connection != null) {
        connection.disconnect();
      }
    }
  }
```

```
void updateEmployee(int empNumber, Employee modifiedEmployee)
                                        throws Exception {
  try {
   URL url = new URL("http://localhost:9090/SpringDemoREST/employee/" +
              empNumber);
    connection = (HttpURLConnection) url.openConnection();
    connection.setRequestMethod("PUT");
    connection.setDoOutput(true);
    connection.setDoInput(true);
    connection.setUseCaches(false);
    connection.setAllowUserInteraction(false);
   connection.setRequestProperty("Content-Type", "application/xml");

    StringWriter stringWriter = new StringWriter();
    jaxbContext = JAXBContext.newInstance(Employee.class);
    jaxbMarshaller = jaxbContext.createMarshaller();
    jaxbMarshaller.marshal(modifiedEmployee, stringWriter);
    String empNewXML = stringWriter.getBuffer().toString();

    System.out.println("Given Employee Record in XML format:");
    printXML(empNewXML);

    OutputStream out = connection.getOutputStream();
    Writer writer = new OutputStreamWriter(out, "UTF-8");
    writer.write(empNewXML);
    writer.close();
    out.close();

    if (connection.getResponseCode() != HttpURLConnection.HTTP_OK) {
      throw new RuntimeException("Failed : HTTP error code : " +
                 connection.getResponseCode());
    }

    br = new BufferedReader(new InputStreamReader(
             (connection.getInputStream())));
    result = br.readLine();
    connection.disconnect();

    if (result == null) {
    System.out.println("Employee record does not match for updation");
    }
```

```
        else {
          System.out.println("Employee record is updated");
        }
      }
      catch (Exception e) {
        System.out.println("Error [" + e.getMessage() + "]");
        throw e;
      }
      finally {
        if (connection != null) {
          connection.disconnect();
        }
      }
    }

    void deleteEmployee(int employeeNumber) throws Exception {
      try {
        // Delete specific employee record
        URL url = new URL("http://localhost:9090/SpringDemoREST/employee/" +
                        employeeNumber);
        connection = (HttpURLConnection) url.openConnection();
        connection.setRequestMethod("DELETE");
        connection.setRequestProperty("Accept", "application/xml");

        if (connection.getResponseCode() != HttpURLConnection.HTTP_ACCEPTED) {
          throw new RuntimeException("Failed : HTTP error code : " +
                                  connection.getResponseCode());
        }

        br = new BufferedReader(new InputStreamReader(
                           (connection.getInputStream())));
        result = br.readLine();
        connection.disconnect();

        System.out.println(result);
      }
      catch (Exception e) {
        System.out.println("Error [" + e.getMessage() + "]");
        throw e;
      }
```

```
    finally {
      if (connection != null) {
        connection.disconnect();
      }
    }
  }

  public static void printXML(String xmlString) throws Exception {
    Source xmlInput = new StreamSource(new StringReader(xmlString));
    StreamResult xmlOutput = new StreamResult(new StringWriter());

    Transformer transformer = TransformerFactory.newInstance()
                                                .newTransformer();
    transformer.setOutputProperty(OutputKeys.INDENT, "yes");
    transformer.setOutputProperty(
        "{http://xml.apache.org/xslt}indent-amount", "2");
    transformer.transform(xmlInput, xmlOutput);

    System.out.println(xmlOutput.getWriter().toString());
  }

}
```

A sample run of the above application results below.

```
Get the list of All Employees
Result of getAllEmployees:

<?xml version="1.0" encoding="UTF-8"?>
<employeeList>
  <employee>
    <allowances>20000.0</allowances>
    <basicPay>50000.0</basicPay>
    <deductions>10000.0</deductions>
    <empName>Mohamed Ibrahim</empName>
    <empNumber>1001</empNumber>
    <netpay>60000.0</netpay>
  </employee>
  <employee>
    <allowances>21000.0</allowances>
    <basicPay>55000.0</basicPay>
    <deductions>10500.0</deductions>
```

```
      <empName>Ajay Kumar</empName>
      <empNumber>1002</empNumber>
      <netpay>65500.0</netpay>
   </employee>
   <employee>
      <allowances>22000.0</allowances>
      <basicPay>60000.0</basicPay>
      <deductions>11000.0</deductions>
      <empName>John Peter</empName>
      <empNumber>1003</empNumber>
      <netpay>71000.0</netpay>
   </employee>
   <employee>
      <allowances>23000.0</allowances>
      <basicPay>65000.0</basicPay>
      <deductions>13500.0</deductions>
      <empName>Anwar</empName>
      <empNumber>1004</empNumber>
      <netpay>74500.0</netpay>
   </employee>
   <employee>
      <allowances>25000.0</allowances>
      <basicPay>70000.0</basicPay>
      <deductions>14000.0</deductions>
      <empName>Mariyana</empName>
      <empNumber>1005</empNumber>
      <netpay>81000.0</netpay>
   </employee>
</employeeList>

EMPLOYEE LIST

Employee No.:  1001
Employee Name: Mohamed Ibrahim
Basic Pay:     50000.0
Allowances:    20000.0
Deductions:    10000.0
Netpay:        60000.0

Employee No.:  1002
Employee Name: Ajay Kumar
Basic Pay:     55000.0
```

```
Allowances:     21000.0
Deductions:     10500.0
Netpay:         65500.0

Employee No.:   1003
Employee Name:  John Peter
Basic Pay:      60000.0
Allowances:     22000.0
Deductions:     11000.0
Netpay:         71000.0

Employee No.:   1004
Employee Name:  Anwar
Basic Pay:      65000.0
Allowances:     23000.0
Deductions:     13500.0
Netpay:         74500.0

Employee No.:   1005
Employee Name:  Mariyana
Basic Pay:      70000.0
Allowances:     25000.0
Deductions:     14000.0
Netpay:         81000.0

===================================

Get specific employee record with empNumber: 1001
Result of retrieving specific record:

<?xml version="1.0" encoding="UTF-8"?>
<employee>
   <allowances>20000.0</allowances>
   <basicPay>50000.0</basicPay>
   <deductions>10000.0</deductions>
   <empName>Mohamed Ibrahim</empName>
   <empNumber>1001</empNumber>
   <netpay>60000.0</netpay>
</employee>

EMPLOYEE

Employee No.:   1001
```

```
Employee Name: Mohamed Ibrahim
Basic Pay:     50000.0
Allowances:    20000.0
Deductions:    10000.0
Netpay:        60000.0

=====================================

Create an Employee record and add it into Employee list
Given Employee Record in XML format:
<?xml version="1.0" encoding="UTF-8"?>
<employee>
  <allowances>28000.0</allowances>
  <basicPay>75000.0</basicPay>
  <deductions>16000.0</deductions>
  <empName>Tammam</empName>
  <empNumber>1006</empNumber>
  <netpay>87000.0</netpay>
</employee>

Employee record is added

=====================================

Get the created employee record [empNumber: 1006]
Result of retrieving specific record:

<?xml version="1.0" encoding="UTF-8"?>
<employee>
  <allowances>28000.0</allowances>
  <basicPay>75000.0</basicPay>
  <deductions>16000.0</deductions>
  <empName>Tammam</empName>
  <empNumber>1006</empNumber>
  <netpay>87000.0</netpay>
</employee>

EMPLOYEE

Employee No.:  1006
Employee Name: Tammam
Basic Pay:     75000.0
```

```
Allowances:    28000.0
Deductions:    16000.0
Netpay:        87000.0

=====================================

Update the employee record [empNumber: 1006]
Given Employee Record in XML format:
<?xml version="1.0" encoding="UTF-8"?>
<employee>
  <allowances>28000.0</allowances>
  <basicPay>76000.0</basicPay>
  <deductions>16000.0</deductions>
  <empName>Tammam Fadal</empName>
  <empNumber>1006</empNumber>
  <netpay>87000.0</netpay>
</employee>

Employee record is updated

=====================================

Get the updated employee record [empNumber: 1006]
Result of retrieving specific record:

<?xml version="1.0" encoding="UTF-8"?>
<employee>
  <allowances>28000.0</allowances>
  <basicPay>76000.0</basicPay>
  <deductions>16000.0</deductions>
  <empName>Tammam Fadal</empName>
  <empNumber>1006</empNumber>
  <netpay>88000.0</netpay>
</employee>

EMPLOYEE

Employee No.:  1006
Employee Name: Tammam Fadal
Basic Pay:     76000.0
Allowances:    28000.0
Deductions:    16000.0
Netpay:        88000.0
```

```
==================================

Delete employee record [empNumber: 1002]
Record is deleted

==================================

Try to get the deleted employee record [empNumber: 1002]
No employee record found with Employee Number: 1002
```

The following client application which invokes the above said RESTful Web Service and it uses JSON as data exchange format. Include library for processing JSON data. I download and included the 'gson v 1.7.1' jar file into the class-path of our client project. This gson jar file can be downloaded from Maven repository (http://mvnrepository.com/) under the group Id: com.google.code.gson and artifact Id: gson.

```
//File Name: EmployeeWSClientUsingJSON .java
package com.springdemo;

import java.io.BufferedReader;
import java.io.InputStreamReader;
import java.io.OutputStream;
import java.io.OutputStreamWriter;
import java.io.StringReader;
import java.io.StringWriter;
import java.io.Writer;
import java.net.HttpURLConnection;
import java.net.URL;

import javax.xml.bind.JAXBContext;
import javax.xml.bind.Marshaller;
import javax.xml.bind.Unmarshaller;
import javax.xml.transform.OutputKeys;
import javax.xml.transform.Source;
import javax.xml.transform.Transformer;
import javax.xml.transform.TransformerFactory;
import javax.xml.transform.stream.StreamResult;
import javax.xml.transform.stream.StreamSource;

import com.google.gson.Gson;
```

```
import com.springdemo.entity.Employee;
import com.springdemo.entity.EmployeeList;

public class EmployeeWSClientUsingJSON {

  HttpURLConnection connection;
  BufferedReader br;
  String result;
  JAXBContext jaxbContext;
  Marshaller jaxbMarshaller;
  Unmarshaller jaxbUnmarshaller;

  Gson gson = new Gson();

  public static void main(String[] args) {

    try {
     EmployeeWSClientUsingJSON restClient = new EmployeeWSClientUsingJSON();

    System.out.println("Get the list of All Employees");
    EmployeeList empList = restClient.getAllEmployees();

    System.out.println("\n=====================================\n");
    System.out.println("Get specific employee record with
                                    empNumber: 1001");
    Employee emp = restClient.getEmployee(1001);

    System.out.println("\n=====================================\n");
    System.out.println("Create an Employee record and add it
                                  into Employee list");
    Employee empNew = new Employee(1006, "Tammam", 75000.0,
                             28000.0, 16000.0);
    String result = restClient.createEmployee(empNew);

    System.out.println("\n=====================================\n");
    System.out.println("Get the created employee record
                                       [empNumber: 1006]");
    Employee empCreated = restClient.getEmployee(1006);

    System.out.println("\n=====================================\n");
    System.out.println("Update the employee record
                                     [empNumber: 1006]");
```

```
      empCreated.setEmpName("Tammam Fadal");
      empCreated.setBasicPay(76000.0);
      restClient.updateEmployee(1006, empCreated);

      System.out.println("\n==================================\n");
      System.out.println("Get the updated employee record
                                        [empNumber: 1006]");
      restClient.getEmployee(1006);

      System.out.println("\n==================================\n");
      System.out.println("Delete employee record [empNumber: 1002]");
      restClient.deleteEmployee(1002);

      System.out.println("\n==================================\n");
      System.out.println("Try to get the deleted employee record
                                        [empNumber: 1002]");
      restClient.getEmployee(1002);
    }
    catch (Exception e) {
      System.out.println(e);
    }
  }

  EmployeeList getAllEmployees() throws Exception {
    try {
      // Get All Employees in XML format
      URL url = new URL("http://localhost:9090/SpringDemoREST/employee");
      connection = (HttpURLConnection) url.openConnection();
      connection.setRequestMethod("GET");
      connection.setRequestProperty("Accept", "application/json");

      if (connection.getResponseCode() != HttpURLConnection.HTTP_OK) {
        throw new RuntimeException("Failed : HTTP error code : " +
                                  connection.getResponseCode());
      }

      br = new BufferedReader(
           new InputStreamReader((connection.getInputStream())));
      result = br.readLine();
      System.out.println("Result of getAllEmployees:\n");
      System.out.println(result);
      connection.disconnect();
```

```
// Bind the result into Value Object and display the values
EmployeeList employeeList = gson.fromJson(result, EmployeeList.class);

  System.out.println("\nEMPLOYEE LIST");
  for (Employee emp : employeeList.getEmployee()) {
    System.out.println(emp);
  }

  return employeeList;
 }
 catch (Exception e) {
  System.out.println("Error [" + e.getMessage() + "]");
  throw e;
 }
 finally {
  if (connection != null) {
    connection.disconnect();
  }
 }
}

Employee getEmployee(int employeeNumber) throws Exception {
 try {
  // Get specific employee record
  URL url = new URL("http://localhost:9090/SpringDemoREST/employee/
   " + employeeNumber);
  connection = (HttpURLConnection) url.openConnection();
  connection.setRequestMethod("GET");
  connection.setRequestProperty("Accept", "application/json");

  if (connection.getResponseCode() != HttpURLConnection.HTTP_OK) {
   throw new RuntimeException("Failed : HTTP error code : " +
                              connection.getResponseCode());
  }

  br = new BufferedReader(
        new InputStreamReader((connection.getInputStream())));
  result = br.readLine();
  connection.disconnect();

  if (result != null) {
```

```
            System.out.println("Result of retrieving specific record:\n");
            System.out.println(result);

            // Bind the result into Value Object and display the values
            Employee employee = gson.fromJson(result, Employee.class);
            System.out.println("\nEMPLOYEE");
            System.out.println(employee);

            return employee;
          }
          else {
            System.out.println("No employee record found with Employee Number: "
                                                          + employeeNumber);
            return null;
          }
        }
        catch (Exception e) {
          System.out.println("Error [" + e.getMessage() + "]");
          throw e;
        }
        finally {
          if (connection != null) {
            connection.disconnect();
          }
        }
      }

      String createEmployee(Employee empNew) throws Exception {
        try {
          URL url = new URL("http://localhost:9090/SpringDemoREST/employee");
          connection = (HttpURLConnection) url.openConnection();
          connection.setRequestMethod("POST");
          connection.setDoOutput(true);
          connection.setDoInput(true);
          connection.setUseCaches(false);
          connection.setAllowUserInteraction(false);
          connection.setRequestProperty("Content-Type", "application/json");

          String empNewJSON = gson.toJson(empNew);

          System.out.println("Given Employee Record in JSON format: \n" +
                                                          empNewJSON);

          OutputStream out = connection.getOutputStream();
```

```
    Writer writer = new OutputStreamWriter(out, "UTF-8");
    writer.write(empNewJSON);
    writer.close();
    out.close();

    if (connection.getResponseCode() != HttpURLConnection.HTTP_CREATED) {
      throw new RuntimeException("Failed : HTTP error code : " +
      connection.getResponseCode());
    }

    br = new BufferedReader(
        new InputStreamReader((connection.getInputStream())));
    result = br.readLine();
    connection.disconnect();

    System.out.println(result);

    return result;
  }
  catch (Exception e) {
    System.out.println("Error [" + e.getMessage() + "]");
    throw e;
  }
  finally {
    if (connection != null) {
      connection.disconnect();
    }
  }
}

void updateEmployee(int empNumber, Employee modifiedEmployee)
                                            throws Exception {
  try {
    URL url = new URL("http://localhost:9090/SpringDemoREST/employee/" +
                                                          empNumber);
    connection = (HttpURLConnection) url.openConnection();
    connection.setRequestMethod("PUT");
    connection.setDoOutput(true);
    connection.setDoInput(true);
    connection.setUseCaches(false);
    connection.setAllowUserInteraction(false);
```

```
    connection.setRequestProperty("Content-Type", "application/json");

      String empNewJSON = gson.toJson(modifiedEmployee);

      System.out.println("Given Employee Record in JSON format: \n" +
                                                          empNewJSON);

      OutputStream out = connection.getOutputStream();
      Writer writer = new OutputStreamWriter(out, "UTF-8");
      writer.write(empNewJSON);
      writer.close();
      out.close();

      if (connection.getResponseCode() != HttpURLConnection.HTTP_OK) {
        throw new RuntimeException("Failed : HTTP error code : " +
                                      connection.getResponseCode());
      }

      br = new BufferedReader(
            new InputStreamReader((connection.getInputStream())));
      result = br.readLine();
      connection.disconnect();

      if (result == null) {
      System.out.println("Employee record does not match for updation");
      }
      else {
        System.out.println("Employee record is updated");
      }
    }
    catch (Exception e) {
      System.out.println("Error [" + e.getMessage() + "]");
      throw e;
    }
    finally {
      if (connection != null) {
        connection.disconnect();
      }
    }
  }

  void deleteEmployee(int employeeNumber) throws Exception {
    try {
      // Delete specific employee record
```

```
    URL url = new URL("http://localhost:9090/SpringDemoREST/employee/" +
                                                       employeeNumber);
    connection = (HttpURLConnection) url.openConnection();
    connection.setRequestMethod("DELETE");
    connection.setRequestProperty("Accept", "application/json");

 if (connection.getResponseCode() != HttpURLConnection.HTTP_ACCEPTED)
 {
     throw new RuntimeException("Failed : HTTP error code : " +
                                  connection.getResponseCode());
    }

    br = new BufferedReader(
        new InputStreamReader((connection.getInputStream())));
    result = br.readLine();
    connection.disconnect();

    System.out.println(result);
   }
   catch (Exception e) {
    System.out.println("Error [" + e.getMessage() + "]");
    throw e;
   }
   finally {
    if (connection != null) {
      connection.disconnect();
    }
   }
  }

  public static void printXML(String xmlString) throws Exception {
    Source xmlInput = new StreamSource(new StringReader(xmlString));
    StreamResult xmlOutput = new StreamResult(new StringWriter());

    Transformer transformer =
            TransformerFactory.newInstance().newTransformer();
    transformer.setOutputProperty(OutputKeys.INDENT, "yes");
    transformer.setOutputProperty(
         "{http://xml.apache.org/xslt}indent-amount", "2");
    transformer.transform(xmlInput, xmlOutput);

    System.out.println(xmlOutput.getWriter().toString());
  }

}
```

The sample run of the above program is given below.

```
Get the list of All Employees
Result of getAllEmployees:

{"employee":[{"empNumber":1001,"empName":"Mohamed
Ibrahim","basicPay":50000.0,"allowances":20000.0,"deductions":10000.0,
"netpay":60000.0},{"empNumber":1005,"empName":"Mariyana","basicPay":
70000.0,"allowances":25000.0,"deductions":14000.0,"netpay":
81000.0},{"empNumber":1003,"empName":"John
Peter","basicPay":60000.0,"allowances":22000.0,"deductions":11000.0,"netpay":
71000.0},{"empNumber":1002,"empName":"Ajay
Kumar"," basicPay":55000.0,"allowances":21000.0,"deductions":
10500.0,"netpay":65500.0},{"empNumber":1004," empName": "Anwar",
"basicPay":65000.0,"allowances ":23000.0,"deductions":13500.0,
"netpay":74500.0}]}

EMPLOYEE LIST

Employee No.:   1001
Employee Name: Mohamed Ibrahim
Basic Pay:      50000.0
Allowances:     20000.0
Deductions:     10000.0
Netpay:         60000.0

Employee No.:   1005
Employee Name: Mariyana
Basic Pay:      70000.0
Allowances:     25000.0
Deductions:     14000.0
Netpay:         81000.0

Employee No.:   1003
Employee Name: John Peter
Basic Pay:      60000.0
Allowances:     22000.0
Deductions:     11000.0
Netpay:         71000.0

Employee No.:   1002
Employee Name: Ajay Kumar
Basic Pay:      55000.0
```

```
Allowances:     21000.0
Deductions:     10500.0
Netpay:         65500.0

Employee No.:   1004
Employee Name: Anwar
Basic Pay:      65000.0
Allowances:     23000.0
Deductions:     13500.0
Netpay:         74500.0
====================================

Get specific employee record with empNumber: 1001
Result of retrieving specific record:

{"empNumber":1001,"empName":"Mohamed
Ibrahim","basicPay":50000.0,"allowances":20000.0,"deductions":10000.0,"netpay
":60000.0}

EMPLOYEE

Employee No.:   1001
Employee Name: Mohamed Ibrahim
Basic Pay:      50000.0
Allowances:     20000.0
Deductions:     10000.0
Netpay:         60000.0
====================================

Create an Employee record and add it into Employee list
Given Employee Record in JSON format:
{"empNumber":1006,"empName":"Tammam","basicPay":75000.0,"allowances
":28000.0,"deductions":16000.0,"netpay":87000.0}
Employee record is added

====================================

Get the created employee record [empNumber: 1006]
Result of retrieving specific record:

{"empNumber":1006,"empName":"Tammam","basicPay":75000.0,"allowances":
28000.0,"deductions":16000.0,"netpay":87000.0}
```

```
EMPLOYEE

Employee No.:   1006
Employee Name:  Tammam
Basic Pay:      75000.0
Allowances:     28000.0
Deductions:     16000.0
Netpay:         87000.0

===================================

Update the employee record [empNumber: 1006]
Given Employee Record in JSON format:
{"empNumber":1006,"empName":"Tammam
Fadal","basicPay":76000.0,"allowances":28000.0,"deductions":16000.0,"netpay":
87000.0}
Employee record is updated

===================================

Get the updated employee record [empNumber: 1006]
Result of retrieving specific record:

{"empNumber":1006,"empName":"Tammam
Fadal","basicPay":76000.0,"allowances":28000.0,"deductions":16000.0,"netpay":
88000.0}

EMPLOYEE

Employee No.:   1006
Employee Name:  Tammam Fadal
Basic Pay:      76000.0
Allowances:     28000.0
Deductions:     16000.0
Netpay:         88000.0

===================================

Delete employee record [empNumber: 1002]
Record is deleted

===================================

Try to get the deleted employee record [empNumber: 1002]
No employee record found with Employee Number: 1002
```